FRENCH PRESSED

FRENCH PRESSED

CLEO COYLE

WHEELER
CHIVERS

LIBRARY OF CONGRESS CATALOGING-IN-PUBLICATION DATA

Coyle, Cleo.
    French pressed / by Cleo Coyle.
      p. cm. — (A coffeehouse mystery) (Wheeler Publishing
large print cozy mystery)
    ISBN-13: 978-1-59722-780-3 (softcover : alk. paper)
    ISBN-10: 1-59722-780-3 (softcover : alk. paper)
    1. Cosi, Clare (Fictitious character) — Fiction. 2. Coffeehouses
— Fiction. 3. Restaurants — Employees — Fiction. 4. Cooks —
Crimes against — Fiction. 5. Large type books. I. Title.
PS3603.O94F74 2008
813'.6—dc22   2008012120

BRITISH LIBRARY CATALOGUING-IN-PUBLICATION DATA AVAILABLE

Published in 2008 in the U.S. by arrangement with The Berkley Publishing Group, a member of Penguin Group (USA) Inc.
Published in 2008 in the U.K. by arrangement with The Berkley Publishing Group, a member of Penguin Group (USA) Inc.

U.K. Hardcover: 978 1 408 41221 3 (Chivers Large Print)
U.K. Softcover: 978 1 408 41222 0 (Camden Large Print)

Printed and bound in Great Britain by
CPI Antony Rowe, Chippenham and Eastbourne

1 2 3 4 5 6 7 12 11 10 09 08

*This book is dedicated to
Roy Snyder*

*For his encouragement, thoughtfulness,
unfailing good
humor, and most of all for his sage
financial advice — a
fundamental asset for any writer who's
crazy enough to
believe that "a room of one's own" is
achievable in one
of the most expensive cities on the
planet.*

*Cheers to you, Roy, for keeping the
dream in play.*

ACKNOWLEDGMENTS

While it is widely recognized that New York City is crowded, costly, competitive, and occasionally downright dangerous, New York is also a foodie mecca. It's the kind of town where you can attend an open-to-the-public culinary talk and find yourself sitting next to a young Cordon Bleu graduate while listening to legendary chef Jacques Pepin speak extemporaneously about such things as butchering a chicken. The aforementioned 92nd Street Y restaurant panel along with my two decades of speaking with restaurant professionals while dining out in New York were among the many experiences that contributed to the backdrop of this novel.

I would also like to acknowledge the gracious help of Douglas Snyder, general manager of Bin Fifty-Four Steak and Cellar. Doug is a consummate professional who chivalrously answered countless questions

7

about running an upscale restaurant, while also giving me one of the finest dining experiences I've ever had.

A succulent shout-out additionally goes to Bin Fifty-Four's executive chef, Andrew Bales, for giving me an after-hours tour of his efficiently run domain, a professional kitchen that consistently produces the most delicious fire-grilled steaks being served in America today.

Dear reader, if you ever find yourself in Chapel Hill, North Carolina, do not miss the dining experience at Bin Fifty-Four. And please be assured that the characters, situations, and murders in this book are completely fictitious figments of my imagination. Although Bin Fifty-Four is *the* scene for fabulous food and wine, it has never been ruled a *crime* scene!

Joe the Art of Coffee and Murray's Cheese Shop, both located in Greenwich Village, New York, have also been great sources of information. My sincerest thanks go out to them, as well. If you are ever in New York's West Village, these first-rate establishments are a genuine delight to visit — you might even see me there.

My special thanks also go out to editor Katie Day, executive editor Wendy Mc-Curdy, and literary agent John Talbot for making my job so much easier.

Last but in no way least, I'd like to thank the roasters at Counter Culture Coffee in Durham, North Carolina, for their inspiration, as well as their superior beans. If anyone knows and loves coffee, it's the intrepid coffee hunter Peter Giuliano, coffee director of Counter Culture. To learn more about the coffees mentioned in this book and the art of making them, drop by my virtual Village Blend coffeehouse at:

www.CoffeehouseMystery.com
Where coffee and crime are always
brewing.

"You can tell when you have crossed the frontier . . . because of the badness of the coffee."

— Edward VII (1841–1910)

"Food and sex . . . what else is there?"

— Wolfgang Puck

PROLOGUE

Stabbing flesh was no big deal. That was the way to think about it. The boy was just another piece of meat . . .

From across the dark avenue, the killer stood, expression grim. There were three stories in the redbrick building, six apartments, a roofless porch. The boy was alone on the highest floor. Through bright windows, the killer watched him pacing. He looked like an animal, like panicked game.

This wasn't something the killer wanted, but the decision had been made. Now time was a slow freeze and the waiting was unbearable on this dank, noisy street. Pub crawlers stumbled along littered sidewalks, Latino teens clustered amid grimy subway girders, and cop cars patrolled too visibly beneath the Number 7 line's elevated tracks.

The killer hugged shadows, tried to stay hidden, maneuver some shelter from the pitiless wind. Glacial gusts continued to whip down

Roosevelt, straight off the East River a mile away. Manhattan had been warmer, the killer thought. Queens was an ice cave, its buildings too low to dull the lash.

Finally, on the street, an opportunity came: a take-out delivery for someone inside. The brown-skinned man in the bright green jacket buzzed the intercom. Behind three pizzas and a liter of soda, the killer slipped in.

Laughter exploded behind a thin door. Some kind of party. A game on TV.

Noise, thought the killer, noise was good.

There were thirty-nine steps to the third floor, thirteen to each landing. The door to the boy's apartment was cheap, nothing more than flimsy wood. The killer loitered quietly in front of it, one minute, two . . .

The breathing must be even, the killer reasoned. The hand must be steady.

The killer knocked lightly, like a neighbor, like a friend. The boy answered fast, expecting someone else. Confusion set in. There'd been no buzzer. No request for entry. His brown eyes went wide. Anxiety. Dread.

"What do you want?"

"To explain," the killer said. The smile seemed to help. "You might have gotten the wrong idea . . . about what you heard last night. Let me come in and talk to you."

The killer's right pocket was a holster now.

Resting inside was the hard silver handle of the ten-inch blade, which poked through the lining. The coat was long enough to conceal the threat, old enough to be discarded after.

"I can quit my internship," the boy pleaded. "I don't have to go back to the restaurant. Not ever. How about that?"

"Did you tell anyone, Vinny? What you heard last night?"

"No! No one!"

"Then let's sit down and discuss it. You don't have to quit. I'll just explain everything, and you won't have to worry anymore."

"Well . . ." the boy said, glancing into the empty hall. "Okay . . . I guess you can come in."

"Thanks, Vinny."

Gloved fingers slipped inside the coat pocket, grasped the silver handle. The French blade was steel, high carbon and stainless, sharp as a surgical instrument, manufactured for the utmost precision.

Precise, the killer thought, I must be precise. No flinching. No hesitation. Thrust down fast. Plunge hard and true . . .

Vinny turned his back, and the knife went in smoothly, past skin, through muscle, avoiding bone. The flailing was minimal, the noise a weak howl. It was done now — over. And so

was Vincent Buccelli. The boy was just another piece of meat.

ONE

"Ugh," I murmured. "This coffee's absolute poison . . ."

No, the lukewarm ebony liquid sloshing around my bone china cup wasn't actually lethal, just bitter, old, and lifeless — the kind of adjectives I would have been mortified to hear uttered about my coffee, God forbid my person.

"It can't be that bad," Madame said. "Let me give it a try."

Sitting across from me at one of Solange's linen-shrouded tables for two, my ex-mother-in-law lifted her cup and sipped. "Oh, my . . ." With a frown, she brought a napkin to her gently wrinkled face, closed her eyes, and discreetly spat out the offending liquid — a routine gesture for an industry cupping, not for one of New York's finest French restaurants.

Up to now, the meal had been astounding. My appetizer of oysters had been poached in champagne, lovingly sauced, and placed back in their shells with a flavor and texture that defined delicate. My entrée of butter-browned lobster — artfully arranged around a flan of porcini mushrooms and earthy foie gras — had danced across my taste buds with savory succulence. And for desert, a modern execution of a traditional tarte Tatin, with spicy-sweet cardamom-laced apples and a drizzle of ginger-caramel coulis, had been presented in a pastry so tender it melted on my tongue like newly spun cotton candy.

The entire experience had been orgasmic, a seduction by color, taste, and sensation, with bite after bite making me shiver. Not that I was a restaurant critic.

I, Clare Cosi, middle-class working stiff, was the manager of a landmark coffeehouse in Greenwich Village, and although my experience with food was long-standing — from my childhood years making stove-top espressos in my grandmother's Pennsylvania grocery to my part-time catering work and culinary writing — it was small-time stuff in light of this four-star establishment.

In short, I was a cook, not a chef. I didn't have the authoritative status to officially declare whether or not Solange's particular take on nouvelle cuisine deserved its place alongside Per Se, Le Bernardin, and Daniel, the highest-flying stars in the Big Apple's culinary circus. But even a long-haul trucker could have judged that Solange's food was exquisite, while its coffee had all the appeal of Mississippi swamp mud.

"It's like a seduction gone wrong," Madame proclaimed. "A princely suitor who shows up with impeccable manners, romances you all night, and escorts you gallantly to the door, then lunges at your breasts with octopus hands and breath foul enough to choke a horse."

A knee-jerk cackle bubbled up in my throat; considering the mannered dining room, I promptly choked it down. "Don't hold back, Madame. Tell me what you really think."

My former mother-in-law rolled her eyes to the chandeliered ceiling. "There's no point in mincing words past your eightieth birthday. What good is being subtle when you might drop dead midsentence? If you've got a point to make, make it, for goodness' sake!" She lifted her hand, and our waiter instantly appeared. "Please take this away. I'm sorry to tell you, it's undrinkable."

René, a somber Haitian gentleman with a heavy French accent, bowed slightly. "*C'est dommage.* I am profoundly sorry." He

19

snapped his fingers, and another uniformed staff member — a young Latino man — swept in to remove the coffee service.

"Perhaps I can suggest a dessert wine," René said.

Madame glanced at me, but I tapped my watch and shook my head. "I've had enough wine. More will just put me to sleep. I still have to lock up downtown."

"Just another bottle of water," Madame told René.

"Of course. Please enjoy it with my compliments."

The young Latino busboy returned to pour our comped container of twelve-dollar water, and we sank back into the buffed leather upholstery to sip our palates clean again.

By now, the hour was late, and few tables around us were occupied. Most of the restaurant's chic clientele had cleared out already: The older couples were making their long drives back to estates on Long Island and north Jersey. The CEOs and brokers were strolling toward their Park Avenue pieds-à-terre to check overseas markets. Even the Yuppsters were gone, running up bar tabs at the Second Avenue pickup marts or the artisanal gin mills of the Meatpacking District.

Observing the now-serene dining room, I could see why Solange had become so popular. Aside from the abysmal coffee and typical astronomical prices of a New York house of haute cuisine, the restaurant truly was adorable. The interior was based on Paris's famous Les Deux Magots café, where Simone de Beauvoir liked to write. There were maroon banquettes topped by polished rails of brass, crystal and copper chandeliers, columns the color of crème fraîche, and even a bit of whimsy in the form of carved wooden gargoyles affixed high on the sunny yellow walls.

The corners held cherrywood end tables with vases of fresh lilies, and the plain white signature china displayed the word *Solange,* handwritten by the restaurant's acclaimed executive chef, Tommy Keitel. According to a note on the menu, the signature had been reproduced from a cloth napkin, taken from a legendary restaurant on the west bank of Paris, where the American-born Keitel had trained and first envisioned his own New York establishment.

Also according to the menu, the name of the restaurant had its roots in a French religious legend: Saint Solange had pledged her chastity to God, then lost her young life fleeing a smitten abductor.

I actually blanched when I'd read that tragic tale, given what I'd recently learned about my own daughter's love life.

"On balance, a marvelous experience," Madame said, interrupting my reverie. "You should be quite proud of Joy."

Of course, I was proud of my daughter. I'd watched her progress from a young teen, struggling to master Martha Stewart's recipes, to an accomplished student at a challenging New York culinary school. The typical intern in a kitchen wouldn't do more than assist a prep cook: wash and cut vegetables, clean chickens, peel shrimp, crack dozens of eggs, and generally fetch and carry. But because of her "special friendship" with Tommy Keitel, Joy excitedly told me that for two dinner services a week she'd been promoted to *legumier;* she was to prepare the menu's vegetables.

Unfortunately, that fact failed to make me proud, because the "special friendship" with her boss was a euphemism. Joy was carrying on an affair with Chef Keitel, a man who wasn't just thirty years her senior but also happened to be married with children.

The subject reminded me of why I was here in the first place: to snoop.

"Speaking of Joy," I said, setting down my leaded crystal goblet of water, "I was hoping I might slip into the kitchen and pay her a visit. Since starting her internship year, I've hardly seen her. Would you like to come along?"

Madame raised a silver-white eyebrow. "So I can referee your next mother-daughter knock-down-drag-out?"

"We've called a truce."

"The terms?"

"We've agreed to disagree about her affair." I shrugged. "If I don't bring it up, she won't — and she'll keep talking to me."

"Is that so?"

"Joy's an adult now," I said with a profoundly distressing sigh, "and, as her father pointed out to me — several times — judging her won't do much more than push her away. Frankly, I'm expecting her to be let down badly by Keitel, and I want our relationship to be intact when that happens."

"In other words, your *only* reason for agreeing to 'butt out' of her business is to make certain that you can be there for her when she really needs you?"

I shifted in my seat, wondering if Madame was about to criticize me. "Truthfully . . . yes," I admitted. "That's exactly my reason."

"Good," Madame said with a little smile. "I'm glad to hear it."

With relief, I leaned back, happy to know she thought I was doing the right thing. Not that I wasn't confident in my own decisions, but Madame Blanche Dreyfus Allegro Dubois was more than my former mother-in-law. For going on twenty years now, she'd been my mentor and friend (not to mention my employer, since she owned the Village Blend). So, of course, I respected her opinion; I also just plain admired her.

Despite her age and the lateness of the hour, Madame's effortless elegance was something to which I — at half her years — could only aspire. Her bearing was all the more impressive to me because I knew her background.

The woman had lost everything in her youth, including her mother and sister. Then she'd remade herself in America, only to lose the young husband she'd passionately loved. Antonio Allegro's death had left her completely alone to raise their son and keep alive the century-old coffee business begun by Antonio's grandfather.

More recently, Madame had lost her older, second husband, a French-born businessman whom she'd highly esteemed. Yet through the challenges of her life, her outlook remained focused and positive, her bearing invincibly regal.

Tonight, for example, her dress of deep violet draped wrinkle-free on her slender form. Her only jewelry was a tasteful necklace of pearls and platinum. Her shoulder-length silver-white hair was swept into a *still* neat chignon, and her big blue eyes continued to appear alert and alive, their lids maintaining their stylishly applied hint of lilac.

As for me, I'd managed to dig a cocoa-colored pinstriped business suit out of my usual wardrobe of khakis, jeans, and hoodies. I'd even managed to jazz it up with a necklace that I'd bought from a local street artisan. As cheap as that sounded, the tiger-eye stones set in distressed gold didn't look half bad with the cocoa suit. Plus I'd done up my own Italian-roast brown hair into a twist, shoved my hastily shaved legs into sheer stockings, my feet into high heels — at five two I needed all the height I could get — and stuck my lobes with earrings that sort of matched the necklace.

Suffice it to say, I was presentable enough to avoid embarrassing my daughter, who was apprenticing behind the double doors at the back of this *très* fashionable dining room.

"You go on, Clare," Madame advised. "Visit Joy at her cook station. New York restaurant kitchens are terribly crowded, busy places. I'll just be in the way. Besides, there might be a very good reason for me to sit here alone for a few minutes."

"Oh, really?"

"Yes . . . there's an intriguing man sitting alone at a corner table."

"A man?" I began to turn and look.

"No, no! Don't do that!"

"Why not?"

"I suspect he may be a bit shy or easily embarrassed. He's been eye-flirting with me for the past half hour, but he hasn't acted. I think perhaps, if he sees me sitting here alone for a few minutes, he'll make his move."

"On the make already?" I teased, since Madame had just broken up with her last boyfriend, a charming oncologist who'd finally retired at the age of seventy-five.

In Dr. McTavish's grand plan, Madame was to have married him and moved immediately to New Mexico, where she was to take up golfing, camping, and trail hiking. Madame gently told him that although she cared for him, she had no intention of uprooting herself from her New York life. And since he'd set his plans in unbreakable stone, he should definitely take a hike — with another woman.

"At my age, dear, one shouldn't waste an opportunity for amour," she said, pausing to drain her water goblet. "And, quite frankly, I've been conjugated too many times to play coy."

"Uh-huh," I said, rising. "I'll be right back."

"No hurry," Madame said with a wily smile. "Take your time."

Resisting the urge to check out Madame's newest potential flame, I instead sought out the maître d'.

Napoleon Dornier was a tall scarecrow of a man in his early thirties. He had narrow shoulders, a beaked nose, and a large head with short, spiked radish-colored hair and long red sideburns. Clearly a fussy, meticulous manager, he'd been breathing down the neck of the waiters and busboys since Madame and I had been seated. It seemed nothing was quite good enough for him, not even the position of his tie's knot, which he'd adjusted twice as I approached.

"Excuse me," I said.

Dornier had been watching a member of the waitstaff deliver a bill to one of the last large tables, a gathering of six businessmen. Behind his catlike amber eyeglasses his dark gaze focused on me.

"Can I help you?" he asked, flicking an

imaginary speck of lint from his black jacket.

"Would it be possible to see the kitchen?" I asked.

The man sniffed, the sort of mildly disdainful gesture that I swear every Frenchman learned to master in maître d' school. "If you're hoping to meet our renowned chef de cuisine," he said, "I fear you'll be disappointed. Chef Keitel is not in the kitchen tonight."

"Oh, thank goodness!"

My outburst obviously surprised Monsieur Dornier, but I just couldn't help myself. I'd met Tommy Keitel exactly once, when Joy had brought him to a Village Blend function a month ago. I'd been caught off guard that evening, learning about their affair in the most in-your-face way possible. (The image of that lecher's fiftysomething arm around my innocent daughter's young waist made me want to strangle him with my bare hands.)

But how was I supposed to explain that to Dornier? *Sorry for the outburst, monsieur. But I'm thrilled to miss seeing a guy I'd like to choke till he turns the color of pomegranate juice.*

Clearing my throat, I decided to keep it simple. "Monsieur, I'm not here to see Chef Keitel. My name is Clare Cosi. I'm the

28

manager of the Village Blend coffeehouse in the West Village, and my daughter is one of your interns. Joy Allegro —"

"Mademoiselle Joy! She is your daughter?" Dornier's demeanor changed immediately. "She is a sweet and lovely addition to our staff." He glanced at his watch. "Dinner service is nearly concluded, and I'm sure we can take a peek behind the veil without being too disruptive."

Behind the veil? Good Lord. This guy's really into the restaurant-as-theater thing. "Uh, thank you."

"Please follow me."

As we walked, I made polite conversation, complimenting the food and service, tactfully leaving out the abysmal coffee.

"Here at Solange, we always strive for excellence," Dornier replied. "Even in the face of our executive chef's *continued* absence."

The critical tone was hard to miss. I decided to probe a little. "Excuse me, Monsieur Dornier? Are you saying that Chef Keitel has been MIA from the restaurant lately?"

The maître d' scowled. "I am unhappy to say that he has been."

"It's, uh . . . hard to believe. I mean, the meal was so perfect. I could have sworn

Chef Keitel finished my plate himself."

Now, I knew very well that an executive chef like Keitel would not have had to finish each plate to guarantee excellence. Sure, he might have designed the dishes on the menu, but the value of a top executive chef was his ability to reproduce that same dish day after day and teach his staff to do the same.

Whenever Tommy Keitel was absent, his executive sous-chef would be expected to step up and fill in for him. I didn't recall Joy ever mentioning the name of the kitchen's second-in-command, so I asked the maître d' about it.

Dornier sniffed again. "Our executive sous-chef is Ms. Brigitte Rouille."

"Oh? Joy's never mentioned Chef Rouille."

"Brigitte comes to us from Chantal, where she was the sauté chef. Before that, she was the sous-chef at La Belle Femme near Lincoln Center. Originally, however, Ms. Rouille was lured to New York from her native Quebec with an offer to serve as executive chef at Martinique's downtown."

The list of upscale eateries was impressive, but Brigitte Rouille's work experience ran like a backward résumé. "From executive to sous to sauté chef?" I said. "Ms.

Rouille's career path seems upside down, doesn't it?"

"Oui," Dornier replied.

"So why was she hired?"

Dornier fidgeted with his expensive cat glasses. "Chef Keitel has known Brigitte for many years. When her life proved . . . how shall I say? . . . *challenging* . . . Tommy was magnanimous enough to offer the woman a chance to redeem her career."

Challenging? What did that mean? I was about to ask, but we'd reached the double doors to the kitchen.

"I'm sure you'll see, Ms. Cosi, that we run an efficient, professional shop."

"Professional," I repeated with a nod.

"Oui. Although our sous-chef has had her ups and downs, Brigitte Rouille is quite capable of handling the kitchen with Chef Keitel away."

Dornier pushed one of the two swinging padded doors, holding it open so I could move through. "Please enjoy visiting your daughter. I'll return in a few minutes to escort you out again."

"Thank you," I said, and stepped inside.

Even though a huge, stainless steel service counter blocked a clear view of the entire kitchen, amazing aromas immediately enveloped me. I recognized the tang of fresh-cut

31

scallions, the piquant bite of garlic, the brightness of wine reduction.

Unfortunately, the riot of appetizing scents was quickly upstaged by the sounds of an *actual* riot. I heard a loud crash, as if a plate had been smashed to the floor. Someone screamed. Another plate was broken, and a woman began shouting in a pronounced French accent.

"Do you hear me?! *Écoutez-moi!* You are an idiot, and your technique is shit!"

"You don't know what you're talking about," a male voice calmly answered.

An echoing clang came next, as if a pan had been thrown down. "If you back talk to me again," the woman yelled, "I will fire you!"

"You can't fire me!" the man replied. "I've got a contract, just like you and Keitel. So screw you, Brigitte!"

Brigitte? I thought. *The woman shouting must be Brigitte Rouille, the executive sous-chef from Quebec.* Obviously, the woman was having a disagreement with her kitchen staff.

I stood by the double doors, frozen like some party guest who'd arrived early to find her married hosts at each other's throats. *What do I do? Go in anyway? Wait till things calm down? Come back later?*

The shouting went quiet for a moment, and I tried to see beyond the large metal service counter, but all I could make out were some cooks moving around in their white jackets. Finally, I heard Brigitte Rouille making angry accusations to another staff member.

This time, a young woman answered in a clear, calm voice: "That's just not true, Chef. I'm sorry, but you're mistaken."

The voice was Joy's, I realized. And my daughter sounded perfectly calm and respectful. I was proud of her for keeping her cool in the face of a professional dressing-down, and I expected Chef Rouille to respond to her accordingly. But the woman's reply was a screaming rant, laced with French obscenities.

I clenched my fists, knowing there was nothing I could do. This was Joy's workplace, after all, and she'd be mortified to have her mommy butting in. So I just stood there, waiting for Brigitte Rouille's tirade to finish.

But it didn't. The French-Canadian woman continued to rage. I understood a fair amount of the French language, but the more she shouted, the less sense she seemed to be making.

Then more plates went crashing to the

floor. A woman screamed, and a Latino busboy in a white smock bolted past me in a panic. I grabbed hold of his smock.

"What is going on back there?" I asked.

"She's gone loco again!" he called to me before breaking away and punching through the dining room doors. "I'm outta here till she comes down!"

Good Lord! I thought. *What kind of hell's kitchen is my daughter working in?*

Two

I hurried around the high steel service counter and finally got a good look at Solange's kitchen. The space was a long, narrow rectangle, with a bank of stoves along the wall and prep tables opposite.

According to my daughter's descriptions, Solange operated no differently than any other busy, upscale restaurant. It utilized the brigade system: basically, a hierarchical food assembly line that was invented in the nineteenth century by the Frenchman Escoffier.

There were supposed to be line cooks here, each one in charge of a different part of the menu (grilling and roasting, sauces, fish, soups, pastry . . .). But the kitchen looked suddenly abandoned, like a creepy ghost ship's galley with pans left simmering on the fire and food still on prep tables.

So where's Joy?! And where's the staff?! I just heard them!

"I have had enough! Enough, do you hear!" Chef Rouille's voice shrieked from the back of the long kitchen.

I moved around obstacles toward the sound of French obscenities, stepping carefully over shattered china, a pan emptied of its contents, and an overturned bowl of asparagus stalks.

Finally, I found my daughter. Her back was pressed against one of the stainless steel doors of the walk-in fridge. A brown sauce was splattered across the front of her white jacket — as if someone had sullied her deliberately. Her chestnut hair was slipping from its dark net. Her green eyes were wide, and her heart-shaped face was crimson with embarrassment.

An older woman was bawling her out, and I assumed this was Brigitte Rouille. She was thinner than Joy and slightly taller. About my age, maybe a few years older, with pale skin, a long nose, and straight hair that trailed down her white-jacketed back in a long ebony ponytail.

"You stupid brat!" Brigitte shouted. The woman's face was flushed with fury. Beneath her tall chef's hat, her forehead was beaded with sweat. "You are a clumsy moron! *Vous écoutez-moi!* If you bump into me *one* more time during service, I will filet your ass so it *fits* into this kitchen!"

"It's not my fault, Chef Rouille. I know about economy of movement from school, but *you* kept bumping me. I was standing still." Joy's quiet defense seemed to further enrage the woman, and she went back to shouting in French, tendons bulging on her neck.

My fists clenched, and I looked around to see what had happened to Joy's coworkers. Finally, I saw them. They'd fled to the dishwashing area: five male line cooks (four small Caucasian men and an Asian guy, their faces blanched as white as their chef's jackets and flat-topped cook's caps). There was also an older Latino swing cook, a younger Latino dishwasher, and an African American pastry chef (an attractive young woman wearing a burgundy chef's jacket). They were all huddled close, like paralyzed swimmers watching a shark circle its chosen victim a few yards away.

Just then, Chef Rouille paused to take a breath from her venomous ranting, and Joy finally snapped out in anger: "If Tommy were here, you wouldn't be acting like this!"

Chef Rouille's body went still. "You little *putain,*" she spat. "*You're* the one undermining me with Chef Keitel, aren't you?"

"No!" Joy's head shook vehemently. "I've

never said a word to him about you."

"You're lying!"

I desperately wanted to stop this horrifying scene. Yet I knew, as bad as this looked, it was still a workplace matter. I could see Joy was starting to defend herself now, and I didn't want to make things worse for my daughter, who'd plainly told me to "butt out" of her business more times than I could count.

But then something happened that tilted my universe.

Chef Brigitte Rouille raised her arm. "I'll teach you!" she cried. Something flashed in her hand, and Joy screamed. That's when I realized this woman was menacing my child with a foot-long chef's knife. *Okay, that's it! Butting out time's over!*

I lunged forward. "Get away from my daughter, you crazy bitch!"

I don't remember exactly how I got myself in front of Brigitte's slashing chef's knife. One moment I was calm, the next livid. One moment I was standing still, the next I was on the move, grabbing a wooden cutting board off a prep table and shouting my own head off.

"Back off!" I cried, raising the cutting board like Lancelot's shield. "I'm Joy's mother! *Je suis la mère de* Joy!"

This failed to impress the woman. She was breathing hard, her eyes dilated, her lips curled into a sneer as she continued shouting in French and making stabs at the board. The line cooks remained huddled across the room; still no help from that quarter!

Before Brigitte could do any real damage, however, Napoleon Dornier crept up behind her, seized her wrist, and twisted it.

Brigitte howled in pain.

"Get hold of yourself, woman!" the maître d' commanded, shaking the chef's knife from her hand.

The heavy blade clattered to the floor, striking a spark when it hit the tiles. I kicked the knife. It slid away and clanged against the base of a metal cabinet.

Brigitte whirled, lashed out with a clawed hand that shredded the flower on the man's lapel. *"Mon Dieu!"* Dornier reared back but continued to grip the sous-chef's arm.

Though she was very thin, Brigitte Rouille was obviously very strong, and it looked like Dornier might actually lose this struggle.

"Ne me touchez pas!" Brigitte repeated again and again. "Do not touch me! Do not touch me!"

"Stop it, this instant!" Dornier demanded. "It is me, Brigitte! *Il est moi! C'est Napoleon*

Dornier! C'est Nappy!"

"Nappy? . . ."

Brigitte stopped fighting, and Dornier released her. She blinked and looked around the room in a daze.

"Brigitte, *what* is going on?" Dornier demanded. "Are you —"

Before he could finish his question, Brigitte burst into tears. Covering her eyes, she fled the kitchen through the back door.

"Brigitte! Brigitte!" Dornier called, and followed the sous-chef into the alley.

With the disturbing scene over, the line cooks returned to their stations, picking up with their duties as if nothing had happened. I turned to face my daughter. Joy's eyes were full of tears as she yanked off her stained chef's jacket.

"Honey, are you okay?"

I didn't know what reaction to expect, but I certainly wasn't expecting the one I got.

"Omigawd, Mom," Joy whispered, then hugged me tight. "Thank you."

My daughter had a good four inches on me, and she had to stoop slightly to bury her face in my neck. I could feel her shaking, and I held on to her, giving her time to regain her composure. The staff worked on, avoiding us with their eyes.

"Joy, what happened?" I asked softly.

My daughter pulled away, swiped at her tears. "Ramon," she called to the older Latino swing cook, "can you take over my station?"

The squat, dark-haired man with a slightly pockmarked face nodded once. "No problem."

Joy thanked him, then took my arm and led me down a narrow corridor lit by buzzing fluorescent ceiling lights. She sat me down in a tiny room next to a stairwell. Inside the room, a bunch of metal folding chairs was scattered around a wooden table. There was a TV, a computer, and a boom box, all of which were off.

"This is our break room," she explained, avoiding my gaze.

My daughter was obviously dealing with feelings of embarrassment. I was feeling a very different emotion. "What's wrong with those people out there?" I said loudly.

"Quiet, Mom, they'll hear you —"

"No. You could have been killed, hurt badly at the very least, by that crazy woman, and nobody in your kitchen moved a muscle! You're lucky the maître d' was there to disarm her!"

Joy closed the door and sat down. "You don't understand," she said, much softer

41

than I was speaking. "Brigitte accused me of messing up some of tonight's plates."

"Excuse me?"

"She said the sea bass should have gone out on a bed of ramps, but I was putting asparagus down instead. I wasn't! I know the difference between a freakin' locally grown leek and a spear of asparagus! She accused me of being incompetent, but I told her that I'd done it right. And since the plates went out already, I couldn't even prove it. I told her nobody sent them back or complained — so she was just making it up to make me look bad in front of everyone. That's when she flung the béarnaise sauce on me."

Joy lifted the soiled chef's jacket in her hand. "And then she said I was purposely bumping into her all night. I wasn't. She was the one bumping me — and on purpose, if you ask me. Anyway, her little fit tonight was nothing new. Chef Rouille's been throwing a tantrum almost every night now."

"I'd call trying to slash your throat with a chef's knife more than a simple tantrum."

Joy sighed. "She probably wouldn't have hurt me —"

"*Probably!?* Muffin, that woman's certifiable. I think someone should press charges.

Surely Brigitte's guilty of assault with a deadly —"

"No!" Joy touched my arm. "My internship's been going really well. I'm not going to mess it up by calling the cops on Tommy's restaurant."

"Okay . . . but you have to tell me more. What exactly has been going on with that woman?"

Joy shook her head. "It's not like Chef Rouille singled me out for special persecution. Last Saturday she screamed at Henry Tso, the sauté chef, and Henry *never* makes a mistake. On Tuesday she came down on Don Maris, the seafood chef, for overbroiling a lobster. Then yesterday, she gave Vinny so much work he had to hide in the walk-in refrigerator until everybody went home last night, just so he could finish. She threatened to have him fired if he didn't have it all done by the morning. You remember Vinny Buccelli, don't you? You met him at that press party last month. It was the same night you met Tommy."

I did remember Vinny. He was a nice-looking Italian boy — a young friend of Joy's from her culinary school class. I had assumed (wrongly) that the quiet, slight young man was Joy's boyfriend, something I still hoped could come true once she re-

43

alized how wrong she was to get involved with Tommy Keitel.

Joy frowned. "Brigitte's got Vinny so rattled he called in sick today. And nobody calls in sick at Solange unless they want to lose their job."

"What kind of a kitchen is Tommy running?" I demanded.

"This isn't Tommy's fault," Joy replied — *too* quickly, I thought.

"Mr. Dornier told me that Tommy hasn't been around much lately," I said. "Dornier doesn't sound happy about it, and I can see why. Tommy's the executive chef. If he's not around, then he's not doing his job."

Joy's face got tight. I recognized *the look.* I'd obviously struck a nerve.

"Is that man still sleeping with you?" I asked bluntly.

"Mom!"

"I know. I'm not supposed to bring it up, but —"

"Please don't start that again, or we'll have to stop talking altogether."

I threw up my hands. "Truce!"

Joy flipped her ponytail over her shoulder, looked away.

"Truce," I repeated, reaching over to squeeze her arm. "Okay?"

Eyes downcast, Joy nodded. "Okay," she

said softly. "And the answer is yes. Tommy and I are still involved . . . romantically."

I tried not to cringe at the word. I found nothing whatsoever *romantic* about their relationship. It was seedy. It was wrong. And it was a testament to my daughter's immaturity that she'd use a word like that to describe what was going on between her and a workplace supervisor thirty years her senior, who was married with kids.

On the face of it, I would have guessed that Joy had been singled out for criticism, if not sabotage, because she was getting preferential treatment from the big boss. But if the restaurant's French-Canadian sous-chef had been torturing poor Vinny Buccelli so badly that he'd called in sick, it sounded like she was routinely targeting different staff members for her wrath. So why wasn't Keitel doing something about it?

"Joy, tell me what's going on with Tommy."

"Well . . . Mr. Dornier is right," she began, leaning closer. "Tommy has been absent — *a lot.* When I first started my internship three months ago, he was practically married to this place. Everyone says he was like that from the very first day. He'd come in early, oversee everything in the kitchen, right through dinner service. He'd stay late, too. After the last customer left, he and Dornier would sit in the dining room with a bottle of wine and go over every detail of the evening — 'tragedies and triumphs' is how Tommy put it. He wanted to be in on every little thing that went wrong or right at Solange."

Joy shook her head. "I really loved that about him, Mom . . . but now he's hardly here. Sometimes he checks in around noon, but then he takes off a few hours later, way before dinner service even starts. And he doesn't come back."

"Where does he go?"

Joy shrugged. "Nobody knows. He won't tell me, and everyone's talking. Everyone has a theory about where Tommy's going, what he's doing . . . even *who* he's do-ing . . ."

My daughter's voice trailed off, and she looked away, her expression hurt and con-fused. *Congratulations, Joy,* I thought but didn't dare say. *Now you know how Tommy's wife must feel.*

I loved my daughter more than anything, but I wanted her to learn from this mistake. Affairs between older, high-powered men and their young interns seldom ended well — and the beginning of the end was the girl getting a clue that her cloud-nine view of

Mr. Big was far from grounded in reality. I was relieved to see Joy at last displaying some ambivalence toward the larger-than-life Keitel.

"It wouldn't be so bad," Joy began to equivocate, "except that Tommy leaves Brigitte in charge."

I forced myself not to roll my eyes. "I can see where that would be a problem."

"You can't imagine how bad it's gotten," Joy said, shaking her head. "Brigitte was just fine when Tommy was around, telling her what to do, but now that he's gone, she can't handle the responsibility. Some of the other cooks are saying she's taking drugs to get through it —"

"Drugs!"

"Mom, please! Keep your voice down."

Oh, God . . . of course . . . That crazed woman had shown all the signs: the dilated pupils, the sweat on her brow, the shaking, the paranoia, the uncanny strength when she'd fought Dornier. *It has to be uppers.* Amphetamines would have caused those symptoms, and they were the drugs of choice in this kind of late-night work. *Stay up! Stay focused! Speed or meth would produce those symptoms, too. So would cocaine . . .*

The very word doused me with horrible

memories.

My ex-husband had become a coke addict during our marriage (and I'm not talking about the stuff you buy in ice-cold cans). The drug use had been "harmless" at first. Or so Matt kept telling me. "Just a few lines" during parties in Central and South America, where cocaine had been used for centuries and was still a cash crop. Then he began doing lines privately "just to combat jet lag." *Right.* Somewhere in there he'd started sleeping around and cleaned out our bank account. Clearly, the drug use wasn't so "harmless" anymore.

Hearing about drug use in Solange's kitchen was my nightmare come true. Ever since I'd caught Joy snorting cocaine with some friends in the bathroom of a down-town nightclub, I worried she'd start traveling the same path her father had: arrested for possession, rushed to the hospital after overdosing, relapsing after rehab.

Joy's use hadn't gone beyond a few casual experiments, out of "curiosity," but I knew it was a short trip to hell if she wasn't careful — because I'd had a front-row seat for Matt's descent.

My ex-husband was clean now, and he believed he'd won out over his addiction. But recovered addicts never really stopped fighting the battle. He'd have to continue resisting relapse for the rest of his life. I didn't want that for my daughter.

Joy cleared her throat. She seemed to take my lengthy silence for disbelief. "I know it sounds crazy," she said. "I mean, who has time to do drugs in Tommy's kitchen? There's too much work, and so much is expected of everyone. You always have to perform to the highest standards, and who can do that while they're high or stoned out of their minds?"

"What are you saying?"

"That Tommy won't tolerate drugs. He's made that clear to everyone. If he ever found out Brigitte was using again, he'd fire her on the spot. I'm sure of it."

I was genuinely surprised by this revelation. I'd assumed Tommy Keitel was a hard-partying guy. But if Tommy was doing drugs at all, it would have been with the young woman he was bedding; and I could see in Joy's eyes that she was telling me the truth.

"Tommy knows something's wrong in the kitchen," Joy continued. "But, for some reason, I don't think he cares. He didn't come in at all last week, and Brigitte was in charge. She's fine for the prep work and most of service, but at the end of the night, she goes ballistic, freaking about any little thing she thinks went wrong. It's been getting worse and worse —"

A knock on the door interrupted us.

"Yes?" Joy called.

"It's Ramon. We're getting ready to close up now."

"I'll be right out," Joy said. She rose, picked up her soiled jacket, and straightened her bangs with her fingers. "I kind of have to go."

"Me, too," I said, rising. "When I left your grandmother in the dining room, she was flirting with a new potential beau." I smiled at my daughter. "They're probably engaged by now. Either that or your grandmother's already broken his heart and moved on to her next conquest."

Joy laughed, and I was happy to hear it.

"Listen, honey," I put my arm around her. "Tommy needs to be told what's going on. Will you let me talk to him?"

"No, Mom. That's ridiculous. This is my workplace. I'll handle the problem. I'll just explain to Tommy what's been happening. I'm sure he'll listen to me."

"Are you, Joy? Tommy Keitel doesn't strike me as the kind of man who listens to anyone."

"You *have* to let me handle this, okay?"

I frowned, my jaw clenching. This wasn't

easy. "So . . . you'll talk to him?"

"Yes. I will. I *promise*."

"Okay, then. Guess I'm demoted back to 'butt out' mode." I forced a smile.

My daughter smiled, too, and we returned to the kitchen.

Joy grabbed a fresh white jacket from a cabinet and buttoned it on as she escorted me past the walk-in fridge, the prep tables, and the cook stations. When we got to the double doors that led to the dining room, I turned to her. "I can wait around, you know. Madame and I would be happy to escort you home. I'm sure it's lonely with your roommate in Paris for the next six months."

Before Joy could reply, the doors pushed inward, bumping my behind. I leapt aside as Chef Tommy Keitel himself swept in.

"Chef," Joy said, nodding. "You remember —"

"Clare Cosi!" Tommy exclaimed. "The coffee lady. Hey, good to see you again!"

He extended his hand, but the doors opened once more, and a member of the waitstaff entered, a tray of dishes on his shoulder. After an awkward moment, Keitel's large, strong hand clasped mine.

"I've got to clean up my station," Joy said, quietly excusing herself.

Keitel looked exactly as I remembered

51

him. He was a tall, fit man in his fifties with arresting blue eyes, salt-and-pepper hair, a slightly crooked nose, and what looked to me like a perpetual smirk of confidence.

He released my hand then slipped off his coat and hung it on a peg. He wore a black silk shirt underneath, opened enough at the collar to show off his curling gray chest hairs, wiry muscles, and a silver chain. He grinned at me as he rolled up his sleeves, revealing the heavily developed forearms of a man who'd probably mixed and whisked and turned dough for thousands of hours in his lifetime.

"So, Clare, how do you like my kitchen?" Tommy asked with undisguised pride.

"Interesting," I said, tightly folding my arms.

Tommy nodded, then cocked his head, shouting at a waiter who'd just pushed through the double doors. "Hey, René! Where the hell is Nappy?"

The Haitian man who'd waited on my table stopped and blinked, as if he was uncertain how to reply. "I, uh, just saw him, Chef," he finally said. "I'm sure he's around . . ."

I cleared my throat. "The last time I saw your maître d', he was chasing your executive sous-chef into your back alley."

Tommy winced. "Again?"

"Yes." I nodded. "And I really think you should speak with —"

"René!" he barked again. "Did Dornier take any calls for me?"

"Your wife," the waiter called as he moved toward the back staircase. "She rang three times during service, looking for you."

Tommy scowled at that.

"And Mr. Wright stopped by. He needed to speak with you about something. Since you weren't here, he spoke with Brigitte."

Tommy's scowl deepened.

"Chef Keitel," I tried again. "Speaking of Brigitte, I witnessed quite a scene with her here earlier —"

"Tommy?" a new voice called from behind me. The voice was deep and male, almost guttural.

Tommy's face instantly brightened as the stranger stepped into the kitchen through the dining room doors. "Hey, there he is!" Tommy cried. "Have any problem parking the SUV?"

The newcomer silently shook his head. He was clad in black from his pointy boots and chinos to his shiny black leather blazer. His sunglasses were black, too — so dark I thought for a second that he might be blind.

"Clare Cosi, this is Nick, a buddy of mine

53

from Brighton Beach."

I extended my hand. "Nice to meet you, Nick."

The man drew his narrow hand out of his pocket and shook mine. His flesh was ice-cold, but then he'd just come in from outside, and it *was* November. Under his dark glasses, the man's complexion was so pale, it looked almost pink. His hair was light brown, and it hung in long, thin strands from an elongated head. His chin had a deep cleft, and his lips were thin and expressionless — literally. He remained silent.

"Well, it was great to see you, Clare!" Tommy said with a dismissive wave. "Nick and I have some work to do."

"But I wanted to tell you —"

"Good night now!" Grabbing Nick's arm, he turned his back to me and swiftly led the man toward the walk-in refrigerator.

Like pale, timid monks, the line cooks watched their larger-than-life boss and his strange friend wend their way to the back of the kitchen. Joy glanced in my direction and flashed a tiny wave.

"Don't worry," she mouthed to me. "I'll speak to him."

I waved back, realizing there was nothing more to do but trust my daughter. I wasn't through butting in. I promised myself that. For now, however, Joy said she could handle explaining things to Tommy, and I had to trust that she would.

With clenched fists, I forced myself to walk away. Though I was sad to say good night to my daughter, I was far from broken up about leaving Tommy Keitel's restaurant. More than anything, I wanted to get back downtown to my Village Blend, where at least I could get a decent cup of coffee.

THREE

The Village Blend occupied a four-story Federal-style town house in New York's historic West Village. To my customers, however, the Blend was more than just a java joint. It was a dependable oasis of calm in a crowded, expensive, stress-inducing city that routinely stripped its occupants of their dignity.

The place was my oasis, too. Behind my espresso bar, I felt capable and in control. After that knife-wielding episode in Solange's cutthroat kitchen, I was relieved to get back to some comfortable, familiar, *sane* surroundings, if only to lock up for the night and head upstairs for a fresh pot of joe and a warm vanilla bath.

As I stepped off the chilly Hudson Street sidewalk and pushed through the beveled glass door, however, I wondered whose coffeehouse I'd just entered.

Oh, it looked the same. Twenty coral-colored café tables sat on a restored wood-plank floor. There was a working fireplace, a colorful collection of antique grinding mills and tin coffee signs, a wrought-iron spiral staircase leading to a second-floor lounge, a line of French doors (which we threw open in warmer weather for sidewalk seating), and a blueberry marble counter fronting a pastry case and state-of-the-art espresso bar. What threw me, however, was the discordant noise reverberating off the exposed brick walls.

The pounding instruments mixed with the barking chant of an angry male voice had all the musicality of construction equipment. And then there were the enchanting lyrics:

> The game's all the same, homey
> Uptown and down
> Cell phones and names, baby
> Bitches, hoes, and goin' down
> Bang, bang, for money, sonny
> That's what she want
> So you bang, bang that booty, sonny!
> Take it from her c—

Ack! I thought with a shudder. *What barista of mine is running rap through the Village Blend sound system?!*

57

It couldn't have been my assistant manager. When he wasn't scribbling one acts or landing small parts in locally filmed TV dramas, Tucker Burton was pulling shots for me to upbeat pop and retro eighties.

There was no way Gardner Evans would be playing rap, either. Gardner was a serious jazz musician who regularly decried "gangstas" making millions on selling "crack music to little crackers whose idea of slumming was going to the fringes of their suburbs for a 7-Eleven Slurpee" (his words, not mine).

The rap fan couldn't have been fine arts painter Dante Silva. His preferences ran to Moby, Philip Glass, New Age, ambient, and space music. And if Joy's father had been pulling shots of espresso tonight (which he did on occasion, when he wasn't traveling the globe brokering deals for the planet's finest micro-lots), opera or classical would have been playing right now. Unless Matt was feeling manic, in which case he'd be blasting the sort of synthpop electronica he routinely partied to in European and Brazillian dance clubs.

Unfortunately, what greeted me as I entered the Blend was none of the above.

Rich man's got his dope, homey

Yo, he need that hit!
All his bitches get a taste
'Cause he think he the shi—

"Okay," I murmured. "This ends *now.*"

I crossed the floor to the espresso bar, which appeared to be abandoned of all human oversight. "Hello!? Hello?!" I slapped my hand on the marble counter. "Is anyone here!"

"Don't start buggin', lady! I'm coming!"

Esther, another of my part-time baristas, emerged from the back pantry area loaded down with paper cups, sip lids, heat sleeves, and coffee stirrers. "Oh, it's just you, boss," she said upon seeing me. Then she dumped the stock on the counter and began to sort it out.

An NYU comparative literature major, Esther Best (shortened from Bestovasky by her grandfather) had untamed dark hair, currently stuffed into a backward Yankee cap; a pleasantly plump figure, now swathed in our blue Village Blend apron; and large brown eyes that were constantly on the lookout for anything that might require her critical observation.

"I'm glad to see you restocking." I folded my arms. "But why are you playing *rap* on our sound system? You know the rules."

"Yeah, yeah . . ." Esther pushed up her black rectangular glasses, rolled her dark eyes, and in an oh-so-droll tone began to recite my playlist playbook. "No rap, hip-hop, heavy metal, or arena rock." She took a theatrical breath. "No polkas, bagpipes, Broadway show tunes, military marches, or anything recorded by Ethel Merman. Oh, and . . . wasn't there one more verboten type of music on your list?"

"Yes," I replied. "Anything by Wagner. But that's not my rule. It's Madame's."

I personally enjoyed Wagner's epic compositions. But if approaching Nazi tanks had forced me and my family to flee our beloved Parisian home with little more than the clothes on our backs, I probably would've banned Adolf Hitler's favorite composer from being played in my coffeehouse, too.

"Look," said Esther in the sort of can't-you-be-reasonable tone I'd heard a thousand times from my daughter, "the CD's only been playing about fifteen minutes. Nobody's complained. There's only one more song. Can't we let it finish?"

I glanced around the room. It was almost midnight, and there were only three customers left in the place. An Asian man and East Indian woman were nursing lattes with heads bent together in a first-date-passionate conversation. They didn't appear to be bothered by the music. Neither did the young white guy in a black leather blazer, lounging near the crackling fireplace, bopping his blond, spiky head to the beat of the rapper's profane chant.

"Fine, Esther," I said. "I'll let it go this *one* time . . . but what the heck possessed you to put it on in the first place?" Like all of my baristas, Esther had a preferred playlist — one that seemed much more aligned with her feminist sensibilities. "What happened to your Fiona Apple, Liz Phair, Siouxsie and the Banshees mix?"

Esther shrugged.

"What does that mean?" I pressed. "You like rap now?"

"My boyfriend's into it. He brought the CD over special and everything, you know? The least I could do was play it for him."

Hold the phone. "Boyfriend?" Ever since I'd known Esther, she'd dated here and there. But never before had she used that "antiquated, *Leave It to Beaver* term" — as she'd once deemed it.

"He's right over there."

Esther pointed across the room toward that wiry young blond man; he was still bobbing his head to the rap. Just then, he looked over at us. He stared for a moment, then winked at Esther and gave her a little wave.

Esther sweetly waved back. "Isn't he cool?" she murmured out of the corner of her mouth. "He's waiting for me to get off."

I raised an eyebrow, more than a little curious about the young man who'd finally cracked Snark Girl's hard-as-a-hazelnut shell.

"Where did you meet him?" I asked. Something about the combination of his angular face, stiff posture, and outer-boroughs clothes told me this little guy was way too street hardened to be an NYU student. And I'd bet the contents of to-night's register drawer that underneath the dude's black leather blazer was a mass of tattoos.

"I met him a few weeks ago," Esther said, "at a Park Slope poetry slam. He read, too. He was awesome."

"What's his name?"

"Actually . . . he hasn't told me yet."

"What?"

Esther shrugged. "He wants me to call him by his handle."

"Which is?"

"BB Gun."

Good Lord. I stepped around the counter and pulled Esther aside. "How much do you know about this guy?"

Esther shrugged. "Enough."

"That's not an answer."

"Oh, boss, you're way too suspicious of people. I appreciate your concern, but you don't have to worry. He still lives with his mother."

"Esther, that's no recommendation! Serial killers live with their mothers!"

What is it with these girls? The more mysterious the "dude," the more irresistible they find him! Joy was no different. And, although it pained me to admit it, neither was I — at their age, anyway. When I was nineteen, I'd known next to nothing about my ex-husband, yet I'd let myself fall completely in love with him.

I'd been spending the summer in Italy with my father's relatives, making a study of Renaissance art. Matt was a few years older. He'd been traveling through Europe, visiting friends along the way. When our paths crossed on an Italian beach, that's all I'd known about Matteo Allegro. Still, I let him take me to bed, again and again — until I'd come home from my European vacation pregnant with Joy and agreeing to wed a young man who believed the "fidelity thing" was an optional rider to any marriage vows.

"Esther, are you hearing me? Am I getting

63

through?"

"Boss, get a grip."

I glanced at the young man again. "Don't you think a nickname like BB Gun should send up a red flag?" I whispered. "Don't you think that boy could be violent?"

Esther rolled her eyes. "It's just a handle. On the Internet, I call myself Morbid Dream Girl, but I don't go around dispensing nightmare-inducing hallucinogens."

"True . . . but you *do* like being morbid."

"Goth's my human condition. I can't help it. Anyway, BB thinks I'm deep."

I frowned. Not sure what to say to that.

"Listen, boss . . ." Esther put a hand on my shoulder. "BB's been crushin' on me since he heard me recite at the slam. He's been taking me to dinners and movies and paying for *both* of us — that's a first. And tonight he brought me the CD. I appreciate your concern and everything, I really do, but would you *butt out* of my love life? It's really not your business."

I bristled for a second, ready to tell her smartly that her love life was *absolutely* my business when it involved playing profane lyrics over the Village Blend's sound system, but I zipped my lip.

I was obviously still in mother hen mode after coming away from my daughter, and while it was true that Matt, Madame, and I all felt that our employees were part of the Village Blend "family," Esther was right. She deserved her privacy, and, frankly, the last thing I wanted to do was drive away a well-trained employee. I was short-staffed as it was, and good technique didn't emerge overnight in this business; it came with hours and hours of repetitive practice. (Top coffeehouses, ours included, required a barista to train at least three months before pulling even one espresso for a customer.)

Despite her occasional crankiness, Esther really had blossomed as a barista. Her espressos were top-notch, and her latte art skills were nearly at the competitive level. And while I didn't like her new boyfriend's taste in music, Esther did seem much less depressed than usual; her jaded eyes were unusually bright, and her pale-as-a-vampire skin was actually flushing with anticipation.

"Okay, you win. I'll butt out," I said, but couldn't stop myself from adding, "Just . . . don't get carried away too fast. Get to know him."

"Duh. Why do you think he's here?"

"Right," I said. "Tell you what, since he's waiting for you and everything, why don't you just get going now?"

"Really?" Esther checked her watch and

pointed to the inventory on the counter. "What about restocking?"

"Don't worry. I'll close."

Amazingly, Esther, queen of the jaded, actually *grinned.* "Thanks, boss!" she said. Minutes later, my love-struck barista and her new boyfriend were off — and so was the rap music.

In blessed silence, I took off my pinstriped suit jacket, rolled up the sleeves of my blouse, tied on my Village Blend apron, and began restocking. I cleaned the tables next, swept the floor, and emptied the garbage cans.

I'd just finished counting the register drawer when I heard the bell over our front door ring. I cursed myself for not locking up after those last two customers wandered out. Looking up, however, I saw it wasn't a customer. The man walking in was *my* boy-friend.

FOUR

The tall, broad-shouldered police detective entered my coffeehouse like he always did, with the commanding authority of a seasoned New York cop. In one sober sweep, he scanned the room to take note of his surroundings, then his arctic-blue gaze came to rest on me and, ever so slightly, his expression melted.

"Hi, Clare."

"Hi, Mike."

In a city that hardened everyone — from little old church ladies to pretty-in-pink sorority girls — cops were the hardest cases of all. Mike Quinn was no exception. A square-jawed New York native, he had a long, powerful physique, short, sandy-brown hair, a dry sense of humor, and a load of street smarts from his years working a uniformed beat.

Like your typical poker-faced soldier of law enforcement, Mike didn't give much away, but I'd been serving him double-tall lattes for well over a year now, and I knew how to read him.

Today, for instance, had been a hard one for him. The shadows under his eyes told me he was coming in here with the weight of a long shift on his shoulders. And the tension in his rugged face told me he hadn't accomplished what he'd set out to.

"You closed?" Mike asked, his expression still stiff as he swept the empty room once more.

"Depends," I teased.

"On what?"

"On what you're here for."

Mike strode across the wood-plank floor. He took his time stripping off his overcoat, a nicely tailored cinnamon-colored garment, which he'd finally exchanged for that battered old trench he wore in warmer weather. Then off came the beige sport coat, revealing a white dress shirt, slightly wrinkled by the leather straps of his shoulder holster. The butt of his service .45 peeked out from beneath his left arm — a turn-on for me; shameful, but a turn-on nonetheless.

He dumped his coats on one of the high chairs at the espresso bar and sat down. Then he glanced back up, right into my openly admiring eyes.

Since his wife had left him for a younger Wall Street whiz, Mike had been working out a lot more. His upper body was looking more muscular these days, and other parts of him were presumably tighter. This was pure speculation on my part, since (to my growing frustration) our first month of dating had remained chaste.

Oh, sure, there'd been kissing and touching (okay, *plenty* of kissing and touching), but although he was legally separated, Mike made it clear that he didn't want us to rush the stages of our fledgling relationship. There were five of these little suckers, according to Mike, and we'd only progressed from stage one to two. What would catapult us to three? I didn't have a clue.

I figured Mike was gun-shy — understandable, given the lying, cheating, and bipolar nightmares his wife had put him through (like the time she'd left a note informing Mike that she'd pulled the kids out of school and used his nearly maxed-out credit cards to fly them to Florida's Disney World for a few days — a passive-aggressive reaction to a morning argument).

One thing I was sure of with Mike and me: sexual chemistry wasn't an issue. Since we'd first met, he and I had flirted openly with each other. He'd been a loyal friend to me during some bad patches, always sticking his neck out to help. In return, I'd tried to be a good listener as he unloaded the problems of his perpetually rocky marriage. Because he was married, however, we'd never pushed for more. But now that he was separated, his wife was living with another man, and we were finally dating, I saw no reason to veil my attraction.

And, clearly, neither did he.

The moment Mike realized I'd been admiring his physique, his sandy eyebrows arched, and he turned the tables, taking his own good time looking me up and down.

Super, I thought, remembering my wretched state.

At the start of the evening, my French-twisted hair had been semi-neat at best. Now I could feel stray strands slipping all over my head. My fitted cocoa suit had been sort of sexy, but I'd taken off the snug jacket to do the closing chores, and I was pretty sure my Village Blend apron held all the allure of a granny smock.

"So, Detective?" My grin turned into a smirk as I loudly blew a loose strand of chestnut hair out of my face. "Make a decision yet? Do you know what you want?"

"The same thing I always want when I

come here, Cosi . . ."

"And what's that?"

A slow, suggestive smile lifted the weariness in his face. "Stimulation."

I blinked, speechless for a moment since the sudden rush of blood to certain parts of my body put a strain on my ability to form words.

"Well, then . . ." I finally managed. "Why in the world are you just sitting there? If you want to be served right, you'll have to come around my counter."

He did. Inside of five seconds, Mike was pulling me into his arms. He kissed me deep and long, his hands roving over me, and I felt something different in him . . . something new. He tugged loose the strings at my neck and waist, yanked the apron off me, and tossed it aside.

My arms lifted high to pull down his head again and get back to the kissing, but the moment my hands locked around his neck, he began dancing me backward —

"Mike?"

With a slight bump, my back end hit the wide work counter beneath the marble espresso bar. He reached behind me, shoving aside two empty milk-foaming pitchers. Then his hands were on my hips, lifting me up. He set my bottom on the cleared

71

counter and stepped between my stocking-clad legs.

"Mike!"

He smiled. "You're serving stimulation, Cosi. Don't hold back now."

This was the most sexually aggressive he'd ever been with me. My skirt was hiked up, his strong thighs between my own, making me understand that there was absolutely no issue with his physically wanting me. With a groan, he started kissing me again, pressing into me.

"Whoa, Mike," I murmured against his mouth. "You know there's a perfectly good bed upstairs."

"I know . . ." His lips moved off mine, trailed kisses along my jaw. "And if I had time, we'd be on it right now."

"You mean it?" I gently pushed at his chest.

He leaned back. "Clare, I've been on duty for the past ten hours, and all I can think about is *you.*"

"Really?"

He sighed, rubbed his bloodshot eyes. "I think about you every day, Clare, and every night. Especially at night. I'm losing sleep. I *had* wanted to wait a little longer, make sure things were right . . ." He paused, letting his voice trail off, as if he wasn't sure what to say next.

"What do you mean *right?*" I pressed.

"Just that . . ." He shook his head. "Forget it. I can't wait anymore, sweetheart. You're messing with my focus on the job. We can't have that."

"No, we can't," I said, practically giddy. "So let's go upstairs."

Mike checked his watch and sighed. "I'm only being spelled for thirty. Not that I couldn't make the earth move in that time —" He smiled. "But there's no way I want our first time to be a quickie."

"Yeah . . . I don't want you leaving me — after. Come back later, when you're off, when you can stay."

"Okay . . ." He nodded, kissed me again. Then he lifted me off the counter.

"Come on up to the duplex in the mean-time," I told him, tugging my skirt back down over my thighs. "I'll press you a pot of my new Morning Sunshine Blend before you have to get back. It's a Full City roast, so it has more caffeine than your regular latte, and stimulation *is* my business."

"You don't have to tell me."

He grabbed his blazer and overcoat off the bar chair, and I picked up my apron. Then I switched off the main lights and, before heading upstairs, *finally* locked the front door, vowing never to tell Esther that, thanks to her genius boss, a Blend customer could have walked in on something a lot more obscene than rap music.

"So what's the job tonight?"

Standing at the marble counter, I pushed the plunger down on the French press. The coarsely ground beans filled the apartment's cozy kitchen with arousing, floral notes. Mike made a show of inhaling the aroma.

"Mmmm . . . nice," he said, his eyes following my every move as I filled our mugs. Then I bent over to grab a carton of half-and-half from the fridge's bottom shelf, and Mike murmured, "Even nicer . . ."

I turned around. "Mike, did you hear me? I asked what's up with your job tonight."

The detective arched an eyebrow. "If you want me to focus, Cosi, then *don't* bend over in front of me."

"Mike!"

"What?" He plucked the carton of half-and-half from my hand and dumped a little splash of light into his pool of black. "You have no idea how distracting that ass of yours is."

O-kay, I thought, *the man's definitely ready to shift us into another gear.* This was fine with me, except for the fact that he was out of here in twenty, and I didn't appreciate being left hot and bothered for the next few hours.

"Go ahead," I warned, "keep up the suggestive talk, and *see* if you make it out of here unmolested. Now *focus,* will you, Detective?"

"I'll try," Mike said behind smiling eyes. Then he downed a few healthy swigs of my coffee and sighed, letting the hot, fresh blend revive him.

MRRROOOOOW!

The sudden jaguar yell echoed off the kitchen walls. I glanced around to find its source, which was not in fact a 300-pound carnivore, but a 10-pound female house cat with the lungs of a famished jungle beast.

MRRROOOOOW!

"Sounds like you forgot to feed Java," Mike remarked, glancing around. "Where is she? Java!"

"I'll have you know I fed her a delicious dinner. She's just protesting now because all she got was cat food."

"Excuse me? She is a *cat,* isn't she?"

I shook my head. "You just don't understand . . ."

White whiskers and two coffee bean–colored paws peeked out from under the kitchen table. Then Java's whole furry form slinked out, and she began to rub herself against Mike's leg. He reached down to scratch her head.

"Watch out," I warned. "She'll think you're a soft touch."

"I am." Mike met my eyes. "Depending on the feline."

He gently picked up Java and set her on his lap. Parts of my body melted as Mike's hand steadily stroked her: long, sweet, gentle strokes. I sighed. *Lucky cat.*

"Okay, I'll bite," Mike said. "If she doesn't want cat food, what does she want?"

"Human food, of course." I folded my arms. "She probably smells the butter-browned lobster on my breath from dinner. Sorry, Java honey, I ate every bite. No leftovers."

MRRROOOOOW!

Mike laughed. "I can see that went over well."

"Here . . ." I went to the cupboard, found a can of Pounce kitty treats. "Give her a few of these. They're lobster *flavor.* Not the real thing, but then she doesn't have the bank account for a Solange entrée. Actually, neither do I. Madame footed the bill tonight. Anyway, they should tame Java's hungri-tude for awhile."

"Hungri-tude?" He popped the can. Java's ears instantly perked up.

"It's what you get when hunger and attitude collide in a self-actualized female tabby."

Java jumped down, and Mike threw her a few of the triangular-shaped treats. My companionable but languorous feline began scampering across the floor like an excited kitten, catching and eating each tiny triangle as if it were a fat mouse.

I might have accused the cat of having no shame, but then I probably would have joined her on the floor if Mike had started throwing out some of those champagne-poached oysters I'd devoured earlier in the evening.

Since Pounce treats were all he was tossing, however, I sat my "distracting ass" down across the table and lifted my own coffee mug. The swallow I took was long and satisfying. My Morning Sunshine was an even cleaner and brighter experience than our regular Breakfast Blend, thanks to my ex-husband.

Matteo had found us an exquisite crop of Yirgacheffe during a trip to Ethiopia, so I decided to make good use of it by creating the special blend. I savored the hints of lemon and honey blossom that the Yirgacheffe brought to the party. They also provided an amazingly juicy finish — the kind of salivation you'd get after a luscious bite of citrus fruit.

It was the perfect cup for my morning customers, because I'd stopped the roasting process at medium, so a healthy mug of it provided a higher caffeine content than a demitasse of espresso.

In my professional opinion, my Morning Sunshine was a superb, eye-opening coffee to wake up with — whatever time of day one needed waking. And I could certainly see, from Mike's weary demeanor, he needed it tonight.

"So . . . what's your duty?" I asked him again.

"I'm supervising three undercover teams at three different nightclubs." Mike tossed Java another treat. This time she rose up on her hind legs and caught the treat with her two front paws.

Mike pointed. "Look at that. Java does tricks."

"She's just showing off for her new boy-friend."

Mike laughed and threw another treat.

"So tell me what's happening at the nightclubs. Drug sales? Assaults?"

"Confidence game," he told me.

"A single perpetrator?"

"At least four, probably six. We're calling them the May–September gang."

"May–September?" I murmured, scratching my head. "They only operate in the summer?"

Mike laughed. "No. Good guess though. Care to try again?"

"Sure . . ."

This was our usual routine. Long before we'd started dating, Mike would come into the coffeehouse as a customer, belly up to my espresso bar, and we would get to talking about his cases, from his theories and interrogations to his methods of trapping an array of criminals. I'd learned a lot about detective work, just listening to Mike as he downed his lattes.

The first week we'd started dating, he'd confided to me how happy it made him that I genuinely cared about his work. Apparently, his wife had changed on him early in their marriage, asking him not to bring his job home.

I'd never met Mrs. Quinn, but I couldn't understand how she could shut down her husband like that. I thought Mike's work was admirable and inspiring, not to mention thrilling. The man routinely risked his life to keep the never-ending New York crime wave from touching me and mine.

How could I not want to hear about it?

"May–September, May–September," I repeated, drumming my fingers on the table. "Is the name some kind of a play on the phrase *May–December relationship?*"

"You're getting warmer."

Mike glanced away from Java and moved his attention fully over to me. I gulped a few more hits of caffeine just to stay focused under his intense blue gaze.

"Okay . . ." I said. "If the gang is May–September, then it must mean a younger person and a middle-aged person are involved somehow. Are younger perps setting up middle-aged victims for robberies?"

"You got it." He put the lid on the Pounce treats. Java got the hint. She licked her brown paws, stretched, then trotted off toward the living room. "Looks like I lost my new furry girlfriend."

"Pop the lid on those treats, and she'll be all yours again."

"I see. It's a superficial thing."

"So . . . how are they doing it exactly? The gang?"

"The MO's been the same a half dozen times now. A twentysomething perpetrator picks up a middle-aged target at a nightclub, brings the target to another location, where accomplices initiate the robbery. Sometimes there's violence, other times just some gun pointing. They always leave the victim tied up. CompStat confirmed the pattern, and my captain asked me to form a task force."

"Does that mean this gang's operating beyond the Sixth Precinct?"

Mike nodded. "Lower East Side, Soho, and here in the Village."

"I guess that makes sense . . . I mean, those are the hot spots for nightlife."

"Three clubs seem to be favorite locations for this gang," Mike said. "We've got personnel undercover, posing as nightclub customers."

"You have them well-dressed, I assume. Flashing cash and jewelry? Looking clumsy and drunk, like easy marks?"

"You got it, Cosi." Mike smiled. "Didn't I tell you to sign up for the Police Academy?"

"You know I'm *way* too old for that, Detective. I may be a long way from December, but I'm definitely pushing September. Are women getting hit on as victims in these nightclubs or just men?"

"Women and men. Both have been targets."

"But you haven't had any bites yet?"

The smile left Mike's eyes; he glanced into his cup. "Nothing."

"That's not unusual, is it? I mean, you

81

just started your operation . . ."

"The robberies are getting more violent: pistol whipping, choking to unconsciousness." He frowned, looked away, sipped more coffee. "If we don't tag a lead quickly, I'm concerned we'll be looking at homicides."

I raised an eyebrow. "Maybe you should use me as a decoy."

"I have a lot of plans for using you, Cosi. *None* involve setting you up as bait for a confidence sting."

"Okay, fine . . . as long as one of your plans involves those handcuffs of yours." I put my wrists together in front of me, hoping to lighten his mood again. "Did I mention the bed upstairs is a four-poster?"

My little joke seemed to perk up Mike faster than another hit of Sunshine. He smiled, rubbing his chin, but he wasn't taking the bait where the handcuffs were concerned.

"So tell me how *your* little investigation ran?" he asked, pointedly changing the subject, which was probably smart, considering we had zero time to act on the other subject.

"My investigation?" I knocked back more coffee, refilled my mug.

"Come on, Clare. You mentioned going to

Joy's restaurant tonight, and I know you didn't choose it for the ambiance. You went to check up on your daughter, right?"

"Right. I admit it. Wasn't that easy? And you didn't even have to beat it out of me."

"Well? How did it go?"

"Not very well, I'm sorry to tell you."

"Why not?"

Mike's brow knitted as I recounted my evening, from the schizoid dinner of perfect food and lousy coffee to my daughter being threatened by a knife-wielding, probably drug-addled sous-chef. When I finally finished, he leaned forward, his mouth tight.

"And *where* was the great Tommy Keitel during all of this?"

"He was missing in action. Joy says he's been disappearing a lot lately, and tonight I saw it for myself. This executive chef came in after dinner service was over — and with this creepy guy named Nick in tow."

"Creepy how?"

"His demeanor, I guess. I mean, I've seen all types in the Village, believe me, but this guy was hard-core intense. His skin was extremely pale, and his brown hair was longish, but not in a trendy way. It just hung there, you know? And he was dressed all in black — which, again, isn't exactly atypical for New York. But these clothes weren't in the least fashionable. He didn't utter a word to me, even after we were introduced, and he wore these pointy boots and a black leather blazer, the kind the outer-boroughs guys wear."

I suddenly thought of Esther's boyfriend. BB Gun had been wearing a black leather blazer that was a lot like Nick's.

"Anything else you remember?" Mike asked.

"Yeah. When Tommy introduced me to Nick, he said the man was from Brighton Beach."

"Brighton Beach, huh? That area of Brooklyn is full of Russians."

"So?"

"So it's a long way from Manhattan. Why's Keitel hanging with a guy like that?"

"I can't imagine."

"Yes, you can, Clare. The black leather blazer's a popular rag with the wiseguys. Do you know if Keitel owns his restaurant?"

"He doesn't." I related what I'd overheard during Brigitte's meltdown. "One of the men on the staff loudly reminded Brigitte that she was under contract just like Tommy Keitel."

"So." Mike paused, put down his cup. "Tommy doesn't own the restaurant. Which means he answers to an owner — or owners. And restaurants like Solange aren't cheap. Starting a place like that must cost a cool million —"

"Six."

"No."

"Yeah. David Mintzer told me it costs around six million to get a-two-hundred seat restaurant off the ground in midtown Manhattan. And to maintain it, the cost is something like five to eight hundred dollars per square foot per month, just for rent."

Mike whistled. "I guess that's why a martini in those joints costs eighteen bucks."

"And a lamb chop is forty-four. Yeah, that's why."

"Well, there you go," Mike said. "The picture seems clear enough to me."

"What picture?"

"Put the pieces together, Clare. Somebody with big money is backing Tommy's restaurant. Tommy goes missing from dinner service. Nobody knows why or where he's gone. Then he shows up late with some creepy guy in wiseguy rags from Brighton Beach —"

"You're saying Nick's attached to the Russian mob? That Tommy got his financing by way of some corrupt gangsters from the eastern bloc?"

Mike leaned back, folded his arms. "You

know and I know the Italian mob has a long history of funding food-related businesses in New York. They practically owned the Fulton Fish Market before Giuliani cleaned it up. And where the Italians have lost ground, the Russians have been moving in to take it up."

"I don't know . . ." I shook my head. "Mob or no mob, the problem from my point of view isn't Tommy and his backers. I mean, factoring out the man's recent neglect of his responsibilities, the real danger to my daughter is Brigitte Rouille, and that's all I care about . . ."

I stood up and began to pace the small kitchen. "If I could just find some way into that restaurant, I could keep an eye on things, make sure Brigitte doesn't freak on my daughter again . . . Maybe I could even help the woman . . . get her to admit she has a drug problem . . ."

Mike cleared his throat. "Uh, Clare . . ." He lifted his coffee cup and pointed to it.

"What?" I stopped pacing. "You want a refill?"

"No." He laughed. "I mean . . . *yes*, I'd love more. But that wasn't my meaning."

"Excuse me?"

"Didn't you tell me Solange's coffee was

abysmal? You said it tasted like . . . What was it?"

"Mississippi swamp mud. Although I've never actually tasted mud from the mighty Mississippi, so it's technically an unfair comparison."

"And didn't you help out David Mintzer this past summer? Setting up the coffee service at his new Hamptons restaurant?"

"Yeah, sure." I shrugged. "I roasted blends especially for his place, created a coffee and dessert pairings menu, and — Oh, yes! I see where you're going! I can do the same thing for Solange!" I started pacing again. "Tomorrow, I can go back. I can make a sales pitch to Keitel and Dornier!"

"Dornier? Who's Dornier?"

"Napoleon Dornier is Solange's maître d' and wine steward." I folded my arms and tapped my chin, thinking aloud. "Since he's responsible for the front of the house, he's got as much say in the beverage service as Keitel, so if I can't persuade Tommy, I'll work on Nappy. He struck me as a prideful man. I can't imagine he thinks it's a good idea to poison a customer's palate at the end of a meal with crap coffee."

Mike nodded. "So there it is. You've got an in."

"I'll give it my best shot anyway. Thanks,

Mike. Thanks for the suggestion."

He smiled. "So how about seconds?"

"Sure. I think you've earned it."

I grabbed the French press pot off the counter, but before I could refill his mug, Mike's strong arm circled my waist. He tugged me onto his lap.

"I meant seconds of something else," he murmured in my ear.

A shiver tore through me as Mike's lips moved down my neck. *Oh, yes* . . . I was exactly where I wanted to be, and if I were a cat, I'd most definitely be purring. There was only one problem —

"Mike . . . I thought you only had thirty."

"We've got at least five left." He tipped his head at the kitchen clock. "Let's make it count." Then his mouth was on mine, and for the next few minutes the only thing I drank in was Michael Ryan Francis Quinn.

FIVE

"I wish you didn't have to go . . ."

Mike and I were standing by the apartment's front door. He was holding me close, stroking my hair, which was now free of its pins and down around my shoulders.

"Three more hours tops, Clare. Then I'll be back."

I nodded, hardly able to believe it. *"Wait,"* I said as he turned to go, "let me get you a key. Then you can just let yourself in and come upstairs, okay?"

"Okay."

Mike smiled as he held out his hand, ready to take that little piece of magic metal — the key to a lot more than my front door. But before it left my fingers, a loud, sharp bang sounded somewhere below us. We froze, realizing a door in the stairwell had opened and closed.

Mike met my eyes. "Are you expecting anyone?"

I shook my head, listened to the footsteps on the staircase. "Could be Joy," I whispered. "She'd be off work by now. Her roommate's in Paris for the next six months. Maybe after what happened tonight, she doesn't want to be alone . . ."

But as the shoes clomped closer, I realized the tread was far too heavy to be my daughter's. Mike and I waited, staring at the apartment's front door as a key scratched into the lock, then came the click-clock of the dead bolt, and the door opened.

"Hey, Clare!"

Oh, no.

Short, black hair on a square-jawed face, Roman nose, cleft chin, and a hard body courtesy of his favorite extreme sports: rock climbing, cliff diving, mountain biking, and meaningless sex (not necessarily in that order). My ex-husband beamed at me through the wedge of swinging wood. He pushed the fissure wider, and his cheesy grin fell.

"Quinn?"

Mike blew out air. "Allegro."

I squeezed my eyes shut, willing away the ruination of my evening. But it didn't work. When I opened my eyes again, Matteo Allegro was still standing in the doorway, his right arm in a white plaster cast, his left shouldering an overstuffed athletic bag. He'd come back to stay.

My ex-husband glanced at me, then glared at Mike Quinn. "What's *he* doing here?"

"Clare and I have been seeing each other for a month now," Mike levelly replied. "And you knew that already, Allegro, so don't be a horse's ass."

Matt flipped his key ring. "Gee, thanks for clearing that up, Detective. Because I thought you might be staking out the place to *arrest* me again."

Quinn shook his head, looked down at me. The warmth had drained from his blue eyes. The chilly cop curtain was back. "I've got to go."

As he began to turn away, I touched the sleeve of his overcoat. "The key," I whispered, holding it out again.

"Can't." He jerked his head toward my ex. "Not if he's here."

I wanted to scream, but it wouldn't have helped. I stood dumbfounded and horrified, watching Quinn's sturdy form stride out while my ex-husband sauntered in. As they passed each other through the doorway, Matt purposely bumped the detective with his bulging canvas bag.

"Grow up, Allegro, will you?" Quinn bit out before continuing downstairs.

Matt moved into the duplex's antique-filled living room and dropped his bag onto the Persian rug. "What's *his* problem?"

"He doesn't have the problem! I do!"

I chased after Mike, following him down to the shop to let him out and lock up again. I tried once more to offer the key, but he absolutely refused to come back with Matt in the apartment. How could I blame him? If the tables were turned, and Mike's estranged wife had appeared with a legal right to use his living space, I would have felt the same way.

"I could come to your place," I offered.

"No." He gently touched my cheek. "It'll be a while before I'm off. You get some rest. I'll drop by tomorrow."

After trudging back up to the duplex, I found Matt in the kitchen, fixing himself a fresh pot of coffee — or at least trying to. With his right arm in that cast, he was making a royal mess of it.

"Clare, this Brita pitcher needs refilling. And the filter needs to be changed." He shook his head at the spilled water on the counter. "How could you not notice?"

"I'll give you something not to notice!" I took off my shoe and hurled it at him.

"Hey!" Matt lifted his cast to fend off my

flying pump. "What's gotten into you?"

"Matt, *why* are you *here?* Four weeks ago, you moved in with Breanne!"

Breanne Summour to be exact, editor-in-chief of *Trend* magazine, aka *Snarks 'r' Us,* as the blogging chef of one snidely reviewed restaurant famously tagged it.

Breanne and Matt had been dating for about a year now. Given my ex's desire for publicity and Breanne's need for a hunky escort to fashionable events, they were a match made in Manhattan, or at the very least the New York tabloids. Every so often, I'd notice their picture in the *Post*'s Page Six or one of the tony glossies at my hair salon: "*Trend*'s top editor is looking especially *perky* tonight on the arm of international coffee broker Matteo Allegro."

Matt continually claimed his "friendship" with Breanne was just "casual," which in Matt-speak naturally included casual sex. But then Matt broke his arm, and Breanne turned into Florence Nightingale. This was perfectly fine with me, since the trashionista's new desire to nest with my ex got him the heck out of my hair for almost a month. So why was he back *now?*

"You can't tell me you got tired of five-hundred-dollar Egyptian cotton sheets and a penthouse view!"

Matt shrugged. "Breanne flew to Milan a few days ago for a trade show. I got lonely."

"You did not. I know when you're lying, Matt. Your eyes go wide, like a begging puppy dog, and you forget how to blink."

"Okay, okay . . ." Matt held up the hand of his good arm. "The truth is . . . ever since Breanne left for Europe, her housekeeper has been hitting on me."

"What?!"

"It was subtle at first, but tonight it got weird. And the housekeeper's a live-in, so there's no escaping it."

"Since when can't you handle a woman making a pass at you?"

"The housekeeper's not a woman, Clare. His name's Maurice."

"Of course!" I threw up my hands. "If it was a woman, it wouldn't have been a problem. You simply would have slept with her until Breanne came back. Problem solved."

Matt's face fell into an "I'm wounded" pout. "That's just not true, Clare. And it's not fair."

"The person it wouldn't have been fair to is *Breanne!*"

"Let's drop it, okay?" he said and pointed to the half-spilled pitcher we used to filter our coffee-making water. "Are you going to help me with this or not?"

"Not!"

I wheeled and limped angrily out of the kitchen, one foot now shoeless, the other clomping loudly along, since I was unwilling to give up a second possible projectile.

Matt followed, his tone more contrite. "I didn't mean to butt in on you, but a decent hotel room in this town is four hundred a night. Breanne's not coming back for a few more days, and in case you haven't noticed, I've been footing the tuition bills for Joy's culinary school. I don't have much extra cash to throw around. Do you?"

"What are you implying? That I should pay for your hotel room because you can't tell Maurice the housekeeper to keep his hands to himself?"

"There's no lock on Breanne's bedroom door. It was creeping me out. You have to believe me."

"I can't *believe* I'm having this conversation!" I checked my watch. "And at nearly one in the morning!"

Matt rubbed the back of his neck. "You mind giving me a massage? My muscles are really stiff."

"You really want the other shoe, don't you?"

"What did I do *now?*"

"God, Matt, you haven't acted like this much of a jerk since we were married. What's happened to you anyway? Did a month of having your every whim fulfilled regress you back to a spoiled childhood?"

"My childhood was anything but spoiled, Clare, and *why* are you so bent out of shape? Because I walked in on your big good-bye scene with the flatfoot? Well, big deal! So what? He was leaving anyway!"

"He was *supposed* to come back. Now he's not."

"You're better off. You can't trust cops. Especially that one."

"Oh, is that right? And who am I supposed to trust? You?"

"I'm not your problem. He is."

"The problem is *you,* Matt. He won't come back with you here."

"Then he's gay."

"Mike Quinn is *not* gay."

"Oh, yeah? Then why didn't he just take you with him back to his place?"

"Because he's not going back to his place. He's going back on duty!" I threw up my hands. "I can't expect you to understand. And I shouldn't have to explain myself, either. We're divorced, Matt. We share a daughter and a business; and because of Madame's bizarre sense of humor — not to mention her delusion that one day we're going to reconcile — we *both* have a legal right to use this apartment. But we're never again sharing the matrimonial bed, and I'd like to find someone who will."

"Oh? So now the flatfoot is more than a passing law enforcement fetish? He's potential husband material? And this happened after a month of his *not* sleeping with you?"

I threw the second shoe.

"Hey!" Matt lifted his cast again, and it bounced off. Then he actually had the nerve to *grin* at me. "Looks like you're out of ammo!"

"Arrrrrgggggh!"

"Come on, Clare. Truce? How about we for call for pizza? Sal's delivers all night."

"I'd rather reload with a closet *full* of shoes!"

I wheeled and stormed out of the living room. My adrenaline had been pumping, and I had no interest in going to bed, but I had to get away from Matt. Unfortunately, he didn't get the hint. Matt's footsteps followed mine right up the duplex's short staircase and into the master bedroom.

Madame had decorated this duplex years ago, when she'd lived here with Matt's father. Not only had she filled the place with amazing antiques, she'd lined the walls —

bedroom and marble bath included — with lovingly framed sketches, doodles, watercolors, and oils that had been created over the decades by artists who'd frequented the Village Blend, from Edward Hopper and Jackson Pollack to Andy Warhol and Jean-Michel Basquiat.

The four-poster bed of carved mahogany was one of my favorite pieces in the master bedroom, and it didn't even completely dominate the space. Commanding just as much attention on the opposite wall was a carved hearth of ivory-colored marble. A century-old, gilt-edged French mirror hung above the fireplace, and a chandelier of pale rose Venetian glass hung from a fleur-de-lis medallion in the center of the ceiling.

The walls had been painted the same pale rose as the imported chandelier, while the door and window frames echoed the same shade of ivory as the marble fireplace and silk sheers covering the floor-to-ceiling casement windows.

It was a stunning room in a spectacular apartment, which was unbelievably convenient for me, since the Blend was just two flights down. And, until this evening, I hadn't seriously considered giving up the use of it. Affordable apartments were scarce in Manhattan and rent-free, fully furnished duplexes in the West Village weren't just unheard of, they were a fairy tale come true.

Unfortunately for me, this fairy tale came with a troll — one who seemed to take delight in popping up at the worst possible times. Matt's constant world traveling usually kept him out of the picture. A few days a month, tops, he'd need to crash in the second bedroom. But since he'd broken his arm, Matt had grounded himself. That hadn't been *my* problem until this minute.

"Come on, Clare," Madame's son cooed to me, "let's not fight . . . There's another reason I'm here, you know, not just Breanne's horny housekeeper —"

"Get out of this bedroom!"

"Not until you hear me out."

Matt took a step closer. I folded my arms and frowned, trying not to notice how well the troll happened to be put together tonight, with black wool slacks that were perfectly creased and pleated, a pale yellow cashmere sweater that was probably softer than kitten fur, and an Italian-made bronze jacket cut from a leather so supple it looked good enough to eat.

Matt wore clothes well. No doubt about it. But for years, as the Blend's coffee buyer, he rarely wore anything fancier than sturdy hiking boots, well-worn jeans, and fraying rock band T-shirts.

Trekking the Third World's high-altitude coffee farms for the choicest cherries was light-years from a fashion show runway, which is why I was sure tonight's obviously pricey outfit had been handpicked by Breanne. This was nothing new, of course. Since they'd started dating, Bree had been dolling up Matt like one of *Trend's* cover models. She'd probably paid for the garments, too, or gotten them gratis from one of her designer friends.

"What is it you want to say to me, Matt? Make it quick."

"I miss you," he declared, his big brown bedroomy eyes wide.

"You do not."

"Do, too."

I folded my arms. "You're not blinking."

Matt pointed to his eyes and blinked. "I miss you, Clare. I miss your . . . down-to-earthedness —"

"My *what?*"

"I miss your smile, your wisecracks, your coffee —"

"You have no shame, you know that? I don't think there's one decent bone in your body."

"No, Clare. There's where you're wrong. I have *one* decent bone." Matt held up his

100

right arm, still wrapped in the plaster cast. He shook his head. "Don't you remember *how* this happened to me?"

Damn. I frowned, recalling Matt's flying Zorro act. I'd been on the trail of a murderer, and I'd roped Matt in to helping me. But when the gun went off, it was Matt who threw himself into harm's way, wrestling the killer to the floor. He'd gotten his arm broken for his trouble.

A wave of guilt doused some of the fury I'd been fanning. "I remember, Matt. I do," I told him with a sigh. "And you *know* I'm sorry about what happened. I hated seeing you get hurt like that . . ."

Matt shrugged. "The cast's coming off soon. No big deal. And it was fun letting Bree play nurse for a while. She and her people took good care of me. But you see, Clare . . ." He continued moving across the bedroom. "Breanne isn't the woman I've been thinking about —"

"Stop it, Matt."

"I've been lying in bed alone these past few nights, Clare, thinking of you —"

"Because Bree's *traveling.* And you're a *child.* Out of sight, out of mind."

Matt stopped right in front of me. "Bree isn't the woman I've been wanting to kiss —"

"Have you been drinking?"

"Just a bottle of Riesling."

"An entire bottle?"

Matt grinned and nodded. "Château Bela, Slovakia 2003. Eric Ripert personally recommended it to Bree during a launch party at Le Bernardin. She scored an entire case. I'll tell you, that woman has one impressive wine collection."

"How long ago did you drink it? The bottle?"

Matt shrugged. "It doesn't matter. It's not the alcohol talking —"

"No . . . It's the part of your anatomy that Bree's momentarily neglecting."

Matt laughed. "Say that three times fast. Anatomy, momentarily neglecting." He laughed again.

"You *are* drunk."

"Why do you think I was trying to make coffee?"

I sighed, wondering if Breanne knew this about my ex. Matteo Allegro could calmly hike through a Costa Rican mud slide or fearlessly fight his way out of a Bangkok bar brawl, but when it came to handling the minor curveballs of domestic living, he often needed a flotation device.

Well, at least this time he turned to a 2003 Château Bela instead of a line of Bolivian marching powder. For that, I have to give him credit.

"Okay, Matt, okay. Let's go back downstairs and get you some coffee." I moved to walk around him, but he caught my arm.

"I *am* sorry, Clare, about messing up your date. I really did figure you'd be at Quinn's place. Will you forgive me?"

I took a deep breath and let it out. It wasn't easy to let go of my righteous anger, but I did owe Matt. The cast alone was a reminder of what he'd gone through for me.

"Yes, Matt. I forgive you. All right? Let's move on . . ."

"Okay," Matt agreed, but his left hand failed to release my upper arm. The heat of his fingers penetrated the sleeve of my sheer blouse. His eyes met mine, and he leaned closer.

I leaned back. "Matt . . . that's *not* moving on."

"Just one kiss? I've been so lonely."

"Oh, *please*."

"*One* kiss. What's the big deal? It'll only take a second. Humor me . . ."

"You're really trying my patience tonight. You know that?"

"I just want to know that you really forgive me. One kiss. *Then* we can move on."

"And you'll grow up?"

103

Matt smiled and nodded. "Close your eyes."

With an irritated sigh, I gave in. Standing stiff and still, I closed my eyes. Matt leaned close again and brushed my lips. I figured that was it. We were done. But before I could open my eyes again, his arm was snaking around me, pressing our bodies together, trying to intensify the connection.

"I knew it! I knew I couldn't trust you!"

"You miss me, too, honey. I can *feel* how much. Your body's humming with it —"

"Your ego's working overtime! Mike Quinn's the one who left me humming."

"Is that right? Well, if he *left you* humming, then he's not here to close the deal, is he?"

My jaw clenched.

"Admit it, Clare. The cop's a hard case, and you miss having *fun*." Matt's voice dropped an octave. "So have a little fun with me tonight. What's so wrong with that?"

"Plenty. You want an alphabetized list?"

He moved to kiss me again; I stiff-armed him. Then I turned and marched out of the bedroom in my stockinged feet. Matt followed me down the stairs but not into the kitchen. He stood, leaning one broad shoulder against the doorway. For long, contemplative minutes, he watched me brew him a fresh pot of coffee in our drip maker.

As I poured him a large, black cup, he moved into the kitchen and began struggling out of his leather jacket. I helped him get the folded-up sleeve over his cast. Then I hung the expensive garment on the back of his chair for him.

"Sit," I commanded. "Drink."

He did. I poured him a second cup and gave him two aspirin.

"Thanks," he murmured.

"You're welcome."

"So . . ." he said, his mind obviously becoming clearer. "You really like the cop?"

"It's more than like, Matt."

He rubbed his eyes and sighed. "I figured by now you would have gotten him out of your system, but I can see you need more time." He shrugged. "So have your fling. Just don't give up on us, Clare . . . not yet . . ."

I closed my eyes. "Please, Matt. It's late. You've had too much to drink. I've had too much . . . *frustration*."

I opened my eyes to find Matt leering at me. One dark eyebrow arched. "So my kiss *did* affect you."

Before I could find another shoe, the phone rang.

"Saved by the bell," I told him, picking up the extension. "Hello?"

"Mom! Thank God!"

"Joy? What's wrong?"

Matt was on his feet before I spoke another syllable. "What's the matter with Joy?"

"It's Vinny!" Joy cried from the other end of the line.

"Vinny?" I repeated.

"Who's Vinny?" Matt demanded, breathing down my neck.

"Vincent Buccelli," I quickly whispered, covering the mouthpiece. "He's Joy's friend from culinary school. They're interning together at Solange this year."

"Mom? I don't know what to do!"

"Slow down, honey. Where are you?"

"I came out to Queens after work, to check on Vinny, see how he was doing."

"You told me he called in sick today."

"I found him on the floor, Mom." Joy began to sob. "And there's blood, so much blood!"

"Blood!" I repeated.

"Blood!" Matt shouted.

"Mom, I can't believe it, but I think Vinny's *dead!*"

Six

Our yellow taxi rolled down a dim stretch of paved avenue that ran under the elevated tracks of the Number 7 line. At one in the morning, not even the flashing red beacons of the police and FDNY vehicles could penetrate the cold shadows beneath the subway's rusty girders.

The three-story apartment house where Vincent Buccelli lived sat between an Irish pub that advertised the best hamburgers in New York City (according to the *Daily News*), and a Sherwin-Williams paint store, now shuttered with a steel mesh gate. The area was a typical working-class neighborhood of Queens, filled with immigrants from an array of countries: Korea, Ireland, India, Ecuador, Colombia, and dozens of others.

Tonight, the front door of the redbrick house was open, spilling yellow light from a gold ceiling fixture in the hallway. The building had white-trimmed windows and a short set of concrete steps that led to a roof-less front porch. That's where the cop was standing, a big Irish-faced officer in his thirties. He wore a dark blue uniform and a bored expression as he guarded the building's entrance. Younger, smaller cops were patrolling the sidewalk, keeping a curious crowd of pub crawlers behind yellow crime-scene tape that had been stretched across the pavement.

"Looks like the national doughnut convention's in full swing," Matt muttered next to me in the cab's backseat.

I tensed. The last thing I needed was for my authority-loathing ex to start a fight with the investigating officers, which could land us all downtown, or crosstown, or wherever the local precinct house was in this part of Queens. As Matt fumbled for his wallet with his good arm, I gripped his shoulder.

"Joy's not a suspect," I said. "There's no reason to get upset."

"Not yet," Matt replied, thrusting a fistful of cash at the Pakistani driver.

Matt had sobered up fast the moment Joy had called for help. Knowing we'd be dealing with outer-boroughs cops, he'd grabbed an old Yankees sweatshirt from his bedroom closet. He ripped the bottom of one sleeve to accommodate his cast and — suddenly no longer needing my help — forcibly tugged it over his expensive cashmere sweater.

I'd found my brown pumps, pulled an older parka over my sheer blouse and tight skirt, and we were off, leaving Matt's cover-model leather jacket back where it belonged, in a multimillion-dollar West Village town house.

Now I swung open the cab's door, and the November chill struck me like a hammer. It felt much colder in the borough of Queens. This wasn't my imagination. Frigid wind blasts flowed down from Canada and across New York's waterways, but the buildings were lower in the outer boroughs. Manhattan's moneyed skyscrapers couldn't shield you the same way here.

By the time I'd climbed out of the backseat, Matt's muscular form was already barreling toward the yellow tape. Two cops near the flimsy barrier saw him approach and tensed. Both officers were so young they had to be rookies, and both were at least a head shorter than Matt.

Behind them, on the apartment house's front porch, stood that big Irish-faced officer. He was younger than Matt, but at least a decade older than the rookies. He also watched Matt's approach, but his expression remained bored.

I hurried to catch up to my ex, which wasn't so easy in high heels, and I cursed myself for not taking a minute to dig out my running shoes.

At the police line, Matt grabbed the tape and lifted it. But before he could step under it, a rookie jumped in front of him, jammed a hand into Matt's chest. "Where are you going, sir?" the baby-faced policeman said. His tone was respectful but insistent.

"I need to get inside," Matt forcefully replied. "My daughter's up there."

"It's a crime scene, sir. No one can go in there until the forensics people are finished."

Matt stared down at the kid. The officer's left hand was still on Matt's chest, his right clutched the top of a long nightstick dangling from his belt.

"I know it's a crime scene," Matt replied. "Now take your hand *away* before you *lose* it, flatfoot."

Oh, damn. Here we go . . .

The big cop, guarding the apartment's front door, tucked his hands into his belt and swaggered down the concrete steps and across the sidewalk. His bored expression had suddenly become animated; in fact, he seemed genuinely pleased by the ugly turn of events.

Great, I thought. *And here he is, for your entertainment! A willing subject for a textbook takedown and arrest! My ex-husband!*

"Flatfoot?" the older cop repeated to Matt with a smirk. His hands were still tucked into his belt, but his chest was puffed out like a bantam rooster. "That's real quaint. Who are you, Damien Runyon?"

The younger cops chuckled. The pub crawlers laughed.

"That's *Damon* Runyon, you *moron,*" Matt snapped.

"Uh-oooooh!" a drunk in the crowd cried. "He's in trouble now!"

"Matt, please —" I whispered, tugging his sweatshirt, trying to get him to back down.

My ex turned and looked down at me. I expected him to bark something nasty. But he didn't. He met my eyes and *winked.* "Go!" he mouthed, jerking his head in the direction of the now unguarded steps.

Matt had purposely lured the big cop away from his post by the building's front door. If I was fast enough, they wouldn't be able to stop me. With Matt distracting them, they might not even *see* me.

The older cop ripped away the yellow tape, and it fluttered to the pavement. He faced Matt, toe-to-toe, thumbs still in his belt. He was younger than my ex, but Matt was just as tall and just as powerfully built.

"You got a problem, buddy?" the cop demanded. Beneath his badge I saw the name *Murphy.* " 'Cause if you keep up the attitude, I can make both of your arms match, if you get my drift."

"Yeah, I get your drift," Matt shot back. "And I also have a *problem* with tin-plated *fascists* like you. I've seen enough of them in the backwaters of this world, and let me tell you something, flatfoot, you're all alike —"

I slipped into the shadows, moving forward, past the knot of policemen and up the concrete steps. No one yelled or followed me. Either they hadn't noticed or were too focused on stopping the big, angry jerk wearing that Yankee sweatshirt in the middle of Mets country.

I shook my head as I moved, realizing Matteo Allegro was a whole lot smarter than I liked to give him credit for; but then the man would do just about anything for his daughter, even put a few extra brain cells to work.

Either way, I was inside. Now I had to find Joy.

There were two apartments on the ground floor. Both doors were shut tight. I hurried up the stairs to the first landing. There were two apartment doors here, and both were open.

Warm air poured into the drafty hallway from the apartments, accompanied by a hiss of steam from a nearby radiator. I glanced inside the first door and saw a uniformed officer speaking with an elderly woman wearing a woolen robe.

"I didn't hear a thing, sorry to tell you. I'm a bit hard of hearing," the gray-haired woman said in a faint but discernable Irish brogue.

Inside the second door, I saw a big African American plainclothes detective standing next to a much smaller uniformed officer. The detective was attempting to interview a young Asian couple who'd been roused from their sleep. The husband rubbed his eyes while he spoke in rapid-fire Chinese.

"What did he say, Officer Chin?" the detective asked.

The uniformed officer shook his head. "He's speaking Mandarin."

"So?"

"So your guess is as good as mine, Sergeant Grimes. My people are from Hong Kong, and they speak Cantonese!"

I crept past the door and moved onto the steps that led to the third floor. A bright

113

photoflash suddenly lit the landing above me. Another flash came, and another. I moved halfway up the stairs and paused, listening to the voices coming out of the apartment.

"Tell me why you came here again. I didn't quite get it the first time," a man demanded.

"You heard the message Vinny left on my cell," a young woman replied between sobs. "You *know* why I came here. Why do you keep asking me the same questions?"

"Joy!" I whispered.

I took the rest of the stairs two at a time, reaching the top landing in under a second. There were two doors on this landing. One was shut tight, newspapers and magazines piled up as if the person had been away. The other door was wide-open. I could see a number of officials inside the apartment: the first was a young man in a dark blue police uniform. He was standing in the small entryway. The second was an older, wider man in a gray suit, but I could only see his back. The third man in a dark nylon jacket was holding a small digital camera and snapping photos. A woman in the same kind of jacket was stooped over something on the floor.

I could only see bits and pieces of the

room from here: there were plants and a large fish tank, some framed posters. I noticed a bank of windows along the front wall were all wide-open for some reason.

Finally, the large man in the gray suit moved aside, and I saw Joy, standing just inside the doorway to the apartment's kitchen. She'd exchanged the chef's jacket and black slacks she'd been wearing at Solange for a white turtleneck and blue jeans. One arm was folded over her stomach. She was wiping away tears with the other, and she was also shivering.

I took a step forward into the short entryway that led to the living room. The uniformed officer who'd been standing there suddenly blocked my path. "Whoa! Where are you going, ma'am?"

"Let me see my daughter!" I shouted.

Joy heard me and called out, "Mom!"

I charged, but the officer blocked me again. "Stop, ma'am!"

"Joy, your father and I came as quickly as we could!" I called to her, trying desperately to get around the cop, but he started moving me backward.

"Back up, ma'am!" the young officer warned, his hand moving to his nightstick. "Back up, or I'll have to restrain you!"

"Lopez! It's all right!" called the older

man, the one in the suit who'd been questioning Joy. The detective turned and moved toward us. He had thick, coarse, slate gray hair with bushy eyebrows and a seventies-style mustache to match. His gray, rumpled suit had lapels as wide as Queens Boulevard, and his loudly patterned green and orange tie was obviously chosen by a man who wore neckwear only because he had to.

I was out on the landing now, just outside the apartment's front door. The detective stepped in front of the young officer and took a hard look at me. I looked at him right back, squarely in the eyes — easily done because he wasn't much taller than I, though he was as wide as a fireplug, with beefy hands and an olive complexion.

"How did you get up here?" he asked. "This is a crime scene."

"I just want to talk to my daughter."

"Let my mom come in!" Joy cried from inside. "I want to talk to her!"

The detective turned his head. "Stay put in that kitchen, Ms. Allegro! And stay quiet!"

He turned back to me. "How did you know to come here?"

"My daughter called me on her cell phone before she called you." I frowned and put my hands on my hips. "*Look,* she's the one

116

who *found* her friend and notified you. Why are you treating her like a criminal?"

The man folded his arms and scowled. "Fifty percent of the time, the person who 'finds' the body is the person who killed the body."

"Then I was wrong." My eyes narrowed. "I *thought* we could trust the police, and that's what I told my daughter. But I guess I should have told Joy to leave here immediately and forget what she saw."

The man's hard expression changed after that. He didn't exactly turn apologetic, but the scowl had lessened considerably. He exhaled, glanced at Joy a moment, and then turned back to me. "I *will* let you speak with your daughter, but I'd like to talk to you first, Mrs. —"

"Ms.," I said. "Cosi. Clare Cosi."

"And Joy *Allegro* here is your daughter?"

"I've gone back to my maiden name — if that's all right with you." I put my hands on my hips. "If not, my ex-husband's downstairs. You *could* consult him."

The man didn't blink. He yanked a big radio off his belt. "Murph? It's Ray," the detective said into the device. "You got a guy down there says he's the girl's father?"

I could hardly hear the reply. "No, don't arrest him. Just keep him there. Lock him

117

up in the car if you have to. Just make sure he doesn't come up here." The detective shot me a dark look. "Like his old lady."

I folded my arms. "That's *ex*–old lady."

"I'll get back to you, Murphy," the detective said, and returned the radio to his belt.

"All right, Detective," I said. "You know my name. Would you please tell me yours?"

"I'm *Lieutenant* Salinas," the man replied. His NYPD badge appeared and disappeared in a quick sleight of hand. "And I'm in charge of this homicide investigation."

I tensed at the word *homicide.*

SEVEN

Lieutenant Salinas cleared his throat. "Did you know the deceased, Ms. Cosi?"

"If it really is Vincent Buccelli, then the answer is yes. I met him a few times."

"You know his family?"

I shook my head. "He moved here from Ohio a few years ago to attend culinary school. As far as I know, any family he has is back in Toledo."

"So you know him because of your daughter?"

"Yes, Vinny and my daughter were friends —"

"Close friends? Boyfriend and girlfriend friends?" Salinas asked.

"Just friends from school and work. Platonic friends. I'm sure Joy has told you all of this."

"She has," he said, "but I'd like to hear it from another source. How well did you know this Buccelli kid, Ms. Cosi?"

"I met him a month ago at a business event. He and Joy came into my coffeehouse several times after that —"

"Coffeehouse?"

"I manage the Village Blend on Hudson Street."

The man paused as if considering his options. He pulled at his loud tie, further loosening the already loose knot. "Maybe you can help us," Lieutenant Salinas said at last.

"I'll try."

"First of all, would you be willing to provide a positive identification? Your daughter refused to look into the corpse's face. Understandable, if they were friends. So would you help us out? Make the ID?"

I frowned. "Right now? This minute?"

"Yeah," he replied with a slightly irked look that said, *When else?*

I took a deep breath. "Okay. Let's go."

Taking my arm, he steered me off the landing and into the one-bedroom apartment. The place was spacious, and the living room looked neat and comfortable with plants and a fish tank. There was a pale green sofa and chair set, a glass coffee table, a small television, and a standing bookshelf filled with cookbooks. All of the framed posters on the walls had something to do with food: an artful photo of fruit, a sidewalk scene at a French café, a colorful day at a farmers' market.

The only sign of violence was a small end table that had been knocked down. Some mail was scattered about, and the phone lay on the floor, its receiver off the hook. I saw a dusting of white powder on the black plastic and realized the police had tested the phone for fingerprints.

An attractive middle-aged woman wearing a dark nylon jacket stood up and approached Lieutenant Salinas. She was petite, with high, prominent cheekbones and dark hair bunched up under a hairnet. She pulled a pair of latex gloves off, exposing long-fingered, mocha-hued hands and fingernails painted a scarlet so deep it was almost black. Behind the woman, the man wearing an identical jacket continued to snap pictures.

"What do we have here, Dr. Neeravi?" Salinas asked.

"This is most definitely a homicide," the woman replied in an East Indian accent. "The victim died from a single blow with a knife to the root of the neck —"

She paused to touch an area of flesh between her neck and shoulder. "The knife was directed downward, coming in at the base of the neck, missing the collarbone, and doing major damage to the great vessels arising from the heart. In short, the victim bled to death."

"You have a time of death?" Salinas asked.

Dr. Neeravi made a face. "That's going to be a problem."

"Come on, Doc," Salinas pleaded. "Give me a ballpark."

"Let me explain. Someone — perhaps the perpetrator — opened all of these windows. Now, perhaps it was done to dissipate any smell from the body, preventing a neighbor from alerting the authorities right away. Or perhaps the perpetrator knew it would help mask the time of the murder. Whatever the reason, the draft streaming through those windows is under thirty degrees Fahrenheit, which means the body's change in temperature is not something I can use to pinpoint an exact time of death."

The doctor tore the hairnet off her head and shook her shoulder-length hair loose. "If pressed, I'd say he was killed one to four hours ago. I'll know more after the autopsy."

"Was the assailant strong?"

I winced, because I knew what Salinas was *really* asking. *Could the killer be a woman?*

"The victim was not overpowered, and there are no defensive wounds because the dead man was struck from behind. Strength wouldn't count as much as skill here, in my opinion. If the blade had struck the victim's collarbone, he probably would have survived."

"*Skill,* eh?" Salinas nodded. "Okay. The assailant may have had knife skills. That's interesting. And there's no sign of forced entry, which means the victim probably knew the person who murdered him."

Dr. Neeravi nodded. "At least casually."

Salinas snorted. "Casually enough to turn his back on his own killer — unless the murderer had a gun or waved the knife as a threat to force the victim to turn."

"Lieutenant," the uniformed officer called. "Look what I found."

Holding it by the edges so as not to smudge any fingerprints, the policeman displayed a copy of a men's magazine — and I wasn't talking *Playboy* or *Maxim.* This was a magazine featuring young, fit men in intimate poses. It was clearly a magazine meant for gay men.

"There's a whole pile of glossy mags just like this one over here, hidden inside this hollow ottoman," the officer added.

"Bag them up," Salinas commanded. "We'll check for prints later. With glossy paper, we might get lucky." He faced me.

"You didn't tell me the victim was homosexual, Ms. Cosi." The lieutenant said this in an accusatory tone, as if I'd been holding it back.

"I didn't know. Joy knew Vinny better than I did. Didn't she mention it?"

Salinas frowned. Said nothing.

"Do you still want my help?" I asked.

"Yes." Salinas turned to Dr. Neeravi. "Can I try for a positive ID?"

The woman nodded. "Sure. The area around the body has been swept and dusted. The ambulance can take the victim to the morgue when you're finished. Just be careful not to step in the blood. It's pretty messy."

Oh, God . . .

Lieutenant Salinas steered me around the couch, and that's when I saw the corpse. Dressed casually in jeans and a T-shirt, Vincent Buccelli lay on his stomach on the polished hardwood floor, sprawled across a brownish-red throw rug. I took a step closer and realized there was no rug, only a drying pool of the dead boy's blood.

"It's him. That's Vinny," I said, pushing my hair back. "I mean . . . That's Vincent Buccelli, Lieutenant." I swallowed hard, steeling my reaction to how violently he'd died.

"You okay, Ms. Cosi?"

I nodded, trying to commit to memory every grisly detail of the crime scene. Vinny's arms were flung wide, though smears of blood on the floor told me he'd flailed around for several minutes.

I looked hard at the knife. Its handle was silver. About an inch of the blade stuck out of Vinny's left shoulder, right at the base of the neck. The rest of the blade had been forced down vertically, deep into his chest. His head was turned, his eyes open but unfocused. The flesh of his face appeared waxy, almost a translucent blue gray; his lips were pale, nearly white; his mouth was gaping and flecked with crusted blood.

I followed the boy's gaze and deduced that Vinny had died staring at the handle of the knife that had killed him — probably in shocked disbelief, if his frozen-in-death expression meant anything.

I closed my eyes, forced back tears.

"The butcher knife went in pretty deep," Salinas observed.

"Yeah," I said, nodding and opening my eyes again. "About nine inches —"

"Huh?"

"That's a ten-inch blade, Lieutenant. And it's not a butcher knife," I corrected. "That looks like a chef's knife . . . more accurately, a *French* knife. It's one of the most commonly used tools in food preparation."

Salinas raised a bushy eyebrow. "And you know this because you're a cook, like your daughter?"

"I know my way around a professional kitchen," I replied, "but I'm not a formally trained chef. I know a lot about knives simply because last Christmas I wanted to buy my daughter a very special chef's knife as a present. And I wanted to find her a really good one."

Salinas opened his mouth.

"And before you ask, this is *not* my daughter's knife sticking out of the dead man."

"You're sure?"

"I'm not an idiot, Lieutenant. It's obvious my daughter's your prime suspect."

"The victim was a cook, right —"

"An aspiring chef," I corrected.

"Yeah, well, he's an *expiring* chef now," Salinas cracked.

The uniformed officer and the photographer both laughed. Even Dr. Neeravi smiled. *Gallows humor,* I thought. Mike Quinn told me it was common at crime scenes — helped relieve the tension. It failed to relieve mine.

"This might be Vinny's knife," I suggested. "You could look around, find his kit, check to see if the chef's knife's missing."

"Thanks for the suggestion," Salinas replied. "But you're a little late."

"I don't understand," I replied.

"We're not idiots, either. We found the dead man's chef kit on the table. All the knives are there."

"So you're telling me that the killer brought the knife?" I asked.

"That's our theory," Salinas answered. "At ten inches, that's not an easy knife to hide. But it's November. People are wearing long sleeves, big coats —" He gestured to my parka.

"I didn't kill him, either."

The lieutenant rolled his eyes, faced the doctor. "What about blood? Would the killer get hit with spray?"

Dr. Neeravi nodded. "Blood would most definitely strike the killer. It's like slicing a tomato — some juice is bound to squirt at you."

Another pleasant image . . . "Excuse me," I interrupted. "But unless I'm completely wrong here, there's no blood on Joy's cloth-ing." I pointed to my daughter peeking out from the kitchen doorway. She'd remained silent and still through everything, sobbing silently and wiping her eyes. "She's wearing a white turtleneck," I pointed out. "Don't you think splattered blood would have been a *tad* obvious?"

"Take it easy," Salinas told me. "There are indications the killer cleaned up after the deed. Towels in the sink, stuff like that. And she could have had a smock or coat, extra clothes and shoes, that she discarded before calling you and us."

"Well, I know my daughter, and I know she could never, not in a million years, do something as brutal as this. I think you know that, too. So I'd like to take her home now —"

"Not yet," the detective shot back.

I stepped close. "Not even if I give you the name of a real suspect?" I whispered. "Someone who worked in close proximity with the victim and had a grudge against him?" I met Lieutenant Salinas's gaze. "Not even if I give you someone who's also been known to attack her fellow workers with a chef's knife, and did exactly that earlier this evening? Because I witnessed it."

The room went completely silent. Salinas and the uniformed cop exchanged glances. Then the detective-lieutenant's bushy eyebrows rose.

"Damn, Ms. Cosi. I'm all ears."

EIGHT

Despite my extremely helpful cooperation with the authorities, Lieutenant Salinas refused to release Joy from informal custody until almost three thirty in the morning. He grilled her, took fingerprints, and had a policewoman search Joy's person and clothing for any clues he could find.

After that, I put my foot down and demanded Salinas release Joy, which he did. To the detective's credit, Salinas realized how hard it would be for Matt, Joy, and me to hail a taxi in this part of Queens in the middle of the night, so he had one of his squad cars give us a lift back to Manhattan.

The driver was Officer Brian Murphy, the big cop Matt had confronted on the street. The policeman didn't say a word on the trip across the Queensboro Bridge and down to the Village. But when he dropped us off on Hudson Street, Officer Murphy did suggest that my ex-husband come back to a certain

Woodside pub and look him up "after the doc cuts that cast off your arm."

Somehow, I doubted the man wanted to buy Matteo a beer.

Joy was too distraught to go back to her empty apartment alone, and I firmly suggested she come back with us to the duplex above the Blend. Matt readily agreed.

By the time we got there, it was four in the morning, and we were exhausted. With Matt's broken arm, I insisted he take the big mahogany four-poster, while Joy took Matt's smaller bed in the guest room. That put me on the downstairs couch.

Matt pulled me aside after Joy went to bed and suggested I join him in the master bedroom. "We can share the bed, Clare. I promise I won't touch you."

His eyes were wide as a puppy dog. He failed to blink even once.

I thanked him very much and headed straight for the living room couch. Now, swathed in flannel pajamas and tube socks, I punched the feather pillow I'd snatched from the closet, pulled a knitted throw over me, and tried to get some sleep.

But sleep wouldn't come. My mind was too agitated. I couldn't let the question go: *Who would want to kill Vinny? Brigitte Rouille might have done it . . .* The woman was obviously unstable, and according to Joy, she'd been picking on poor Vinny so badly that he'd called in sick. But I knew there was a huge gap between picking on a subordinate at work and actually killing him. On the other hand, Brigitte almost slashed my daughter, an event I saw with my own eyes.

As crazy as she'd behaved with Joy, however, I frankly couldn't see Brigitte Rouille bolting out of Solange and hopping a train to Queens to take out her frustrations on Vincent Buccelli in a homicidal bender. That assumption made me feel a little guilty about giving Salinas her name — but only a little.

If Brigitte wasn't guilty of murdering Vinny, then she had little to fear from some police questioning. In fact, maybe a visit from the authorities would inspire the troubled woman to seek some professional help before she did hurt someone.

So who else could have done it? I'd been asking myself this for hours, of course, and after Salinas released my daughter, I'd specifically asked Joy about Vinny's friends or a possible boyfriend. She said he was a loner, and it was totally news to her that he was gay. On the other hand, she confirmed that he'd never talked about having a girlfriend or liking any girl, and he'd certainly

131

never made a pass at her.

If Vinny Buccelli was in the closet, could he have been carrying on some kind of secret gay affair that went badly?

By the end of the evening, Lieutenant Salinas had started asking questions around that exact theory. Vinny could have been the victim of a crime of passion, a gay lover or encounter that had turned deadly. If so, the young man's secret affair could have been with another student at the culinary school or a fellow cook at Solange. Who else would carry a ten-inch French knife around with them?

As I lay there in the living room, watching the slowly breaking dawn lighten the world beyond my French doors, I considered calling Mike Quinn.

I'd thought about Mike earlier, too, while I was waiting for Joy to be released in Queens. But I'd decided not to bother him. He'd been leading his own important task force into the wee hours, and there was little he could have done to influence a man like Salinas anyway. I figured it would be better to let things play out, let Salinas see for himself that there was no reason to suspect Joy of murder.

I'll be seeing Mike soon enough, anyway, I told myself. *I'll ask for his advice when he drops by the coffeehouse.*

Finally, just before five, I dozed off.

Around nine I awoke to the sound of a coffee grinder. I moaned, rolled over on the couch cushions, and pulled the throw up to my neck. Technically, this was my morning to sleep in because Tucker was opening the Blend, but when I heard the sound of laughter a few minutes later, and smelled the aroma of my freshly brewing Morning Sunshine Blend, I sat up.

Voices and another laugh came from the kitchen. I got to my feet, wrapped myself in my baggy terrycloth robe, and approached the kitchen doorway.

"Okay, muffin," Matt's voice declared. "You made coffee for me, so I'll cook breakfast for you."

"With one arm?" Joy replied.

"I can cook an egg with one arm. Just watch me."

I smiled, pausing just outside the room to eavesdrop a little more.

"Step aside, Dad, and I'll cook you the *best* egg you've ever tasted!"

"Better than my famous peppers and eggs?"

"*Much* better," Joy said.

"Then I defer to your expertise."

I heard a chair move and then a clank as a

133

pan hit the stove top. The refrigerator door opened next.

"That's how I got my job at Solange, you know." Joy said. "For my audition, Tommy told me to cook him an egg."

"That doesn't sound like much of a test," Matt said.

"You're wrong, Dad. According to Tommy, it's the simplest ingredients that truly test a chef's skill and imagination — not to mention technique."

I continued to listen, feeling only a little guilty for spying. It was a charming domestic scene that would have warmed my heart a decade ago, when it would have counted. Now it only made me sad and maybe a little resentful, too.

It was so easy for the two of them now. But then Matt always had been the yearned-for parent. Oh sure, he showed for the important moments: birthday parties, school plays, high school graduation. He'd arrive laden with presents and stories about exotic, faraway places. For Joy, those were the good times, with a doting, if temporary, father. And then Matt was gone, before the return of the disappointments, arguments, and frustrations of normal, messy, everyday living.

During Matt's absences, I raised my

daughter as well as I could, but I resented having to be the sole authority figure, the de facto disciplinarian, the spoilsport, the stickler. I was the miser who vetoed things that were too costly, the prude who said no to activities a teenager didn't have the maturity to handle.

"You know, I can make a pretty good egg," Matt said.

"Sure. Uh-huh," Joy said skeptically.

"Don't you remember those peppers and eggs I cooked for your eleventh birthday?"

"That was my *ninth* birthday, Dad. And the answer is yes, I remember —"

"Doesn't seem that long ago."

"That's because you're old now."

"Excuse me, little girl, but those eggs must have been pretty good for you to remember them."

"How could I forget such a disgusting, greasy mess?"

"You've got to be kidding! My peppers and eggs are world famous."

"You should have drained the peppers before you added the eggs."

"Drain the peppers? But that's where the savory flavor is —"

"It's *grease,* Dad. Artery-clogging, cottage-cheese-thigh-creating grease. All it does is make you fat."

"Fat? Do I look fat to you? No, wait, don't answer that. I've been living pretty easy with Breanne, and this arm has interfered with my workouts for the last few weeks."

"Is that why you're getting a paunch?"

I covered my mouth to stifle the snort.

"I do not have a paunch," Matt replied, sounding appropriately irritated. "What are you, size four?

"Six."

"In my opinion, you should eat more. You don't want to end up like the skinny models in Breanne's magazine. They wolf down the catered lunch, then throw it back up right before the shoot."

"Gross," Joy said. "I could never do the bulimia thing, which is too bad, because I love to eat. And my butt's too big."

"Your butt is *not* too big," Matt rightly affirmed. "In fact, you look skinny to me, and nobody trusts a skinny chef. You should pack on a few pounds, just enough to show you like to eat. Look at your *mother* —"

"Ahem!" I exclaimed, deciding it was a good time to cut Matt off.

Walking into the kitchen, I found Joy standing by the stove in sweatpants and a T-shirt, and my ex-husband lounging at the table, his hand around a mug, a floor-length silk Japanese kimono swathing his muscular body (Breanne again. No doubt).

Matt brightened when he saw me. "Clare? How did you sleep?"

"Sleep?" I muttered. "What's that?"

"Come here, Mom," Joy said, looking serious.

"What?" I said. "What did I do now?"

My daughter's arms opened wide. "You only *totally* came to my rescue *twice!*" she exclaimed, and before I knew it, Joy was hugging me like she used to when she was a little girl. "Thank you, Mom," she said, swaying back and forth with me in her arms. "You were so great, coming to Vinny's last night and standing up to that detective! I don't know what I'd do without you! I love you!"

My eyes met Matt's. He was smiling so big I thought his face was about to split.

"Am I dreaming?" I whispered to him.

He shook his head. "Your daughter loves you. You don't believe her?"

"Joy," I said, "your dad helped last night, too. I never would have made it up to Vinny's apartment without your father's innate ability to act like a big, dumb jerk."

Matt rolled his eyes.

Joy laughed. She released me and stepped back. "Daddy told me what he did. I thanked him already."

"I see."

"So, sit down!" Joy insisted. "I'm about to cook you both the best eggs you've ever tasted."

I took a seat across the table from Matt. Joy poured me a fresh cup of Morning Sunshine. Then she returned to the stove, where she added a second frying pan and a tiny sauté pan to the clutter on top of the range.

"I was telling Dad about Tommy asking me to cook him an egg for my audition," Joy explained. "Of course, I realized that a four-star chef would expect a four-star egg, so I prepared it in the style of Fernand Point — he's the man who invented French nouvelle cuisine."

I glanced at my ex. "Are you paying attention? This is what you paid for, you know."

"Yeah." Matt smiled, rubbed the dark stubble on his chin. "I think it was worth it."

Joy took two small china dishes and immersed them in a hot water bath. Then she lit the gas under the pair of frying pans and dropped a pat of butter in each. "We start with butter in a gently warming pan —"

"Butter?" Matt said. "I thought nouvelle cuisine was supposed to be light, not full of butterfat."

Joy shrugged. "Monsieur Point had a saying about butter. *'Du beurre! Donnez-moi du beurre! Toujours de beurre!'* "

"Butter, give me butter, always butter?" Matt translated.

"Exactly," Joy said. "A lot of fine cooking can be done without butter, but nothing from the great syllabus of French classics — and nouvelle cuisine is no different. Okay, Dad, let's move on, shall we?"

Matt's eyebrow rose at his daughter's pedantic tone. I laughed into my coffee cup.

Joy checked both pans. "Now that the butter is just warm enough to spread, but not hot enough to foam, crackle, or spit, I take two eggs —" She displayed the tiny white orbs to us in a fair imitation of a magician presenting his beautiful, delicate doves. "I crack each one into its own saucer. Then I slide the egg carefully into its own buttery pan."

I watched as she deftly slipped the eggs into the melting butter, first one, and then the other. She adjusted the flame until it was barely more than a blue glow under each pan.

"At this low temperature I slowly cook the egg until the white barely turns creamy, and the yolk heats up but doesn't solidify."

With a knife, Joy plopped another lump of

butter into the sauté pan, turned on the gas. "In a separate pan I melt more butter."

Matt glanced at me and whispered, "When will these eggs be done? Next Friday?"

"I heard that, Dad!" Joy snatched the china from the hot bath, dried each plate. Then she glanced into the pan. "Perfect," she announced. "Now I slip the egg onto a slightly heated serving plate and pour the fresh, warm butter over it. Then a touch of ground sea salt and fresh cracked pepper."

Joy turned to face us, a plate in each hand. "Voilà! The perfect egg."

She set the plates down in front of us, handed me a fork. I touched the yolk with the utensil, and then tasted it. It was sweet, like butter, and silky, too. I'd never tasted an egg quite like it. I took a bit of the white. It was creamy and delicate.

"Wonderful," I cooed.

"Absolutely amazing!" Matt declared. "Delicate and buttery and perfectly seasoned."

"So I guess Chef Keitel must have been impressed," I said.

"Well, I got the job," she replied with a shrug.

"How about Vinny?" I asked. "Was he given the same challenge?"

Joy's face fell. She nodded silently. "Vinny

was so talented. Tommy told me his eggs were amazing, even better than mine."

"I can't imagine that," Matt said, licking his fork.

"Vinny didn't even let his egg get near a *pan.* He separated the white from the yolk, cooked them both in buttered saucers set over boiling water, then reunited them at the moment of cooked perfection. He used sea salt for seasoning — and *white* pepper so no dark spots would spoil the look of the finished dish." Joy looked away. "Vinny was such a great cook . . . and he was a really good friend to me . . . I can't believe how I found him last night, lying there that way . . . in all that blood . . ." She wiped at a tear with the neckline of her T-shirt. "I can't believe he's gone."

I took a fortifying sip of coffee and then carefully said, "Joy, I'd like to ask you a little more about all that. About what happened last night."

She shook her head. Turning, she started cleaning up the pans. "I don't want to talk about it anymore. It's over now and —"

"*No,* Joy," I told her firmly. "Honey, listen to me. This isn't over. Whoever killed Vinny is still out there. You have to talk about it, help us understand, so we can help find whoever hurt him."

141

"Why? Why can't you just let the police handle it? Why can't you —"

"Butt out," I interrupted. "That's not an option. Not anymore. Not with Lieutenant Salinas on the case. I have no doubt he still suspects you of something, Joy — if not hurting Vinny, then maybe knowing something about who did or helping to cover it up."

"But that's crazy! Don't you think so, Dad?" Face flushed, Joy stopped trying to clean up. She looked to her father. To my surprise, Matt was shaking his head in agreement — with *me!*

"Your mother's right, Joy. You have to tell us whatever you know. *Everything,* you understand? Even if you think it's something we won't like hearing. We're your parents, and we love you. If you can't trust us, who can you trust?"

Joy frowned. She was quiet a long moment. Finally, she exhaled and nodded. "Okay," she whispered.

Matt glanced at me. His expression had gone from firm and parental to almost helpless. He'd gotten Joy to cooperate, but he clearly had no idea what to ask her next.

That's okay, I thought, *because I do.*

142

NINE

"Joy," I began, after clearing my throat. "Tell us exactly why you went over to Vinny Buccelli's apartment in the middle of the night. I'm still a little fuzzy on the details . . ."

My daughter folded her arms and leaned her back against the granite sink. "If you want the whole story, then I've got to start at the beginning."

"Fine." I glanced at Matt. "We're not going anywhere."

"Well, Mom, after you and Grandma left the restaurant last night, I talked to Tommy. I told him about Brigitte and all the trouble she's been causing. But it seemed to me he was barely listening. Didn't say a word, you know? Then I thought maybe he'd want to go out with me after work; we did that a lot when we first started seeing each other. But Tommy just blew me off."

Joy scowled and looked away, obviously still upset by his treatment. "He was doing something with his friend Nick, or so he said. He promised we'd have 'a talk' tomorrow, which is today, I guess."

A talk, I repeated to myself, feeling a buoyant lift of hope. When one lover told another they needed to have "a talk," it usually meant *a talk* about breaking up. I could only hope Keitel was about to do just that with my daughter.

"Were you upset with Tommy?" I asked Joy. "Was that why you went to see Vinny?"

"I was upset, yeah. But that's not why I went to Queens. I went because Vinny left me a cell phone message asking me to come over and see him after work."

Matt spoke up. "You played that phone message for Lieutenant Salinas, right?"

Joy nodded. "He impounded my cell phone, too. 'Evidence,' he claimed. He gave me a voucher, told me I'd get it back in a few weeks."

"What did the message say?" I asked. "Try to remember exactly."

Joy stared at the ceiling. "Well, Vinny sounded kind of weird. Mysterious, you know? I mentioned that he called in sick yesterday, right?"

I nodded.

"That was weird, right there. For Vinny, going to work at Solange was like a kid going to Disneyland. He totally loved it —"

"And the message?" I interrupted.

"Vinny said he needed to talk to me. He said he wasn't really sick, but that he couldn't come back to work until we spoke. I knew he was on prep today, which meant he'd miss two days if we didn't talk. So I knew whatever he had to say was *really* important."

"And he left this message when?" I asked.

"Around nine thirty. Tommy won't allow the staff to use cell phones during service, so I didn't retrieve the message until after midnight. I was already changed into my clothes to go home."

"Who else was in the kitchen when you were getting ready to leave?"

"Tommy and his friend Nick were there . . . and Ramon was finishing the cleaning with Juan, the dishwasher."

"No other cooks were hanging around?"

"No. Everyone was gone by then: the sauté chef, Henry Tso; the pastry chef, Janelle Babcock; everyone. The waiters were gone, too."

"What about the executive sous-chef, Brigitte Rouille?" I asked.

Joy shook her head. "Brigitte never came back after she ran out the back door."

"And the maître d'? Did he disappear with her?"

"No, Monsieur Dornier came back to the restaurant. Then he and Tommy had a talk in the back of the kitchen, which to me sounded more like an argument. Then Dornier left, too. That was weird, because those guys are really tight. I never saw them fight like that before. But then the whole night was pretty intense, with Tommy skipping out on yet another dinner service and Brigitte freaking like she did."

I nodded and sipped more coffee, considering how long Brigitte had been gone from the restaurant. But then Dornier and the cooks had left before Joy, too. Any one of them could have gotten to Vinny before her.

Who else did that leave? I closed my eyes and replayed a memory of Tommy Keitel shaking my hand in the restaurant's kitchen, his creepy friend Nick walking in behind him. That had taken place around ten thirty.

Dr. Neeravi's lilting Indian accent replayed in my head. *"Someone — perhaps the perpetrator — opened all of these windows. Now, perhaps it was done to dissipate any smell from the body, preventing a neighbor from alerting the authorities right away. Or perhaps the perpetrator knew it would help mask the time of the murder."*

Could Tommy Keitel have killed Vinny? I wondered. He certainly could have done it, given Dr. Neeravi's ballpark guess on the time frame. But what in the world would have been Keitel's motive to murder an innocent kid like Vincent Buccelli?

I was silent so long Matt cleared his throat and tried to jump in with the questioning: "So, let me get this straight, Joy. You were hanging around later than everyone because you were waiting to speak with Tommy? And you wanted him to go out with you?"

"Yeah." Joy nodded. "Until he dismissed me like some kind of servant —"

Or employee, I couldn't help thinking. *Which you still are, even when you're sleeping with the boss.*

I was dying to underline that point to my daughter, but I held my tongue. The last thing my distraught offspring needed right now was another sermon from Mom, especially when Tommy himself was pretty much making my point for me.

". . . so then I left the restaurant and called Vinny back," Joy went on. "I got a busy signal, and I figured he was home on the phone. I took the R train to Times Square, switched to the 7, and got to his place around one, I guess."

I thought about that busy signal. "I sup-

147

pose Vinny could have been using the phone then. Or the killer could have knocked the phone off the hook by that time."

"Yeah," Joy said softly. "I know that now."

I frowned, remembering how Joy had looked in Solange's kitchen last evening with all that béarnaise sauce splattered on her chef's jacket. Vinny's pooled blood wasn't that much different in color, and I shuddered, sick with the idea that my daughter could have just missed walking in on Vinny's brutal murder. What would have happened then? Would Joy have been stabbed to death, too?

"Okay . . ." I said, my voice sounding a little shaky. I paused to drown my dread with more coffee. "Then what happened next? How did you get through Vinny's front door and into his apartment?"

"Easy." Joy shrugged. "I had a key."

"A key?" Matt said, surprised. "Why did you have a key? Were you sleeping with Vinny, too?"

It was an unsavory question to ask your own daughter: Was she cheating on her married lover with her gay best friend? Matt managed it without blinking an eye.

"I wasn't seeing Vinny on the side," Joy said. "Vinny had no interest in me as anything but a friend — I guess now everybody knows why."

Matt blinked. "Oh."

"I mean, Vin was a quiet guy, but he was really cool and really talented. He gave me this impression that he liked someone back in Ohio, and that's why he wasn't seeing anyone here. Maybe that was true, or maybe it was just a line he gave everyone. Maybe he just wanted to keep his private life private."

"So why did you have a key to Vinny's apartment?" I asked.

"Because sometimes me and Tommy . . ." Joy scratched her head, looked away.

"What?" Matt pressed.

"This is just too weird to tell you guys." Joy shook her head, started to walk out of the kitchen.

"Honey, please." Matt stood up, caught her arm. "You need to remember we're on your side."

"We *are*." I nodded. "And you do need to tell us everything, Joy."

After studying the floor for almost a minute, she finally admitted, "Tommy and I . . . we were sort of using Vinny's place. You know, *romantically.*"

Oh, Lord. That word again. I rubbed my temples, feeling a headache coming on. "How often?" I whispered.

149

"A few times a week, in the beginning. There's this wholesale cheese importer just around the corner, Newton's Fresh Market, and Tommy took me there my first week working at Solange. Tommy's really into cheese, and he thought it would be a real education for me to visit one of the places that imports it for him."

A real education? Right. I tried not to visibly cringe.

"It was great. We had a lot of fun tasting these amazing European cheeses. Tommy was flirting with me, and . . . Well, I had the key to Vinny's place because whenever he visits his family in Ohio, I feed his fish and water his plants. So I suggested to Tommy that we go around the corner and use Vin's apartment to . . . you know . . ."

Joy shrugged. She still hadn't looked Matt or me in the face. Matt sat down again, exchanged glances with me. My ex-husband appeared to be as surprised as I was.

"Joy, did we hear you right?" I asked. "Are you telling us that *you're* the one who suggested taking Tommy's flirtation to the next level? Tommy wasn't the one to seduce you?"

Joy shifted her feet, obviously uncomfortable. "You have to understand . . . I've been really into Tommy for a long time . . ." Her gaze moved from the floor to the window to the ceiling, anywhere but on us. "Ever since I read his book two years ago, I thought he was amazing. And then he taught a class at my school, and I totally wanted to work for him. But what really blew me away was when he flirted with me my first day on the job. Tommy never touched me or sexually harassed me or anything like that. He just gave me this amazing private tour of Solange's wine cellar and cheese cave —"

"Cheese cave?" Matt interrupted.

Joy nodded. "Tommy's really proud of his cheese plates. He changes the choices every week, and he picks the selections out personally. The cave's just this small refrigerated room in the basement, where the temperature is constant. Anyway, we got in there, and he started feeding me cheese and joking with me. He was totally flirting. After that, just being around him was a high for me. I couldn't stop thinking about him."

"But Tommy never actually suggested sleeping together?" I pressed. "*You* did?"

"Oh, Mom, stop looking at me like you're *so* disappointed in me! I know you are! And I *hate* that you are . . . And, the truth is . . . I'm disappointed in me, too." Joy rubbed her eyes, let out a weary sigh. "I know it was wrong, throwing myself at a married man like that, not to mention my boss. I *know* it was wrong, okay?"

"Joy, honey," I said softly, "it's not too late to end it."

"You just don't understand what it feels like, Mom!" Joy threw up her hands. "Tommy Keitel wanting *me?!* Tommy Keitel! I couldn't believe it! I still can't!"

Matt glanced at me. "Did I miss something?" he whispered. "When did young women start treating chefs like rock stars and ballplayers?"

"Give it up, Matt. You're old."

Matt grunted.

I focused on my daughter again. As wrong as Joy was in her actions, I knew how incredibly easy it must have been for her to fall for a man like Keitel. An infatuation burned bright as the sun at Joy's age. It blinded you to everything else. Tommy, on the other hand, was older and presumably wiser. If I could get him to see that what he was doing wasn't fair to Joy (not to mention his wife), maybe he'd act like a grown-up and end the affair.

Of course, I knew my grown daughter's love life was none of my business. But as Joy's mother, I believed my daughter's happiness and well-being were very much my business. If I could privately persuade Keitel to cut Joy loose, at least one ugly aspect to this catastrophic mess would be over. As far as the other aspect, that was going to be much trickier.

"Let's get back to Vinny," I said. "Did he know that you and Tommy were using his place for sex?"

"Not the first time, but I told him about it right after. He said it was okay with him if we used his apartment, as long as I left the place clean and stuff."

"And when was the last time you and Tommy used it?"

Joy frowned so deeply I thought she might cry. "The last time was the afternoon of Uncle Ric's decaf coffee–tasting party at the Beekman Hotel — you remember, Mom, that's when I introduced you to Tommy for the first time? Ever since then, Tommy said he was just too busy. He keeps saying, 'We'll do it again soon' . . . but we haven't done it since . . ."

Good. "Okay, so it's been about a month since you and Tommy were there together." I nodded, thinking through the forensics. "From what I saw, Vincent Buccelli kept his apartment spotlessly clean. A lot of the fingerprints and DNA were probably already washed away. But you did unlock the door last night, Joy, which means your fingerprints are on the knob, right?"

She nodded silently.

"And the key?" I asked.

"Lieutenant Salinas confiscated it."

"More evidence," I said, sighing. I went back to massaging my temples. Joy turned around and started cleaning the dishes. Matt drank his coffee in silence. Finally, another question occurred to my ex-husband — a good one.

"Joy, did you *tell* Lieutenant Salinas about you and Tommy using Vinny's place for sex?"

"No, Dad." Joy stopped cleaning and turned around. "All I told Salinas was that I had a key to water Vinny's plants and feed his fish. I didn't mention Tommy at all. I didn't see any point in bringing his name into it."

"But Tommy may mention it when the police interview him," I pointed out. "That's not good, Joy. It'll make it look like you held back information, which you did."

"It was my private business!"

"That's not how Salinas will see it."

"But —"

"How about the murder weapon?" I asked, hoping she might be able to recall whether she'd seen it before. "Did you get a good look at it?"

"No. I just couldn't . . ." Joy closed her eyes, hugged her stomach. "I couldn't look at Vinny long enough. Not after seeing him in all that blood."

"Well, I took a long look at Vinny's corpse and the weapon that killed him." I glanced at Matt. "It was a ten-inch chef's knife."

Matt blew out air.

Joy nodded, opened her eyes. "I overheard you talking about that to the lieutenant."

"You weren't by any chance carrying your Shun Elite last night, were you?"

"No way, Mom." Joy shook her head. "I keep the Shun in my locker at Solange, along with the rest of my knives."

"Good." I'd saved up for months to buy that knife. It was probably the finest in the world: hand-forged and machine-edged by a Japanese manufacturer in Seki City, Japan, the samurai sword–making center for over 700 years. Maybe it was a venal concern, but I would have hated to find out my special Christmas present to my daughter had been confiscated by Salinas, too.

"Believe me, Mom, if the police found a knife on me last night, I would have been booked for murder already. Anyway, what about the knife? Was it one of Vinny's, do you think?"

"The police say no. They checked his kit

155

and said all his knives were in it. I *can* tell you that the knife that killed Vinny had a silver handle —"

"Then it's not Vinny's, for sure," Joy said. "Vinny liked the feel of German-made knives because they have a curved edge for economy of motion. He used Henckels, and they all have wooden handles. My Shun's like that, too."

I searched my own memory. Though most of the blade was embedded inside that poor kid's corpse, I saw enough of it to know the sharpened edge was flat, not curved. I asked Joy about it.

"If it's flat, then it's a French-made knife," she said, "like the ones at Solange. Tommy had those knives made special in Thiers; that's the knife-making center of France. They all have flat edges and silver handles, like the one Brigitte almost used on me last —" Joy froze. "You don't think Brigitte really did it, do you?"

"It's possible," I said. "You know I've already given the woman's name to Lieutenant Salinas."

Joy nodded. "I gave him Brigitte's name, too, Mom. And that's what I'm afraid of."

Matt spoke up. "What do you mean, muffin? What are you afraid of?"

"Dad, if Brigitte is guilty, and the police

don't nail her, she'll know I accused her —
and then there'll be real hell to pay in Tommy's kitchen."

I glanced unhappily at Matt. He was
scowling.

"Joy," he said firmly, "I want you to quit."

"Quit?!" Joy violently shook her head. "No
way! My internship's going well — and it's
not because Tommy's given me a break or
two. I've worked my *butt* off in that kitchen!"
Joy's face reddened with fury as she loomed
over her seated father. "I was at the top of
my class in school! That's how I got the
chance to work for Tommy in the first place,
and I'm holding my own with that professional staff! If I quit, I'll fail. And I *won't*
fail! I've come too far. I've worked too hard.
Quitting is *not* an option, do you understand?"

Matt's eyes had gone wide; his mouth was
gaping. He'd obviously never seen this fero-
cious side of his daughter. Well, I had. And,
frankly, I was proud of Joy. Without that
fighting spirit, she'd never survive in the
backbreaking, unforgiving, male-dominated
world of the culinary arts.

I stood up, put my arm around my girl.
"We understand, Joy. We do. Tell you what,
why don't you let me and your dad clean
up those dishes, okay? You go upstairs and

take a nice, long bath." I led her into the living room. "I've got some really nice scented oils up there, vanilla and jasmine . . ."

Joy took a breath, let it out. "Okay, Mom."

When she was finally out of earshot, I went back to the kitchen and faced Matt. "Our daughter doesn't have to quit. I'm going to deal with Tommy's cutthroat kitchen personally."

Matt folded his arms. "And how are you going to do that?"

"Well, first I'm going to call up Solange's maître d' and tell him his coffee sucks."

"Excuse me?"

I explained to Matt my idea. Actually, it was Mike Quinn's idea, but my ex didn't need to know that. "I'll pitch a contract to improve Solange's coffee service. It's a way for me to get into Keitel's kitchen and figure out what's going on."

"How are you going to pull that off, Clare?"

"Easy. I did it already for David Mintzer in the Hamptons. The restaurant should go for it. They won't need to buy any equipment, because we have dozens of French presses stored in our basement for catering already. I can consign a portion of them to Solange for the time being. And I have more than enough roasted beans on hand to sell them for their dinner service. Tucker and Dante wanted more hours this month because they need the money, so they can take over my shifts."

Matt sighed. "I can't see how you're going to convince Tommy Keitel to hire you. The man doesn't drink coffee. I don't think he even *likes* coffee."

"That's the beauty of it. I don't have to convince Tommy. The man I'm going to pitch is Napoleon Dornier, the restaurant's maître d'. He's in charge of the front of the house. And the front takes care of the wine and beverages."

"What about Joy?" Matt asked. "How's she going to feel about your doing this? She might freak, accuse you of horning in on her territory."

I frowned, hoping my daughter was more understanding than that. "She was happy to have my help last night."

"True, and she might be happy to have you around the kitchen now that things are dicey. But still . . ." Matt shook his head. "Let's keep it from her until you're sure you can even *get* a contract with the restaurant. Then we can both tell her together. It'll sound more like a business venture for the Village Blend, rather than, you know . . ."

"Another way for me to spy on her?"

"You're not spying on her," Matt gallantly pointed out. "You're spying on everyone *around* her. That's a very important distinction."

"Thanks, Matt. I mean it." It was a big leap for him, considering his jaundiced view of my previous forays into amateur detective work.

He nodded, rubbed his eyes. "I guess even if Joy quit her internship this morning, she'd still be a suspect on Lieutenant Salinas's list, right?"

"Right. I have to find out how that knife got into Vinny's neck. And to do that, I've got to get into Tommy Keitel's kitchen."

"Okay, fine, get into his kitchen," said Matt, rising from the table. "But after hearing Joy's little tale of falling for Keitel, I think I've got the man's number."

"What do you mean?"

"When it comes to this snooping stuff, Clare, I may not be as good as you. But as a man, I can give you one good piece of advice."

"What's that?"

"Stay the hell out of Tommy Keitel's cheese cave."

"Mooooom!"

I left the kitchen to find Joy standing at

160

the top of the stairs. She was wrapped in a towel.

"What is it, honey?" I called. "Can't you find the scented oils?"

"No!" she called back. "I mean, yes, I found them. I was calling you because I heard your cell phone go off — twice. Whoever's trying to reach you, it might be important."

"Thanks, honey!"

I bolted up the steps and grabbed my handbag off the hall table. As Joy returned to the bathroom, I ducked into the master bedroom and shut the door. My phone listed three missed calls in the last thirty minutes, all of them from Detective Mike Quinn.

Mike.

Just seeing the man's name on my cell's tiny screen did something to my central nervous system. I couldn't wait to talk with him, tell him everything that had happened last night, ask him for his help and advice and support.

I was about to hit my speed dial when I saw he'd left a message. I punched the buttons and listened, eager to hear something sweet and sexy.

"Clare, it's me, Mike . . ."

By now, my body's reaction to the deep,

gravelly timbre of Mike's cop voice was Pavlovian. Like a love-struck teen, a shiver went through me. I could practically feel his arms around me again. His mouth on mine —

"I can't imagine why you're not picking up . . . Actually, with Allegro in the apartment, I can, which is what's eating me. So, uh, *look* . . ." There was a pause, followed by an audible exhale. "I'm going to be blunt with you, Clare. I don't think things are going in a direction I like with us, and . . . I'm sorry, but I need to have *a talk* with you. Don't call me back when you get this. I'm going on duty, and I'll see you later anyway. I'll drop by the Blend this afternoon."

"A talk . . ." I repeated. My legs didn't feel so sturdy all of a sudden, and I sat down heavily on the four-poster's mattress. First Tommy Keitel wanted "a talk" with Joy. Now Mike Quinn wanted one with me?

" 'Don't call me back,' huh?" *Oh, hell no!* I hit speed dial. Mike's cell phone rang and rang, and then sent me to voice mail. *Great.* I snapped the phone shut.

"This day just keeps getting better."

TEN

"Are you ready, Ms. Cosi?" Napoleon Dornier called from the kitchen doorway.

"Yes! Please, come in," I replied. "Sit down."

It was just after noon. I was dressed to kill in a conservative forest-green business suit that I'd hastily appropriated from Madame's Valentino collection. With borrowed emerald studs in my ears, a stunning emerald necklace encircling my throat, green silk heels, and my dark brown hair smoothed into a neat French twist, I looked like a vendor worthy of pitching a four-star establishment.

I'd set up five French presses on one of the large round tables in Solange's empty dining room. There was no lunch service today, a result of the police interviews, which had taken place all morning, according to Dornier. So the dining room's cherrywood tables were still stripped of their white linens.

Back in the kitchen, the prep cooks were hard at work starting sauces and braising meats for dinner. The smells of a mushroom duxelles suffused the air with sautéing shallots and fresh tarragon as the leather-padded double doors swung wide on their hinges and Nappy Dornier swaggered out.

With six hours to dinner service, I wasn't surprised to find him not in his formal evening wear but in comfortable street clothes. He looked less like a scarecrow in his loose beige khakis and untucked polo. The lime green color was a bold statement, given the bright red color of the man's short, spiky hair, but then Dornier, with his pricey amber cat glasses, didn't strike me as the kind of guy who was willing to fade into the woodwork.

Getting the appointment with the man had been remarkably easy. The moment I'd dropped David Mintzer's name, Solange's maître d' couldn't have been more accommodating.

"Name-dropping only matters when it serves an end," Madame liked to remind me. "Use it stupidly, and you'll be seen as an unctuous idiot. Use it judiciously, and you'll go far."

Well, so far, it had worked like a charm to

get me in this restaurant's door. But then New York was the sort of town that thrived on networking and connections. I hadn't come to this burg with a pedigree or e-Rolodex, but over the years I'd gotten to know the customers of the Blend, and the natural relationships that developed were often very helpful.

David Mintzer, for instance, was well-known in New York as a successful and influential entrepreneur. Lucky for me, he maintained a town house in the Village and loved my espressos. That connection led to an offer to spend last summer in the Hamptons, setting up the coffee service for his newest restaurant — an experience that couldn't have come in more handy at the moment.

"Let's start with a Kenyan," I told the maître d' as he settled into a chair. Dornier was one of the city's most accomplished and respected wine stewards, so the Kenyan Single Lot medium roast was a natural choice. I'd already coarsely ground the beans and steeped them for four minutes in the press. Now I pushed the plunger down and poured Dornier his very first sample of Village Blend coffee.

"Please take in the aroma first, monsieur. And then taste it as you would a fine wine.

Slurp it with some air so that you can spray the coffee on your entire palate."

Behind his amber cat glasses, Dornier appeared skeptical but curious as he brought the cup to his nose and then his lips. With one slurping sip, an eyebrow rose.

"Hmmmm," he said as if he couldn't trust his own taste buds. He tried another sip. "It's quite good, Ms. Cosi. I must say, I'm favorably surprised."

I noticed that, out of his maître d' uniform, Dornier's French accent was barely detectable, but then he wouldn't have been the first front-of-house worker in a French restaurant to pump up the Gallic show for his customers.

"Now close your eyes," I told him. "Sip again and tell me what you taste."

Dornier nodded, clearly game for the experience. He dropped his eyelids and sipped once, twice, three times. "There's a striking fruitiness in this coffee. I'm tasting notes of raspberry and lemon. Very nice. But I think the strongest flavor is black currant . . ."

"Anything else?"

Dornier took a few more slurping hits. "There are most definitely umami characteristics here . . ."

I smiled at his use of the term. It was a

popular adjective in culinary circles, describing one of the basic tastes sensed by the receptor cells on the tongue: sweet, salty, sour, bitter . . . and *umami,* the Japanese word for a savory or meaty flavor.

"I detect a hint of sun-dried tomato. Yes . . . and an earthy steak flavor in the finish." Dornier's eyes snapped open. "My goodness, Ms. Cosi. I'm absolutely flabbergasted. This coffee is reminiscent of a Grand Cru!"

"Exactly, monsieur. Quality coffee beans, if processed, roasted, brewed, and served correctly, will show off as much complexity as a fine wine."

The sound of one person clapping echoed across the empty dining room. I looked up to find Chef Tommy Keitel himself doing the honors. He was leaning near the doorway to his kitchen. There was a hint of superior amusement in his expression. Apparently, he'd been standing there awhile, watching me conduct the tasting.

"Tommy!" Dornier waved him over. "You *must* come here and sample this."

It was difficult not to remember how I'd first met Keitel — at the Beekman Hotel, with one of his heavily muscled forearms around my daughter's young waist. But I forced the image from my mind. I had to sell Dornier on my services, and I wasn't going to score any points by being hostile to the restaurant's executive chef. For my own daughter's well-being, my issues with Keitel had to be put on hold.

The larger-than-life chef pushed himself off his leaning position and moved across the dining room. He was wearing black slacks and running shoes, a plain gray T-shirt beneath the chef's white jacket, which he buttoned up as he strode toward me.

"I heard you were coming, Clare. How are you?" He extended his hand.

"Fine, Chef Keitel." I placed my hand in his. "And you?"

"I've had better days." His large hand shook mine and held it, his piercing blue eyes staring into me. "You've heard about Vincent Buccelli?"

I nodded, stepping back, tugging my hand free of his hold. "Joy and I found out last night. Did the police come by this morning to talk to you and your staff?"

"Yeah, they did. They questioned every-one."

"For *hours*," Dornier sniffed unhappily. "I'm terribly sorry for young Vincent, but no one here knew a thing about what hap-pened to him or why. I believe the police were wasting their time. They should have been spending it in Queens searching for the crazed thug who murdered him."

Dead silence ensued after that little speech.

I nearly started grilling Dornier at that moment, asking him where he'd gone after he'd left Solange last night — and, more importantly, where Brigitte Rouille had gone, and where the woman was now. Was she back there in the kitchen? I'd been let into the restaurant through the front door, and Dornier instructed me to set up in the dining room. He hadn't allowed me into Keitel's kitchen.

That was a bad break to start. Joy was due to begin her shift in two hours. More than anything, I wanted answers. But I wasn't a member of the NYPD, I didn't have a PI license, and unless I could convince these men to sign a contract with me, I was going to be out on my ear in the next five minutes.

Keitel cleared his throat. "So, Clare, what have you brought here that's got Nappy so excited?"

"This Kenyan coffee to start." I poured Chef Keitel a cup.

He sipped, paused, and drank more.

"You're sampling the legendary SL-28," I informed him, "probably the most respected coffee varietal in the world."

"Is that so?" Keitel exchanged glances with Dornier. "And how did you get hold of it?"

"Well, most coffee farms in Kenya are small. They form cooperatives and auction their lots on a weekly basis, primarily to big exporters, which is why most Kenyan coffee ends up in blends. But Matteo, our buyer, doesn't rely on a big exporter. He goes directly to the bidders at the Nairobi Coffee Exchange to score pure, uncut lots for our coffeehouse business."

I refilled the men's cups. "Matt samples the lots personally to make sure we're getting the crème de la crème of the Kenyan coffee experience. The green beans are shipped to New York, and I personally roast them in our basement. The moment a bean is roasted, it begins to lose flavor, so I roast regularly to ensure superior quality with every cup."

Chef Keitel exchanged another glance with his maître d'. The chef's expression remained neutral, but from the single nod and arching of one eyebrow, I got the idea he was favorably impressed.

"I brought four other wonderful coffees for you to sample today." I forced a smile. "Shall I prepare them?"

"I don't think so." Keitel folded his arms and regarded me. "Look, this Kenyan coffee is good enough, and I appreciate the trouble you've gone to, but — as I understand it — this little presentation came about as a result of your *own* coffee experience here last evening?"

Dornier visibly tensed. "Please, Tommy. Let's not go there."

"No," he said. "I want Clare to understand why she was given whatever swill she was served last night."

Dornier let out a tortured sigh and waved his hand. "You explain."

"Nappy here has trained his waiters to provide the highest-quality service possible. So when a customer asks for something that's not on the menu, his server — in your case, René — will attempt to supply it so that the dining experience is not a disappointment."

"I see."

"No, you don't," said Keitel. "Coffee is not on our menu. And it never was. Since you ordered it, René took it upon himself to brew you some from our *employee* coffee-maker."

Dornier appeared to sink down farther in his chair.

"Let me guess," I said. "The machine's

old. It's dirty. And the coffee that's brewed inside it comes in preground aluminum packets with unspecified expiration dates."

"I had no idea this was going on," Keitel said. "Now — thanks to you, Clare — I *do.*"

"And now you can do something about it," I countered.

"Yes. I can." Keitel's blue gaze speared Dornier. "I can make *sure* we never serve *employee* coffee to our paying customers *again.*"

"*Or* you can put quality specialty coffees on your menu," I pressed.

Keitel shook his head. "Why would I want to go to the trouble?"

"For profit, of course."

"My customers don't order coffee."

"If it's not on your menu, how *can* they order it?"

"You're arguing an unsubstantiated point."

"I can substantiate it in two seconds flat. Do you know what your customers are doing after they leave your restaurant?"

Keitel frowned. "What does that have to do with —"

"They drive to Long Island and north Jersey. They check the overseas markets. They head downtown to party into the wee hours. I grant you that a portion of your clientele would be only too happy to continue drinking port, ice wine, or cognac on top of the substantial amount of vino they've already consumed with their food, but this is New York. The night is just beginning at nine or ten o'clock when they leave your dining room. Offering coffee is a way to wake up for the drive home, the ongoing business deal, even the lovemaking that goes on, after dinner is concluded."

Keitel stared at me for so long, I thought perhaps he'd been flash frozen. Did the man think I was completely nuts? I glanced at Dornier. He was still sipping the Kenyan, apparently waiting for his chef de cuisine to make the decision.

"Look . . ." I pressed, "why not at least try a dessert pairings menu with my coffee? Give it one week. I promise you'll not only sell my coffee at premium prices to people who would have declined more alcohol anyway, you'll sell more desserts."

Dornier sat up a little straighter. "Did you hear that, Tommy?"

Keitel grunted once. He stared for another few silent moments, then without any discernable articulation of words, turned and stalked back toward his kitchen.

Crap.

I figured that was it. I was dismissed. Time

to pack in my French presses and go —
until I realized Keitel hadn't disappeared
through the swinging gateway to his domain.
Instead, he was holding one door open and
sticking his head through it.

"Janelle!" he bellowed into the busy
kitchen. "Come out here!"

An attractive, full-figured, African American woman answered the command. She
wore a burgundy chef's jacket and a flat,
burgundy baker's cap. Beneath the cap, her
shoulder-length ebony hair was styled in
rows of beautiful tight braids. Her skin was
mocha, and her roundish thirtyish face
displayed Creole features.

"What is it, Chef?" she called, wiping her
hands on the white towel that was thrown
over her shoulder.

Keitel held the door open for her. "Come
with me, please," he said, his voice softer
and much more polite as she moved toward
him.

"Janelle, this is Ms. Clare Cosi," he said,
leading her to our table. "Ms. Cosi is Joy
Allegro's mother. She also happens to manage a coffeehouse downtown, and she's
proposing a contract with us to supply
gourmet coffee."

Janelle's face immediately brightened.
"Are you asking my opinion, Chef?"

"I am."

"By all means, let's taste what she's brought!"

He speared me with his gaze. "Clare, I'd like you to meet Janelle Babcock, our pastry chef. If you're proposing a dessert pairings menu with your coffee, you'd better win her over."

I held out my hand. Janelle shook it with surprising fervor. "I'm very pleased to meet you, Ms. Cosi —"

"Please call me Clare." I smiled at the woman, realizing this was the Janelle that Joy had mentioned to me weeks ago. She was a graduate of Le Cordon Bleu in Paris and had come to Solange not from France but from the pâtissier position in a New Orleans restaurant that had been destroyed by Hurricane Katrina.

According to Joy, Janelle had been the kindest to her of all the line cooks in Tommy's kitchen. The woman had lost everything in the storm: her job, her home, her dream of opening her own bakery. Apparently, when Tommy Keitel had heard about her plight from a colleague, he'd gone out of his way to make a place for her on his staff. She'd started as an assistant to the existing pastry chef but quickly assumed the lead position when that chef moved along.

According to Joy, Janelle was saving up her money to move back down to Louisiana and start again. But she was beginning to get nervous, because the desserts at Solange weren't moving — the very reason her predecessor had left.

From my own sampling of her cuisine the previous evening, I knew the quality of her confections wasn't the issue. Her desserts were being sabotaged, it seemed to me, by the lousy, palate-poisoning coffee that the waiters had been permitted to serve with those amazing creations.

I pressed another pot of the Kenyan for Janelle. Then I pressed the Yirgacheffe as a single-origin. The brightness, floral aroma, and citrus finish blew her away. But she hadn't tasted anything yet. Next came the Colombian, a micro-lot produced by the indigenous Guarapamba tribe.

"They live on a reservation high in the Colombian Andes," I explained.

Janelle sampled the coffee. Dornier did, as well.

"I taste layers of vanilla in this one," Janelle remarked, her voice betraying only the slightest traces of that syncopated New Orleans lilt. "Sweet cherry and raisin . . ."

"There's a dark chocolate in the finish, as well," Dornier added. "Very nice, Ms. Cosi."

"The coffee's grown from older plant varieties," I explained, "and the tribe of fifty families that grows it uses traditional agricultural methods, planting and harvesting by the phases of the moon."

Janelle's long-lashed eyes widened. She faced Keitel, who'd been watching in silence, declining to taste anything more. "Chef, we *have* to serve this."

Keitel rolled his eyes toward the dining room's laughing gargoyles. "Don't get yourself sweet-talked by some tale of ritual harvesting. The proof is in the pudding."

"But you haven't *tasted* the pudding," Janelle pointed out.

I cleared my throat. "Chef Keitel, I'll make you a deal," I said, summoning the bravado of a serious salesperson. "At least try this next coffee. If it doesn't impress you, even a little bit, I'll pack up my things and leave you in peace."

Keitel folded his arms. "Bring it on."

I ground the beans coarsely and measured them into the bottom of a clean press (two tablespoons of coffee for every six ounces of water). Then I poured in the hot water (just off the boil) from my electric pot, stirred the grounds to begin the brewing process, and set my digital timer to four minutes.

"Mmmmm," Janelle said. "I already smell something floral . . ."

"It's *lavender,*" Keitel said.

I nodded. "You're right."

"Of course I'm right, Ms. Cosi. Who do you think you're dealing with?"

A man with an ego the size of New Jersey?

I cleared my throat. "This coffee comes from a family farm in the mountains of Honduras called Finca el Puente —"

"The Bridge Farm," Keitel abruptly translated.

"A colleague in the trade, Peter Giuliano of Counter Culture Coffee roasters, calls this coffee the Purple Princess, and it's the perfect moniker. This coffee is elegant enough to be served to a princess, and it's greatly desired at coffee auctions."

My timer went off, and I pushed down the plunger, forcing the spent grounds to the bottom of the glass press. Then I began to pour out the sample cups. "It's a testament to the savvy of our own Village Blend buyer that he's been able to secure lots of the Purple Princess for us year after year."

Keitel grunted. "Quite a speech. But let's sample it, shall we?"

I nodded and zipped my lips, knowing the

taste of this coffee alone would sell it for me.

"Oh, my goodness," Janelle said after a few sips. "I didn't know there were coffees like this."

"It's full-bodied, and there's a juiciness to the finish," Dornier described, his voice quick and excited. "But I'm especially impressed with the level of lavender aroma and flavor. It's absolutely bursting with it . . . and there are other fruit flavors here, too."

"Plum," said Keitel. He sipped again. "And grape . . ."

"With a note of something else, I think," Janelle said.

"Raspberry," Keitel added flatly.

I shouldn't have been surprised by Chef Keitel's spot-on description of the underlying flavor characteristics. You don't get to be a world-class chef without a world-class palate — and, apparently, a world-class ego.

"Coffee gets its character from thousands of aromatic chemicals," I pointed out. "This Purple Princess is probably the best illustration I've ever come across for that particular notion."

"It's a remarkable coffee," Janelle said. She glanced hopefully at Keitel. "Don't you think so, Chef?"

Keitel sipped more of his coffee, said nothing.

Damn. The man was one tough sell. But I refused to go down in flames.

"These and other Village Blend coffees can be paired beautifully with items on your dessert menu," I pointed out. "The Guarapamba tribe's Colombian, for instance, would have paired very nicely with Janelle's modern take on the tarte Tatin that I enjoyed last night. My dinner companion ordered the profiteroles; the Kenyan would have been delightful paired with that. Its note of black currant would have resonated magnificently with the blackberry sorbet inside the pastry and black currant flavor in the casis coulis. And, of course, you can also offer a tasting of cheese and coffee pairings. If you sold an entire table on the idea, you could move as many as four presses of coffee to go with your cheeses."

"Excuse me? You did *not* just suggest that coffee and cheese go together." Keitel shook his head. "Too bad, Cosi, and I was just beginning to give you the benefit of the doubt on your gastronomic judgment."

"Excuse *me,* Chef Keitel, but when it comes to coffee, you're out of your depth."

Keitel's flummoxed expression was priceless.

180

"Hear me out," I quickly added. "People have been eating fresh cheese and coffee for a long time. A cup of java with a morning bagel and cream cheese is practically an institution in this city, and who eats a New York cheesecake without a hot pot of joe?"

Janelle giggled.

Dornier murmured, "She has a point."

Keitel shot them both unhappy glances.

"Not every cheese pairs well with every coffee," I admitted. "But like wine and beer, there are coffees that pair beautifully with certain cheeses. Given the right pairing, a cup of coffee can highlight special notes of flavor in a cheese, helping it shine like a jeweler putting a black backdrop behind a white diamond."

Keitel said not a word. He simply stared at me like he had before. Then he turned abruptly and began striding toward his kitchen.

Dornier exchanged a disappointed glance with Janelle and sighed. Then he faced me. "Well, Ms. Cosi, I'm very sorry, but —"

"Sign her up!" Keitel bellowed over his shoulder.

Dornier's eyes widened. He turned his head. "For how long?"

Keitel stopped at the kitchen doors and spun to face us. "Seven weeks."

"No more?" Dornier asked.

"Seven weeks from Monday," the chef called. "After that, who knows . . ."

Then Tommy Keitel pressed his back against the swinging doors and disappeared into his kitchen.

Eleven

Napoleon Dornier suggested that I come back again the next day to discuss the contract details.

"I just can't do it now," he told me, checking the digital schedule on his PDA. "I have a vintner coming in twenty minutes, reservations to review, specials to go over with my staff —"

"Of course, I understand how busy you are. Perhaps I can just take a look around the kitchen on my own —"

"Oh, no," Dornier said. "Janelle here will show you around." He turned to the pastry chef. "You don't mind, do you, Janelle? You two will be working together soon enough anyway."

Janelle smiled. "I'd be happy to show Ms. Cosi the ropes; she probably just saved my job."

"Great," I said. *This is going well. Now I just need Janelle to agree to one more thing.*

"I'm actually looking forward to meeting the kitchen staff. You know, getting the lay of the land."

"Of course!" Janelle said. "Just give me a moment to wrap up my *pâte sucrée* and get it into the fridge."

"No problem," I said, nodding. "Sweet pastry dough is so much easier to work when it's cold." That much I knew from my own trial and error — *a lot* of error.

As Janelle headed back into the kitchen, I slipped off my suit jacket, hung it on a chair, and began to clean up the table. Loud voices caught my attention as two men slammed through the kitchen doors and into the dining room. One was Tommy Keitel. The other I didn't recognize. He was younger than Keitel by at least ten years. Shorter, too, but not by much. The man was fit, tanned, and far more polished than Keitel. He had thick black hair styled into a perfect coif, and his attire was obviously expensive. The charcoal gray suit appeared finely made and sharply tailored to his tall, lean form. He wore no tie, just a white dress shirt, open at the collar.

"Tell me again, Tommy," the man was practically shouting, "because I can't believe it!"

"Don't take that tone with me, Anton. You

184

may own this place, but it's a shell without me. I run the kitchen. I hire the personnel. I make the decisions about who stays and who goes. That was the deal five years ago. That's always been the deal!"

Anton? I thought. *So this is the owner of the restaurant.*

The men's voices were loud, and they didn't appear to care who was listening. I stepped back and stayed quiet, hoping to hear more.

"Brigitte Rouille was your second-in-command," Anton said. "She knew every recipe. She was running your kitchen —"

"She couldn't hack it. She was cracking under the pressure. I did her a favor and let her off the hook."

"You fired the one person who can run your kitchen when you're not here!"

"That's not true," Keitel said. "I've just promoted someone who's quite capable of doing Brigitte's job — without the drama."

"Who?"

"Henry Tso."

"The sauté chef?" Anton shook his head.

"Henry's a graduate of Cordon Bleu London. He trained under Marco Pierre White, and he knows every single dish in my recipe book."

"But aren't there issues with Henry? He

185

worked only eight months as executive chef for Petite Bouchée, and they let him go."

"The only *issue* Henry has — and I hate to say it — is his lack of aptitude in creating new dishes. That's really the only reason he couldn't hack it as a chef de cuisine. But that's not a problem here, because this is *my* kitchen, and all he has to do is re-create *my* dishes. Nobody's better than Henry in repetition of technique. He's the best mimic I ever met. No one will ever know I'm not in this kitchen."

Anton sighed, ran a hand over his face. "I'd like to see him in action."

"Then come back for dinner service. I'll let him run the show."

"You're bailing again?"

"Not tonight. I'll be here to back him up, take care of any problems. We'll call it a trial run."

Anton rubbed the back of his neck. "Listen, Tommy. About that other matter —"

"You know how I feel. End of story," Keitel said, cutting him off.

"I still don't understand your problem with it, Tommy. All of the marquee chefs are doing it. It's the wave of the future."

"Not *my* future," Tommy replied. Then he turned on the man and strode back into his kitchen.

Anton hesitated a moment, shook his head, and followed his chef through the double doors. A second later, the doors opened again, and Janelle Babcock came out, smiling.

"So, are you ready to meet the staff, Clare?"

"First, I have a question for you." I leaned close, dropped my voice. "Is it true what I overheard? Was Brigitte Rouille really fired?"

"Uh-huh, girl," she whispered, her professional tone loosening for a little old-fashioned gossip. "I can't say as I'm broken up about it, either. That woman was a holy terror. But you already know that, don't you? I saw you in the kitchen last night, defending Joy."

"When was Brigitte let go?"

"I'm not sure. Tommy and Nappy got into a hell of a row about her. Dornier was defending her. Why? I don't know. But it's Chef Keitel's kitchen, and he made that clear. He must have called her late last night or pretty early this morning to tell her she was fired, because Brigitte, she hasn't been back since she ran out of here last night."

Janelle held the kitchen door open for me, and I walked through. Savory scents enveloped me as I moved around the high service counter: simmering wine reductions, freshly cut vegetables and herbs, yeast breads baking in the oven.

Four Latino men in white aprons were moving quickly around the banks of heavy gas stoves and metal prep tables, yelling in Spanish to one another. They carried trays of chopped vegetables, pots of sauces and extractions, delivering them to the various cook stations that needed stocking or replenishment.

I recognized a short, squat man directing the Hispanic workers. It was Ramon, the gracious swing cook who'd filled in for Joy the previous night while she'd spoken to me in the break room.

"These guys are the prep crew," Janelle explained. "They come early in the morning, and most of them will be gone by the time we open for dinner, usually to shift jobs at other restaurants and cafés. Ramon here is our prep supervisor, swing cook, and unofficial translator."

"Hello," he said.

"Ramon. Nice to see you again." I smiled. "Don't you ever go home?"

He laughed, revealing a gold tooth. "If I ever left this place, it would fall down around all of their ears. That would be sad, because then I'd have to get a job with Robbie Gray."

Seeing the way Ramon ran his staff, I had no doubt what he told me was absolutely true.

Next, Janelle led me over to a commercial sausage machine and pointed to a line of black plastic ring binders on the shelf above it. All the volumes were dated and covered a six-month period from the day Solange opened to the present. I counted ten of them.

"These binders hold the daily menus and recipes for every dish ever served at Solange," Janelle explained.

I was shocked. "You mean the recipes Tommy spent years perfecting are just sitting out here, where anyone can take them?"

"The line cooks need to be able to prepare what the chef wants on a given day. When in doubt, they look it up."

"But someone could steal these so easily."

Janelle shrugged. "What would they do with them if they did? Tommy would sue the pants off anyone who stole his signature dishes and tried to pass them off as his own" — she laughed — "if he didn't kill them first."

Next she led me to a slight, pale man in his late twenties with adorable dark curls peeking out beneath a flat-topped cook's cap. He was furiously stirring two pots at once.

"Yves Blanchard, this is Clare Cosi. Starting next week, Clare's going to bring premium coffees to the menu here at Solange."

The man glanced over his shoulder at me, his lips lifting into a smile. "Good," he said in a very discernable French accent. "Something better than that merde they provide for the staff."

"You're a man after my own heart, Monsieur Blanchard," I said.

"Yves, if you haven't guessed, is our saucier," Janelle said. "And we better let him get back to it."

We moved deeper into the kitchen, past the prep tables and the refrigerators. Suddenly I heard a loud voice.

"Don't be afraid to use your knife! It's just a piece of meat, for God's sake. Stab first, really cut deep into the flesh. Then start to slice. Otherwise you'll make a total mess of it."

I stepped forward, observed a table-sized cutting board, a pile of small hens piled on one side. Beside the birds, an intense Asian man in his late thirties circled around a young man who was clutching a silver-handled chef's knife.

"You're really making a mess of it, dude,"

the Asian man said, a note of exasperation in his voice.

"Sorry, Chef Tso," the young man replied, dropping the bird.

"Don't be sorry. Just do it *right*."

So this was Henry Tso, I realized, the man who'd just been promoted to executive sous-chef, the second-in-command of Solange, the man Tommy himself picked to replace Brigitte Rouille.

Joy had talked about Chef Tso, always with a little awe. She said he was the best chef on the entire line. That was important because, unlike the roasting chef, the vegetable chef, or the saucier, who had the luxury of preparing many of their courses in advance, the sauté chef prepared dishes that were made to order. He had to be on top of his game all the time and possess the ability to juggle two, three, or even four tasks at once.

Joy also said that Henry had the best technique she'd ever seen. And it appeared I was about to see a demonstration.

"Watch closely," Chef Tso said. He took the eight-inch blade from his young apprentice, pushed the mangled bird to the side. Then he reached for a fresh chicken from the pile. He slapped the fowl onto the board, belly side down.

"Remove the spine first, cutting here and here," he said, flicking the blade twice. "Cut on both sides, as close to the bone as possible."

With quick, smooth motions, Henry Tso sliced through the pink flesh on either side of the spine, extracting the bones so fast I barely followed his moves.

His movements were sure, economical, and precise. In under a minute, Chef Tso removed all of the bones except the tips of the legs and wings. At one point he flipped the knife in the air, caught it blade up, and used the handle to break a joint for easy extraction. When he was finished, he placed the perfectly deboned chicken on its belly and set the knife down.

"Think you can do that?" he asked the apprentice.

Gamely, the young man lifted the knife and tried again.

"Chef Tso," Janelle interrupted. "I'd like you to meet Clare Cosi. Clare is going to help us add premium coffee to our menu."

Henry Tso faced me. Under his high chef's hat his hair was shaved so short I could see his scalp. He was a lot taller than I, but his hands were small, his fingers long and delicate. His brown eyes scrutinized me with intensity, and he moved with a contained energy that reminded me of Chef Keitel. Something else reminded me of Tommy Keitel: Henry Tso's ego and a radiated confidence that bordered on arrogance.

"Coffee, huh," Henry finally said. "Sorry, I prefer tea."

"No worries," I replied.

Henry suddenly noticed another transgression by the new young apprentice and cried out. "Cut the meat; don't rip it!" he said. "If I served that bird, I'd look like an asshole!"

The apprentice quailed.

"Is that your job description?" Henry asked, getting into the young man's face. "Make Chef Tso look bad?"

"Yes, Chef . . . I mean, n-no, Chef," the apprentice stammered.

Janelle touched my arm, tilted her head, and we moved on.

"Is he always like that?" I asked when we were out of earshot.

"Like what?" Janelle asked. "An arrogant, superior perfectionist who'd do anything to get ahead?"

I blinked.

"Let's just say that if you get between Henry and his ambition, you'll probably end up like one of those chickens." Janelle froze, closed her eyes, and shook her head. "God.

I shouldn't have said that, not after what happened to poor Vinny."

"It's okay," I said, and we continued moving through the kitchen. "Janelle, since you've brought it up, did Henry and Vinny get along okay? I mean, did you ever notice any hostility between them? Or maybe there was something else in play. Did they have an especially close friendship by any chance?"

"That's funny," said Janelle. "The police basically asked me the same thing this morning."

"It's a pretty standard question when someone's found murdered. The detectives want to know if that person had any enemies . . . or intense relationships."

"I can only tell you what I told them. Vinny was a quiet kid. Very private. Didn't talk much at all. Except for Brigitte picking on him, I didn't see much in the way of hostility directed toward the boy by anyone, Henry included. And as far as Henry and *friendship* —" Janelle shook her head. "He's pretty much all business around here. The other line cooks go out sometimes to hang after work. It's fun, and I usually go, too. But Henry never joins us."

Finally, we arrived at an island away from the chaotic activity everywhere else. "Well, here we are. My domain," Janelle declared proudly.

In the center of the space stood a large prep table, now wiped clean. A gas stove and array of ovens hugged the wall; beside them stood a bakery rack on wheels, holding freshly baked rolls and baguettes. Janelle offered me a high metal stool. She pulled up another to sit beside me.

"I have to tell you, Ms. Cosi, I'm very excited about your coffees. My mind's already spinning with ideas."

"Café au lait and beignets, by any chance?"

Janelle laughed. "Joy must have mentioned I come from the Big Easy."

"Yes." I smiled. "She really likes and admires you."

"Well, that's very sweet. And Joy's a very sweet girl, very accomplished, too, and at such a young age. You should be proud."

"I am."

"It's funny you should mention the beignets," Janelle said. "My mother made them all the time, so I practically grew up on them. You can tell, can't you?" She laughed, patting one ample hip. "And while I do believe it would be fun to offer something as simple as a classic French doughnut, Chef Keitel would kill me if I proposed it.

He won't allow retro to come out of his kitchen. He's all about fusion, *loves* new spices, combinations of flavors, aromas, and textures. Explore! Experiment! That's Chef Keitel's credo."

"Is it? *And here I thought it was 'Sleep with your young intern on the side.'* "

"It's no joke, Clare. It's your entire professional reputation on the line. You start putting traditional chocolate mousse and crème brûlée in your dessert selections, and the gourmands will declare you zombified and send a body bag back to the kitchen."

"I suppose the same dish, prepared the same way for years and years can be numbing — for the diner and the chef," I conceded. "Then again, there's something to be said for paying tribute to the classics. I love what you did with the tarte Tatin, for example, deconstructing it on the plate, adding the cardamom and ginger to the apples. And what you did with the profiteroles, using blackberry sorbet instead of the same old vanilla ice cream. Drizzling casis coulis instead of chocolate sauce."

"Yes, if you really love something, then it's worth looking at it with new eyes."

"Now there's a credo I can agree with: *loyalty.* I had this coq au vin recipe that I loved. It was hard to admit that it was getting pretty tired after fifteen years. But instead of throwing it out, I woke it up — literally — by infusing coffee into the braising process."

Janelle paused a moment, tapped her chin in thought. "You know what, Clare? I could do that with my desserts. I've wanted to do chocolate pots de crème — except it's so retro that Chef Keitel would be unhappy with a one-dimensional approach. But if I were to infuse the heavy cream in the recipe with some of that wonderful Colombian coffee you brought today, I could create a mocha pot that would resonate with the coffee itself. I could serve the dessert in an espresso cup with praline crème Chantilly standing in for the macchiato froth, and place two vanilla-pecan *sablés* on the side of the saucer."

I nodded. "My mouth's already watering."

"Or . . ." Janelle searched the ceiling, "what do you think of a *tartelette* of framboise and chocolate ganache with a pistachio crust? Wouldn't that be delicious served with fresh raspberries and a French-pressed pot of your Kenyan?"

"It would, but I'd want to give the Kenyan to you in a French roast for that pairing. The darker roast carries a bolder flavor that will stand up better to the chocolate ganache. A darker roast also changes the flavor profile of the Kenyan beans so the fruity notes you tasted in my medium roast will become caramelized. Then you'll have a cup with flavors closer to a chocolate-covered cherry."

"Excellent! I can't wait to try it. And how about this pairing with the Purple Princess? I could do those little ol' beignets after all, but keep them small, about the size of a profiterole, inject each one with a filling of lavender-ginger-plum crème pâtissière and on the plate drizzle a bit of plum coulis—"

"Janelle," a voice interrupted.

The pastry chef and I looked up to find Tommy Keitel looming just a few feet away, legs braced, arms crossed. It was clear he'd been standing there, quietly listening to us.

Janelle tensed a bit. "Yes, Chef? Did you have any problems with what we were discussing?"

"No." He stared at us for a silent moment. "Have you taken Ms. Cosi downstairs yet?"

"No, Chef."

"I'll do it." Keitel said, then abruptly turned and began moving toward the back of the kitchen. "Come with me, Ms. Cosi!"

Janelle shot me a glance, but I couldn't read it.

"Where am I going?" I whispered to her.

She arched a dark eyebrow. "Oh, you'll see . . ."

"Clare!" the man called, his legs continuing to stride toward the stairwell doorway. "Come see what's in my cellar!"

TWELVE

Chef Keitel led me down a set of creaking wooden steps and into the restaurant's dim, cluttered basement. With my high heels and skirt, I had to step carefully. Extra tables and chairs were stored here along with boxes of dry goods and cleaning supplies. There were four doors along one wall: three wooden and one metal. He waved me over to the metal door, pulled a ring of keys off his belt, and unlocked it.

"Come in . . ." he said, moving into the shadowy room.

I took one tentative step, a little wary about sharing the small space with such a monumental ego. On the other hand, I knew this could be the best chance I'd ever have to speak with Keitel in private, talk to him about Vinny's death and his relationship with my daughter.

"Come all the way in and close that door," Keitel said. "The temperature and humidity are kept at a constant level in here, and I'd like to keep it that way."

I shut the door. The second the steel handle clicked, he hit the light switch. A single bare bulb provided a golden illumination to the interior. Standing wooden shelves lined the walls, each one stacked with large and small wheels of white and yellow.

"Welcome to my cheese cave."

I couldn't believe it. Keitel had actually led me into the very room where he'd started his flirtation with Joy. That thought alone made it difficult for me to concentrate on the patter of words flowing out of the man's mouth.

Take it easy, I told myself. *This isn't Bluebeard's secret room. It's just a stupid closet full of cheese.*

He'd already started talking about the imported dairy products in the refrigerated space — from France, Spain, Switzerland, and Italy. Clearly, the man was proud of the collection, and he selected a few to sample, bringing them onto a small butcher block table set up against one shelf.

"So, what do you think? Are you game?"

I cleared my throat. It was very humid in here; warmer than a fridge but still downright chilly at fifty-seven degrees, if I could trust the thermometer hanging by the chef's head.

Keitel was in a nice, thick chef's jacket. I was in sheer stockings and a skirt. I'd left my matching green jacket upstairs, and my silk, lace-edged blouse only had half sleeves. I wasn't freezing *yet,* but I wasn't exactly comfortable, either. And I suddenly recalled what I'd said about Janelle's ball of sweet pastry dough. *It's so much easier to work when it's cold.*

"Sorry, Chef Keitel?" I said, folding my half-bare arms. "Game for . . . ?"

"Taste the cheese and tell me what you think it should be paired with. Nappy can do it blindfolded with his wine list. You *claim* coffee and cheese can be paired, too. If you really do have the palate, I'd like to see what we're paying for."

"Not all cheeses go with coffee," I warned. "Blues and runny cheeses, anything with strong ammonia notes, won't work. But there are plenty of fresh cheeses that will pair fabulously."

"So you *are* game?"

What is this? Some kind of test? Who does he think he's dealing with?

My eyes narrowed. "Bring it on."

From my work in catering, I knew plenty about cheese plate presentation. A proper

202

plate positioned the portions in a circular pattern, starting with the mildest cheese at twelve o'clock, then moving around the plate with increasingly stronger flavors, the final cheeses being the most pungent. As a world-class chef, Tommy was well aware of how to handle a palate, and he started me with a mild one.

"What do you think of this?" Keitel had sliced a wedge of semisoft cheese onto his wide-edged, bell-shaped cheese knife — a knife with a silver handle, I noticed, like the ones Joy said Keitel had imported from Thiers. Like the one found inside of Vinny Buccelli's corpse.

I moved to take hold of the knife's silver handle, but he pulled it high, out of my reach. "Close your eyes, Clare. I'll feed it to you."

I folded my arms, already not liking the direction of this little tasting.

"What?" Tommy smirked. "You're not afraid of the challenge, are you?"

The man's condescension was absolutely infuriating. "I hate to burst your bubble, Chef Keitel, but I'm not intimidated by you."

"Then close your damn eyes."

With an aggravated sigh, I did. And Keitel fed me the first cheese. "All right. Talk."

203

I let the soft morsel pass over my receptor cells, and I had to admit it was pretty amazing. "This product has an almost unctuously creamy mouthfeel, like a rich piece of cheesecake — without the sugar and eggs, of course. There's a thin rind and a mousse-like interior. It's very seductive, this cheese. Voluptuous . . ."

"Have another bite."

I savored and swallowed once more, my eyes still closed. "It comes into the mouth like a dense cake then dissolves into a creamy liquid without any trace of ammonia. It's obviously very high in butterfat, definitely a triple crème, and that's very good for a coffee pairing. I'd put this with the Ethiopian Yirgacheffe or the Purple Princess. The bright acidity of those coffees would cut the heavy fat of the cheese and make the gastronomic experience balanced and absolutely delightful."

I opened my eyes. Chef Keitel was staring at me with a veiled expression. "That's good," he said simply. "What you were tasting, by the way, was a Brillat-Savarin from île-de-France. It's one of my favorites."

"Brillat-Savarin? That's the name of the *cheese?* Isn't that the name of the eighteenth-century French food writer?"

Keitel regarded me. "You know, most of

my line cooks didn't even pick that up." He winked. "But I let them work for me anyway."

"So it really was named after the writer?"

"The cheese maker who conceived the product back in the 1930s was a big fan. His son Pierre carries on the tradition."

"Well, I guess a high-fat cheese is appropriate, since Brillat-Savarin was never one to deny himself."

Tommy grunted, presumably in agreement. "Try another?"

"Why not?"

"This cheese was aged by Hervé Mons outside of Roanne," Keitel informed me as he brought out a cheese corer to penetrate the wheel for a sample. "Okay, close 'em."

I dropped my eyelids, and something extraordinary was slipped into my mouth. *Oh, my* . . . This product was firmer than the Brillat-Savarin but still mild in flavor. "There's a nice nuttiness here. But it isn't overpowering. It's subtle and amusing . . . and the caramelized flavor is very delicately handled."

I paused, thinking it over. "I could see this paired with a fine red wine, so I'd have to go with my Kenyan medium roast, which, as your maître d' pointed out upstairs, has those umami characteristics of a really good burgundy in the finish. It would highlight but not overcome the flavor."

Keitel was actually smiling when I opened my eyes this time. "Did you know what kind of cheese you were eating?"

"Wild guess? Petit Basque, but I've never had one that good."

"Of course not." Tommy snorted. "Most Americans think a Petit Basque is a yellow wedge of industrially produced sheep milk coated in yellow wax."

"Welcome to *my* world."

"What do you mean?"

"Most Americans think coffee is supposed to come preground in a tin can. It's not always easy persuading people to pay premium prices for a premium product."

"True." Keitel paused, considering my point. "But it's easier in this city, you have to admit."

"I suppose. Of course, my customers only have to come up with an extra dollar or two for a transcendent experience. They can sip a cup slowly at one of my café tables and spend an hour on a beautiful piece of real estate. Your customers have to cough up well over one hundred to hang out in your house."

"Spoken like a proud member of the proletariat."

"I am. The democratization of luxury is my credo."

"I come from the working class, too, Clare. My father was a Navy cook who bought a diner. My mom worked in a bakery. I *get* where you're coming from, but I'm a man who's learned to appreciate the finer things; not having grown up with them makes them all the sweeter to savor, no?"

The man had a point.

Tommy shrugged. "Anyway, I have no problem with the markups on my menu. My customers come here for a four-star experience, and they get one."

"Except for the coffee."

Keitel shook his head. "You're one pushy female, you know that?"

"You have no idea."

"And you probably have no idea just how cutthroat my world is. People don't just want *good* anymore, Clare. They want *new*. They want fresh, novel, invigorating experiences. And, you know what? I can't blame them, because so do I. Solange is going to be five years old in seven weeks, and there are younger, flashier restaurants opening up every season, trying to seduce her customers away."

I found Keitel's characterization of Solange as a "her" intriguing. He'd trained for over a decade in France, so assigning a gender to something like a restaurant was understandable. Then again, from what Joy told me, Chef Keitel had acted "married" to the place since it opened.

Given his increasing and unexplained absences, however, I'd have to conclude that Tommy Keitel had been straying, not just on his wife and my daughter, but on his other mistress, Solange. The question was *why?* Wasn't this his big dream come true, the restaurant he'd envisioned over a decade ago on the west bank of Paris?

"Chef, I overheard you speaking with someone named Anton?"

"That would be Anton Wright, Solange's owner."

"It sounded like you two were having a disagreement about something."

"Let's do two more cheeses," Tommy said, completely ignoring my query. "Then we'll have a complete cheese-and-coffee pairings offering to try next week. That'll give the regulars something new, eh?"

My eyebrows rose at that. "You want to put the tasting we're doing *right now* on your menu?"

"That's what I just said, isn't it? Now, close your damn eyes."

And he calls me pushy?

Keitel slipped a Proosdy into my mouth. The cheese was from north Holland and had the characteristics of a really fine Gouda.

"It's hard on the initial bite, yet soft as the tooth penetrates. The flavor is much stronger than your previous offerings, but I'm a real sucker for muscular cheeses like this one."

"Really?"

"Yes, my grandmother ran a little Italian grocery, so I grew up on this kind of sharpness: aged provolones, pecarinos, and asiagos. The first taste can be overpowering, but I love a cheese that's been well-aged."

"Is that so?"

"I'm tasting some caramelized notes in this product . . . butterscotch, I'd say . . . and also some satisfyingly salty bursts — I'm assuming from tiny crystallized curds within the meat. I think that's what's so tantalizing about this one. The coarse little bursts provide big surprises. They catch you off guard with these unexpected explosions of intensity. The effect is highly stimulating."

"Well, then. Open up for more."

Keitel fed me another slice, and I continued to chew and swallow blindly. "I'd definitely want to pair this one with an espresso."

"My kitchen doesn't have an espresso machine."

"Oh, right. Of course. We're using French presses exclusively, so I'd fall back on our Italian Roast; that's the next best thing to an espresso for that dark, caramelized flavor. The Italian is also luxuriously full-bodied."

"Full-bodied." He grunted softly. "Now that's something I can appreciate."

"And there's a level of smokiness in the Italian that can take on the power and sharpness that's present here. Really stand up to it."

Keitel was quiet a long moment as he fed me another bite. "It's good to have that bite in there, don't you think, Clare?" His voice sounded lower and softer all of a sudden. "It's something I think a woman like you, with such well-developed senses, can appreciate. The pungency awakens that mature palate of yours, am I right? Excites it? Challenges it?"

I swallowed uneasily, my eyes still closed. Up to now, I thought we were talking about *cheese.* But now I was getting the distinct impression that Tommy Keitel was talking about something else.

THIRTEEN

I opened my eyes. In this small space, the chef's larger-than-life presence felt even larger. His muscular forearms appeared sculpted in granite. His confident energy was almost palpable. Without even touching me, I felt an unnerving infiltration of my personal space (but then, of course, the man *was* hand-feeding me with my eyes closed).

All things considered, I could actually understand why Joy had been so taken with the accomplished chef. He was arrogant, true, but he was intelligent, witty, and extremely magnetic. Unfortunately, he was also completely wrong for my daughter.

"Chef Keitel —"

"Call me Tommy, Clare. You're not one of my line cooks."

"Okay, Tommy . . . I'd like to say something to you that I don't want you to take badly."

Keitel laughed. "What? You don't like my

cheese cave?"

"Your cheese cave is magnificent. It's your taste in young women I'm having a problem with."

"Oh, is that right?" The chef's laughing blue eyes suddenly appeared far less amused.

"Joy mentioned to me that you two haven't gotten together in a while, and I thought that maybe you were having second thoughts about your relationship with her?"

Tommy rubbed his jutting chin and studied me for a long, silent moment. "Clare, do you by any chance remember the night you met me? It was at the Beekman Hotel, during that coffee-tasting party last month?"

"How could I forget?"

Tommy snorted. "You looked like you wanted to slap me — or strangle me with your bare hands."

"What are you? Psychic? That was my exact thought."

"I didn't have to be psychic to know what you were thinking. I could see it in your face — and, to be completely honest, I was shocked at how young your face was."

"What?"

"When Joy told me we'd be meeting her mother at the party, I expected a little old gray-haired lady, like my own mother back in Phoenix. When I saw how young you were, not to mention how attractive, I started to realize just how young Joy was. I know that probably sounds like a monumental cop-out on my part, but . . ." Tommy shrugged. "After that night I couldn't quite see her the same way anymore. I actually got to thinking you were more my speed."

"You've got to be kidding."

"Take it easy. I'm not hitting on you . . ." He raised an eyebrow. "Not unless you want me to."

"I want you to end your affair with Joy."

"Is that so?" Tommy leaned back against a wooden shelf and crossed his arms. "Normally I wouldn't take a directive like that seriously. I wouldn't even take an order like that from my wife seriously."

"Then I feel sorry for you — and your wife."

"Well, you don't know my wife, Clare. I'm just a paycheck to her. Not that it's your business."

"I know it's not. But I am Joy's mother, and even though she's a grown woman now, I feel I have a right to protect her from —"

"Stop." Tommy held up his hand. "Don't lecture me. I've already made the decision to break it off. So you can save your sanctimonious speech for Joy's next inappropriate suitor."

"Really? You're going to end the affair?"

"Really."

I closed my eyes with extreme relief. "Thank you, Lord."

"You're welcome, but I already told you to call me Tommy."

I opened my eyes. The man was smirking again. "You know, Keitel, you may have the biggest ego of any man I've ever met — including my ex-husband. And believe me, that's not an easy feat."

Tommy laughed. "I'm going to take that as a compliment."

"Well, it wasn't meant that way."

"How do you think I got here, Clare? By being consumed with self-doubt?"

I frowned. How could I argue with that?

"Stop fretting, okay?" he said. "I'm telling Joy today. I actually can't stand it anymore. She just won't stop hitting on me. It's embarrassing."

Despite my relief at hearing the end was near, I couldn't help feeling offended by Keitel's words. "Listen, mister, you're talking about my daughter, and —"

"You're taking offense. Don't. She's a lovely girl. But she's just that: a girl. I'm not interested in romancing her. I'm way be-

214

yond that crap. Frankly, I forgot how needy young women at Joy's age are. She wants continual reassurance. She wants constant attention. She wants things I can't begin to give her . . . so I'm sending her to Anatomy."

"What?" My head was spinning with the multiple bull's-eyes the man was hitting. This guy was way more evolved than I gave him credit for. "Say that again? Where are you sending her?"

"To Anatomy," he repeated. "You haven't heard of Robbie Gray's three-star downtown?"

"Yes . . . of course I've heard of the restaurant. It's just that . . . Joy's been so happy working here at Solange. Are you telling me that you're *firing* her?"

"I'm relocating her, that's all. Robbie's a good guy and a brilliant chef — not as brilliant as *me,* you understand." He gave me a little wink, presumably to take the edge off his unbridled arrogance. "He'll take over her internship year. I talked to her school an hour ago, told her Vinny's death was too much of a shock since they were friends. And it's better for her to relocate. They agreed. I'm going to give her top grades for her work so far. There won't be any problems."

I knew this would be very hard for Joy to

215

take. She wouldn't get the breaks at Anatomy that she'd gotten under Keitel, but then it wouldn't be the first time in history that the end of an affair on the job would end the job, as well. It wasn't the worst thing in the world for Joy to learn that early in her working life.

"So." Tommy smiled. "Are you going to slap me now?"

"No."

"Too bad. It might have been a turn-on — for *you*."

I rolled my eyes. "You're sick, you know that?"

"I'm just an uninhibited package of self-actualized testosterone. You can't condemn me for that."

"Yes, I can. And, the truth is, I'm relieved that Joy's leaving your restaurant. For a lot of reasons. You *do* know that Vincent Buccelli was killed with a knife from your kitchen?"

"What?" Tommy's confident mask suddenly fell. He looked genuinely horrified. "I *didn't* know that. The police never mentioned it."

"They will. My guess is today's interviews were only the first round. And since we're being truthful here, I'll be truthful, too. I only came here today because of Joy. I

wanted to get in here to keep an eye on her
— more precisely, the people around her.
The way Vinny was killed suggests someone
with knife skills did the deed. The knife's
handle and blade shape resemble the ones
you've got here at the restaurant, and I
believe someone here at the restaurant killed
that boy."

Tommy's eyes narrowed. "Who?"

"I don't know. But I'd like to find out.
Did you know Vinny was gay?"

"No."

"Did he have any kind of special friendship or relationship with anyone at your
restaurant?"

"The police asked me that, and, frankly, I
don't know . . . If he was, it wasn't obvious.
He certainly kept it under wraps."

"And did you say anything to the police
about you and Joy using Vinny's apartment
for sex?"

"Merde." Tommy closed his eyes, took a
breath. "How do you know about that? Did
Joy tell you?"

I nodded. "But she didn't tell the police."

"I didn't, either." He ran a hand through
his salt-and-pepper hair. "I didn't think it
was smart to give them a reason to look
harder at her — or me, frankly."

"Should they have?"

"You think I killed that boy?" Tommy met my eyes and held them. "I'm an ambitious prick, Clare. And I can be cutthroat in my business decisions. But I'm not a murderer . . . with maybe one exception." His fists clenched. "When I think of an innocent kid like Vincent Buccelli being stabbed to death, it makes me want to kill whoever did it."

Either Tommy was very good at faking honesty, or he was actually being honest with me. In this close proximity, I leaned toward the latter.

"If you didn't hurt Vinny, then who did?"

"I told you, Clare, I don't know. He was a quiet kid. He didn't have any close friends here, apart from Joy, or enemies — apart from Brigitte picking on him constantly, which is only one of the reasons I let her go."

"There are other reasons?"

"Brigitte's back on uppers again. I don't know which kind, but she knew the conditions of my hiring her. No drugs. She's using again, so she's fired."

I nodded, knowing Brigitte may or may not have been responsible for Vinny. Either way, I had to consider other possibilities — and fast. Tommy's patience could run out on me any second in his chilly cave. And I

218

was close to freezing. But now was my best shot at getting some answers.

"Not to change the subject, Tommy, but is Anton Wright the only owner of Solange?" I had to ask the question, if only to put to rest Mike Quinn's theory about organized crime being involved with the restaurant.

Tommy's brow knitted. He was obviously confused by my question. "Yeah, Wright's the only money man. Why do you care?"

"I was just curious."

"No, you weren't." Tommy's jutting chin lifted. "I can see it behind those bright green eyes of yours. You have an ulterior motive. What is it? You plan on hitting the man up for backing to open your own restaurant?"

"No. Nothing like that. I was just wondering if maybe he was involved with some shady partners. My father was a small-time bookie back in PA, so I'm not exactly an innocent about the way organized crime works. I know they can infiltrate legitimate businesses pretty easily, operate around them. Vinny's violent murder with a knife right out of your kitchen could have been a warning of some kind."

"That's a hell of a leap. You think Vinny was whacked?"

"It's a thought."

"It's ridiculous."

"So someone from the mob isn't threatening you or the owner, pressuring you or Anton Wright for more money, a bigger cut?"

"Listen, Anton's the son of a Brooklyn butcher. He doesn't like to admit that, but he grew up just like us. Then he became a stockbroker and made a few million on Wall Street, but it was always his dream to go into the restaurant business. Opening Solange was a big deal for him. It's the third Manhattan restaurant he's backed but his only successful one — due to *me,* of course. There's nothing more to it than that. Hey, are you shivering?"

"I'm okay."

"No, you're not. I should get you out of here if you're cold."

"Is there anyplace else we can be alone to talk?"

"Not really, but does that matter?"

"Yes." I put my hand on his chest, an automatic gesture as he moved to leave. "Just a few more questions —"

"You sure, Clare? Look at you. You're covered in goose bumps." The back of his hand moved to test my cheek. "Your flesh is like ice!"

"It's okay. Really. I'm fine."

"No, you're not." Before I could stop him, he'd stepped close and began to rub his large hands up and down my freezing arms. "How does that feel?"

I smirked up at the man. *"Inappropriate."*

Tommy laughed. "You really are a pistol, you know that? Too bad I didn't meet you before your daughter —"

"Tommy? Are you in there? They said you came down —" The door to the cave cracked open. And so did my world. My daughter stood there with a look of complete devastation on her young face. "Mom?"

Oh, no.

"Mom? And Tommy? I don't believe it."

I backed away from my daughter's lover. "Joy, this isn't what you think —"

"Yes it is," she whispered. "I'm not an idiot."

She bolted. I chased her. But her feet were in running shoes, and mine were in high heels. She was up the steps and out that restaurant's back door faster than Brigitte Rouille.

I moved as quickly as I could through the shade of the concrete alley. By the time I reached the open sidewalk, the afternoon sun was blinding. I'd spent too much time in Tommy's dim cellar. It had wrecked my vision.

I shaded my eyes and searched uptown

then down, but bodies of pedestrians obstructed my view. I darted and moved one way then another. But it was no use. I had no idea where my daughter had run.

"No! I *can't* have lost you!"

Tommy strode up behind me. "Clare, I'm sorry that happened."

"You and me both!"

We stood together on the sidewalk, squinting against the sun's glare as we spent another minute peering up and down the street.

"Don't sweat it, Clare," Tommy finally said.

"She's my daughter, you jerk! Of course I'm going to *sweat* it!"

"Look . . ." he said, his voice tight but conciliatory, "she left everything behind back there. Her knives are out of her locker and all over her prep table. I'm sure she left things in her locker, too. She'll be back. And when she comes, I'll talk to her. I'll explain that you and I were talking about Vinny and what she saw was completely innocent."

"Will you even *be* here when she gets back?" My eyes narrowed. "You're not taking off again?"

Tommy stiffened. "I'll be here at Solange all day and all night, likely into the wee hours. Brigitte's gone, and I've got some catching up to do." Hands on hips, he braced his legs, like a ship's captain readying for a storm. "Her replacement is very good, and he's as cocksure of himself as yours truly, but I still have to make sure Henry can handle his promotion. It's important that he's able to take care of things when I'm not here."

That sounded ominous to me. "So you plan on going AWOL again?"

Tommy looked away, glanced at his watch. "I have lots of work to do, Clare."

"But you *will* tell Joy about going to Anatomy?"

"Yes, by the time she leaves here tonight, she'll be only too happy to leave Solange. She'll be cursing my name, too."

"What exactly are you planning to do?"

"I'm going to break up with Joy publicly, in front of the entire staff."

"Does it have to be that brutal?"

"Hating me is the best thing for her," Tommy said. "And I want the best for your daughter. Don't you?"

I closed my eyes, steeling myself against the pain and shame in store for Joy.

"Believe me, Clare, in cases like these, the cleanest cut is the best."

FOURTEEN

"You what?!"

"Calm down, Matt."

"What did I tell you, Clare? Did I *not* tell you to stay out of the man's cheese cave?!"

"I know you did. I know. But it was my one chance to speak with Keitel privately . . ."

I was on my cell phone with Matt, pacing Solange's back alley. There'd been no more talking with Tommy after we returned to Solange's kitchen. The second he hit the back door, he went into extreme chef mode, shooting orders to cooks, tasting sauces, checking and rechecking ovens, and taking call after call on his cell phone — from vendors, colleagues, and the occasional VIP.

I hung around for another hour, waiting for Joy to return. I'd tried her cell phone and home phone, and got her voice mail on both. So I waited some more. Then I could tell I was in the way, and I ducked into the

alley to make the call that I was dreading —
to my ex-husband.

"I never meant for Joy to see us," I told
Matt. "She wasn't even scheduled to arrive
for another hour."

"Obviously, she got there early to talk with
Tommy."

"Well, now she's over an hour *late*." I
checked my watch again. It was almost three
thirty. "I'm worried about her. Are you sure
you checked your cell's messages? She
hasn't tried to call you?"

"Believe me, she hasn't. And if she does,
it'll have to be from a pay phone. Salinas
confiscated her cell phone last night, don't
you remember?"

"Of course, right . . ." With so much happening, I'd forgotten. "Well, if she does call
you, let me know, okay? And it's important
that she report back to the restaurant. I just
found out that Brigitte Rouille's been fired
so she's no longer a threat to Joy —"

"Wait, slow down. Brigitte's been fired?
That's good news, isn't it?"

"Yes, but I still want our daughter out of
this kitchen altogether, and that can't happen until Tommy fires her."

"What do you mean fires her? Run that
by me again . . . ?"

I brought Matt up to speed on Tommy's

225

intention to break up with Joy — and not with roses and a farewell poem. It was going to be ugly. Matt swore a few times upon hearing the plan, but he calmed down when I pointed out that the result of all this was getting our girl out of Solange's kitchen and over her infatuation with Tommy Keitel in record time.

"Tommy's going to give her high marks for her work under him —" I closed my eyes, choking for a second on my own Freudian phrasing. "*Anyway,* she can finish her internship at another great New York restaurant. That's not a bad ending."

"No," Matt grudgingly admitted. "It's not."

"You just have to help me with Joy. You have to explain to her that you and I agreed to pitch Keitel on a coffee contract with the Blend. She'll believe you. And hopefully she'll understand what was going on wasn't anything more than my helping the man create a pairings menu."

"If I were you, Clare, given what she saw, I wouldn't put Keitel and you and *pairing* in the same sentence."

Oh, God . . . I squeezed my eyes shut. "Please, Matt, if she comes back down to the Blend, let me know."

"I'm not at the Blend."

226

"Where are you?"

"The top of the Empire State Building."

"Excuse me? You're not jumping, are you? You can't miss Breanne *that* much."

"Koa Waipuna is here with his wife and kids for a shopping and sightseeing excursion," he said flatly. "I promised to show him and his family around New York today. I mentioned it to you earlier —"

"I guess I was distracted. You can't get out of it?"

"No, Clare. You know very well the Waipunas' coffee farm is one of our best sources for Kona on the Big Island. Don't you remember how well Koa's parents treated you and me on our honeymoon —"

I gagged. "You mean back in the Paleozoic?"

"I know it's ancient history, but I can't bug out on them —"

"Okay, okay. You're right. I'm sorry. I'm just upset. But please phone me if Joy contacts you."

"Will do."

"Ms. Cosi?"

A man had called my name. I closed my phone and turned in the alley to see a familiar face. It was René, the waiter who'd served Madame and me the previous evening. He was standing in the back door

227

of Solange's kitchen.

"Yes, René?"

"I'm sorry to bother you, Ms. Cosi, but Monsieur Dornier would like you to pack up your French presses. We are preparing for dinner service."

"Of course! Of course!"

I walked through the busy kitchen and into Solange's dining room. Waiters in white aprons and black jackets were bustling around the room, shrouding tables with linen, putting down place settings, arranging fresh flowers.

I quickly packed up my presses, beans, grinder, paper cups, and electric hot-water pot into my carrying case. I was just crouching down to zip up the little Pullman when I heard Tommy Keitel coming into the dining room.

"Nappy? What is it? René said you wanted to speak with me?"

"You got another one of those notes, Tommy. I found it in our mail slot."

Another note? I repeated to myself. I was still crouched down with my Pullman case, but I wanted to see what was happening, so I rose up just enough to peek up over the edge of the cherrywood table.

Napoleon Dornier was handing Chef Keitel a glossy black envelope at least eight by eleven inches large. Tommy examined the outside label a moment, then ripped open the end. He glanced at the single white page inside and swore.

"That son of a bitch! It's him again. Just burn it, Nappy, like all the others."

Keitel tossed the envelope to Dornier then strode away and slammed back through the doors to his kitchen.

What the hell was in that envelope? As I watched Dornier walk off with it, I tried to come up with a way to finagle a look at its contents or persuade Dornier to tell me what was going on. But I never got the chance to do either, because my cell phone went off.

Hoping it was Matt, I quickly flipped it open. The digital screen said the Village Blend was calling. Praying that my daughter had gone down there and was now trying to reach me, I answered.

"Hello?!"

"It's me, boss."

Damn. "Esther? What's up?"

"Houston, we've got a problem!"

"What's wrong?"

"Gardner's not coming in. He's stuck on the road between D.C. and New York."

"Is he okay?"

"His friend's piece of crap car broke down

outside of Philly, and I can't find anyone to take his shift. Tucker's long gone, and Dante's due to leave at four. I'm fine flying solo for a little while, but a very thirsty NYU Law study group just came in, half of a Dance 10 class is waiting for their lattes, and pretty soon it's going to be a *zoo* here with the after-work crowd."

Crap.

"I need backup, boss! You know what those people are like in the afternoons. Most of them haven't had their caffeine fix since lunch. They're animals!"

"Calm down, Esther. I'll be down there in thirty. Just hold the fort alone for now."

With a sigh, I snapped closed the phone. Joy hadn't shown up yet, Napoleon Dornier and that black glossy envelope had disappeared, and one purse-lipped waiter, holding an armload of folded linen, was now giving me that look of strained politeness that clearly said: *Excusez-moi, Madame. But would you mind getting the hell out of my way!*

"Okay, okay, I'm going," I mumbled. Then, yanking my little wheeled case of French presses behind me, I headed for the door.

The rest of the afternoon and evening went by in a blur. It was Friday, an electric night for the Village, and the crowds of coffee drinkers and pastry eaters just kept on ringing the little bell above our front door.

After the office and hospital workers left, the pre- and postdinner crowds flooded us: couples on dates, NYU students hanging out, older acquaintances having long talks, cold, tired tourists hoping to warm up and wake up with a hot beverage. And though Saturday and even Sunday evenings were the biggest of the week for the bridge and tunnel crowd, Friday had its fair share of business from the residents of New Jersey and the other four of New York's five boroughs.

Esther and I worked well as a team. The faster the crowds came in, the faster we turned them over with espressos, lattes, cappuccinos, muffins, cookies, cannoli, tarts, and, bizarrely, even a few icy coffee frappes — a chilling choice on a frosty November night, but who was I to judge a paying customer's coffee craving?

By ten o'clock, the pace at the bar finally slowed, although dozens of customers were still lounging on the shop's first and second floors, mostly clustered around the warmth of the fireplaces. By eleven fifteen, we were getting ready to start cleaning and closing.

"Do you want me to shoo the rest of the

231

customers out?" Esther asked, wiping her hands on a dish towel.

I shook my head, wiping my own hands on my jeans — I'd changed back into work clothes after leaving Solange. "I'll do it myself. You did a great job today, Esther. If you've finished restocking, you can hit the road."

"Thanks, boss." Esther yawned. "I've got to sack out fast and recuperate before BB takes me out tomorrow. I'd hate to be wrecked for our big date."

"You're still interested in that rapper?" I asked, too weary to mask my skeptical tone.

"Am I *still* interested?" Esther gawked at me through her black-framed glasses as if I'd just asked her if the Earth was flat. "I'll have you know that boy *rocks* my world. And unless a dirty bomb goes off somewhere in the tristate area mañana, he'll be rocking it at exactly this time twenty-four hours from now."

I sighed. Esther was about the only person I knew who'd even consider bringing a nuclear fallout reference into her anticipation for a Saturday night date.

"Then I'm happy for you, Esther," I told her sincerely. "Have a good night."

"Ciao, boss!"

■ ■ ■ ■

By midnight, my Goth girl barista was long gone, and I had shooed the last of the customers out, too. I was about to twist the key on the front dead bolt when I noticed a familiar figure in a long, cinnamon-colored overcoat negotiating the traffic across Hudson Street.

The lanky, broad-shouldered detective strode right up to the Blend's entrance and stood there, looking down at me through the beveled glass. I cracked open the heavy door.

"Hi, Mike."

"Hi, Clare."

"Can I come in?"

"Yes . . . of course . . ."

I stepped back and let Mike Quinn step through. A bone-chilling blast of damp air swept in with him off the river just a few blocks away. I shuddered, remembering that humidified cave of Keitel's that had led to the misunderstanding with my daughter.

I *still* hadn't heard from Joy. And I'd checked in with Matt so often, he'd told me to cool it already because his cell's battery was about to die, and he still had a long night ahead squiring Mr. and Mrs. Kona

Coffee, Jr., around.

While the Waipuna kids were with a sitter at the hotel, Matt had taken their young parents to a Broadway show and a late dinner. Now they were on their way to the first in a long list of nightspots that they'd read about on the Internet and wanted to visit.

"Did you get my voice mail message?" Mike asked. His tone was flat, his face impassive. The man had all the life of an ice sculpture.

"Your message?" I repeated weakly. "You mean the ominous one that said you wanted to have 'a talk' with me?"

Mike nodded. "I stopped by twice earlier, but Tucker told me you were uptown on business."

"Yeah. That was your idea, if you recall. I pitched Solange on serving coffee from the Village Blend."

"Oh, right . . . How did that go?"

"They want the contract, but it was still a catastrophe . . ."

I had so much to tell Mike: Joy's close friend being murdered, Joy being looked at as a suspect, my infiltration of her workplace in search of the boy's killer, the disastrous misunderstanding when my daughter found me in the arms of her married lover. *Oh, where to begin?*

234

"So . . . do you want your usual latte?" I asked, turning from the door. I began walking toward the espresso bar, but Mike didn't follow.

"I can't stay long, Clare," he said sharply.

I turned back around. His face was still a stark plane. And his eyes, which were always so alive when they gazed at me, were now still, blue stones. There was no sentiment in them, no playfulness, no affection, hardly a bit of life.

"You don't have time for coffee?" I said weakly. "Not even one cup?"

"It's Friday, and the clubs are crowded," he said. "We've doubled the number of undercover officers tonight."

"Oh, right . . . the May–September gang. Still no bites?"

"Nothing yet. And they struck twice last night; a man and a woman were victimized after leaving two different clubs. We missed them both."

I could see that failure had been hard for him. Really hard. It was there in his tense jawline, his weary posture. "Well, hang in there," I said gamely. "The biggest clubbing days are tonight, tomorrow, and even Sunday. I bet you'll nail them before the end of the weekend."

"Yeah . . ." Mike said, but he failed to

buck up. Then his dead expression became downright grim. "Listen, Clare, I don't have much time, and I didn't want to do this over the phone."

Oh, God. "The talk." Oh, God . . .

"I'm sorry, Clare. I really am . . ."

I stepped back, closed my eyes. *He's really going to do this. He's going to break us up.* I could feel tears already welling up in my eyes and throat, choking me.

"Just say it, Mike."

"Okay." He took a breath. "I want you to kick Allegro out of your apartment."

I opened my eyes. "What?"

"I want you to take away his key, throw out his pants and his shirts and his shoes. I want you to evict him from your living space."

"I can't do that, Mike. My ex-husband has a legal right to live there. His mother owns the duplex, the entire building, and she had us sign papers —"

"Then *you* need to leave, because I can't go on like this. I want a relationship with you, Clare. I do. And I know you want more from me. Believe me, I'm willing to give it. But I need to know the woman I'm falling for isn't going to make a fool of me."

"Mike, I don't know why you think —"

"Hear me out, Clare!"

His sharp tone floored me. Mike rarely raised his voice. And when he did, it was a holy terror — the kind of intensity that came from years of cowing defiant criminals and taking command at crime scenes.

"Okay," I said softly. "Talk."

"I'm not a kid anymore, some Dudley Do-Right in a uniform that I was at twenty-six when I met my wife. I won't just stumble along in a relationship again, letting things happen to me, hoping things just work themselves out. I've been through too much craziness already in my marriage. So you take the time you need to think about what you want —"

"Stop, Mike. Please!"

Quinn did. And I was stunned to see the look of pure dread come over his face. I'd never seen him scared before. *My God, he thinks I'm going to choose my ex-husband.*

"Mike, I don't have to think about it," I said quickly. "I *know* what I want. I want you. I want us to give this relationship a chance. If I didn't, I never would have said yes to a first date, let alone a second, third, fourth — what are we up to now?"

"We've been out nine times, Clare. Believe me, I've kept count. Nine agonizingly arousing necking sessions followed by a number of extremely long, lonely hours alone in bed."

"Well, you won't have to be alone much longer. And neither will I."

"Are you sure, Clare? You're really prepared to move out of that beautiful, convenient duplex upstairs?" He jerked his thumb towards the ceiling.

"Moving out isn't the problem," I said with a sigh. "It's where do I move in? Rents are crazy steep in the West Village. Maybe I should try Alphabet City, too. It isn't too far. How did you get your place? I never asked you about it, but it seemed like you found it pretty fast."

"The landlord held an opening for me in the building."

"He what? He *held* an opening? In Manhattan? Were you blackmailing the guy?"

Mike's grim expression finally loosened a little. His chilly gaze began to warm. "The landlord's a retired detective. I was his partner for a few years there. He inherited the building, and he's been renting to divorced cops ever since."

"Only divorced cops?"

"The rookies are usually still living at home. The married guys get houses in the boroughs. It's the older guys whose marriages break up that need the camaraderie.

We even get together once a week to hang out, shoot the breeze."

"So you belong to a divorced men's group?"

"We don't think of it that way."

"Of course you do. That's why you never mentioned it until now." I stifled a laugh.

Mike rolled his eyes, checked his watch. "I've got to get going . . ."

"Okay, but . . . can we make a date to meet? At your place? I promise I'll move out of the duplex the first chance I get. Is that good enough for you?"

Mike smiled for the first time since he walked in my door. "Yeah," he said, leaning in. "It's good enough."

His hand caressed my hair, and he pulled me close, brushed my lips with his. But the light kiss wasn't enough for either of us, and we locked pretty tightly for a few minutes.

"How about we get together Monday afternoon?" Mike suggested softly when we finally parted. "If you can take off, I can arrange a little picnic on the floor of my one-bedroom."

I smiled. "Let me guess; it's a *picnic* because you still don't have actual furniture yet."

"You're right, Cosi. I admit it. See that?

And you didn't even have to beat it out of me." Mike's eyes were laughing now; his voice was warm. I'd finally melted him down to the human race.

"I told you before, Lieutenant, many times. You should let me help you detect some furniture. I promise I'll go easy on your credit cards."

"Okay, okay. I'll give in soon. In the meantime, you'll be happy to know I do have a nice big bed in the bedroom. Is that good enough for now?"

"That's more than good enough, mister. That's *I'll be there with bells on.*"

"Really . . . just bells, huh?" Mike's eyebrow arched. "Kinky."

I swatted him. He laughed. And then we heard a bell for real; the front door was opening again.

"Hello, hello!" Matt's mother waltzed in, bundled in a floor-length fur.

"Madame?" I checked my watch. "It's almost twelve thirty. What are you doing here?"

"I wanted to talk to you in person, Clare. It's rather important."

Mike smiled down at me. "I have to get going." He squeezed my shoulder. "I'll call you."

I nodded. "Be safe."

Mike winked at me, gave a polite nod to Madame, and then he was gone.

"I remember that young man," Madame said as she waved me over to a café table. "He's that nice detective who fixed your traffic violation last month."

"You mean the BOLO that resulted from the police chase that ensued after you told me to run that red light in Brooklyn?"

"Yes, that one."

"Mike's handy that way." We both sat down. "So what's up? Do you want some coffee?"

"No, dear."

I threw up my hands. "I can't give it away tonight."

"It's just that I don't have much time. My young man is picking me up here in" — she checked her watch — "fifteen minutes."

"Your *young* man?"

"He's only just turned sixty-six, quite a difference in our ages, but I couldn't resist his charms."

"Is this the man who was 'eye-flirting' with you last night at Solange?"

"The same. We're going to a nightclub downtown. I haven't done anything like that in years. And I'm quite looking forward to it!"

"Well, I'd love to hear more about him,

but I don't want you to keep him waiting. So what's up? Why are you here so late?"

"It's Joy."

My breath caught. "You've heard from her?"

"I just left her, Clare. We spent the evening together. Now she's on her way uptown."

"Uptown? Why?"

"She's going back to Solange, of course."

FIFTEEN

Inside of six minutes, I'd gotten the entire story out of Madame and was waving down a taxi on Hudson. Then I was off, my driver heading uptown, transporting me back to Tommy Keitel's hellacious house of haute cuisine.

Madame stayed behind to lock up the Blend, and I was indebted to her for that. But I was even more grateful to her for telling me the one thing I'd been waiting all night to hear:

"Joy wasn't upset with you, Clare, not in the least."

According to Madame, when Joy had bolted away from that cheese cave and out of the cellar, she hadn't been running from me. She'd been running from Tommy Keitel . . .

"She was mortified by Keitel's behavior," Madame had told me. "Seeing his hands on you in that small room, she knew instantly that he was making a pass. It was a tremendous blow to her ego. But she didn't blame you. She blamed him."

Apparently, after Joy's long, tearful walk, she'd returned to her job. But as soon as she started working at her prep table, Tommy Keitel delivered the final cut.

"He loudly told her in the open kitchen that he'd made a decision. He no longer wanted to see her romantically. They were through. Not only that, as of Monday, she was to report to Robbie Gray at his restaurant downtown, where she'd serve out the remainder of her internship year."

Listening to Madame's tale, my whole body went rigid. I'd already known what Tommy had planned for Joy, but hearing the blow-by-blow made me sick to my stomach.

"Our girl was humiliated, of course," Madame went on. "The entire kitchen brigade heard Tommy toss Joy away like a piece of substandard produce. Rather than break down in front of her colleagues, she fled the restaurant and took a cab to my apartment to cry it all out."

My shoulders sagged upon hearing that. "Why didn't she come to me?"

"Because, Clare, down deep Joy knew you were right all along about Tommy. Now she's humiliated. But most of all, she's ashamed. She didn't want you to see her crying over Tommy. That's what she told me. She simply wants you to be proud of her again —"

"But I am proud of her! She made a mistake. But for so many reasons, I'm still so very proud of Joy. She should know that."

"She knows you love her, Clare. That much I can promise you. She only came to me because she knew I wouldn't ask questions. I'd just let her cry it out. And my goodness, she did. She cried herself to sleep on my sofa. When she woke up, she told me the whole story.

"I invited her to stay the night, but she said no. She washed her face, brushed her hair, and announced she was going back to Solange to retrieve her knives and personal items. I thought it was rather late to do that, but she was quite determined. And she assured me that someone would be there . . ."

Of course, *someone* would be there — Tommy Keitel himself — which was why I was speeding toward his restaurant now. Joy wasn't going back there to pick up her knives and personal items. I was certain she was really going there to see Tommy one more time, either to tell him off or make a last desperate attempt to win him back.

But if Joy was going up there looking for closure, explanations, or any kind of comfort, she was about to be severely disappointed because Keitel's singular goal tonight was to leave her emotionally bloodied. I couldn't let her go through that alone, but there was an even more vital reason I was speeding north. Solange was a minefield, and I didn't want Joy anywhere near its ticking bombs, especially at this hour.

Tommy Keitel and Anton Wright were feuding about something. Who knew if that would lead to violence? And even though Brigitte Rouille had been fired, it didn't preclude her returning to the scene to vent some rage. Then there was that glossy black envelope that made Tommy crazy. What was inside that thing? Was someone blackmailing the man? Would there be deadly repercussions if he failed to comply?

And what about Tommy's creepy Russian friend Nick? The mysterious man in black from Brighton Beach had arrived at the restaurant late the previous night. If he really was a mobster, then any number of shady things could be going on in Solange's kitchen after hours.

As my taxi sped uptown, I continued to fret, hoping the least I would find when I entered the premises was some petty scene — like my daughter in tears, begging her inappropriate lover to take her back; or Tommy Keitel desperately dodging Joy's own personal choice of flying cutlery.

I can handle the situation either way, I told myself. *I'll just pull my daughter into my arms, and we'll both wave good-bye to Chef Tommy Keitel for good.*

Thankfully, traffic was light, and within fifteen minutes we were rolling up to the curb beside Solange's signature burgundy awning. I paid the cabbie and approached the glass door. Beyond the window, the reception area was dimly lit, the only illumination a menu set on a glowing brass pedestal. My gloved fingers closed around the front door's long handle. I pushed, and the door opened.

A little surprised that it was still unlocked, I stepped into the restaurant. With a quiet *swish,* the door swung closed behind me. I unbuttoned my coat.

"Hello?" I called into the darkness of the empty dining room.

The large, shadowy space carried a slight funereal scent of decaying lilies. With the crystal and copper chandeliers extinguished, the sunny walls now looked a sick, pasty yellow. The tablecloths, once the color of crème fraîche, now looked like gray ghosts. The gargoyles weren't so whimsical anymore. From their high perches, their carved faces had turned grotesque, like cackling spies from the underworld. Their wooden eyes wouldn't stop following me as I stepped around the gathering of shrouded tables.

My low boots were halfway across the room when a shrill scream froze me in place. The cry had come from the kitchen, and I instantly took off for the double doors. As I pushed from murky dimness into bright fluorescence, I heard a young woman's voice wail.

"Oh, no! Noooo! God, no . . ."

The sound of sobbing came next, and I blinked against the glare, hurrying forward around the high service counter.

"Joy!"

"Mom, stay back!" my daughter cried, rushing to my side.

There was moist heat in the room, the scent of simmering stock. *Why is someone cooking at this hour?*

As Joy gripped my arm, I finally spied a figure in the center of the kitchen. The man was sitting on a metal stool, his body slumped all the way over a cutting board covered with purple cubes of freshly cut beets, coated now with his own blood. The victim had been stabbed in the same manner as Vincent Buccelli. Someone had plunged a chef's knife deep into the shoulder at the base of his throat.

I gently removed my daughter's clinging grip, stepped closer. I knew who the man was before I saw his face. I recognized the salt-and-pepper hair, the thickly muscled forearms under rolled-up sleeves.

The corpse was Tommy Keitel.

I swallowed and took another step forward, just to make sure.

When I saw the wide, sightless blue eyes, I knew he was gone. And I recognized something else. The murder weapon had a black handle and the familiar Shun symbol on the blade. This was a ten-inch Shun Elite chef's knife, I realized with a jolt. It retailed for hundreds of dollars and was forged from powdered steel, allowing for an exceedingly sharp and durable edge.

It's crazy the kinds of things that pop into your mind at a time like this. But these facts were stored in my memory because I'd purchased this very knife the previous December.

The evidence was undeniable. Tommy Keitel had been murdered with my child's own personal chef's knife, the one I'd given her last Christmas Day.

"Mom, come away," Joy insisted, tears streaming down her cheeks.

"In a second," I replied.

A knife kit was open on another prep table next to Tommy's corpse. The knives were stored in a fiery red canvas bag with a luggage ID tag and plastic cat charm dangling from the zipper. All the knives were in their sheaths except one.

I faced Joy, who had her back against the swinging double doors.

"Your knife kit is here, Joy," I said, trying to remain steady. "Were you packing up when this happened?"

I couldn't believe it, but I was actually asking my daughter if she had just killed her lover.

Joy shook her head, used the long sleeve of her pink jersey to swipe at the unceasing flow from her eyes. "I just got here five minutes ago . . ." she said between gasping sobs. "The doors were unlocked . . . so I knew Tommy was . . . probably back here . . . in the kitchen . . . I came back here and found him . . . like that . . ."

"Call 911," I said.

Joy took a step toward the phone on the wall.

"No!" I cried. "Don't touch that phone! Don't touch anything! Use your cell."

"I can't. Lieutenant Salinas took it last night."

"That's right. Okay . . ." I put my arm around my daughter. "Come with me, honey. I have my cell. We'll call the police from the dining room."

Then, with a final glance at the late Tommy Keitel, I led Joy out of his kitchen.

Within minutes of my 911 call, two uniformed officers arrived. One man waited with us — although I suspected he was really guarding us. The second man went into the kitchen, and almost immediately came out again. These two were followed by more men in uniforms, and a pair of plainclothes detectives who sat us down at a table.

Someone turned on the lights, and the dining room was bathed in a golden glow. The walls were sunny yellow again, the room warm and welcoming. But the laughing gargoyles hadn't changed for me. From their balcony seats, they appeared to be grinning at the officious activities of police personnel as if Chef Keitel's grim, brutal murder had been staged entirely for their amusement.

I closed my eyes, said a prayer for Tommy's soul. Yet the prickly feeling of dread was still chilling my skin. Beneath the buzz of conversations, I could almost hear a quiet, demonic cackling. Something terrible was still to come. Even the gargoyles knew it.

I took a breath, blocked these dark thoughts, and tried to avoid looking up.

In a burst of sound and movement, new arrivals entered the premises, a horde of men and women in overalls, clutching rolls of yellow crime-scene tape. The forensics team streamed in through the dining room and into the kitchen.

A short time after that, the two detectives on the case introduced themselves. Eugene Lippert and Ray Tatum were part of the Nineteenth Precinct's detective squad. Lippert was probably fifty, his beige suit slightly rumpled. He had thick ankles and wore Hush Puppies on his large feet.

His partner, Tatum, was a decade younger, African American, and much more stylishly dressed in black slacks, a black turtleneck, and a tailored gray jacket. Lippert was the senior man, but he was the quiet, reserved one. Tatum was the one who radiated outgoing authority, shooting reminders or instructions to the uniformed officers and asking questions of the forensics people.

The two men worked well together. When

they got around to us, they were both very cordial. They were also very professional, gently separating Joy and me before I even realized what was happening. I was speaking to Lippert, looked up, and Detective Tatum was already guiding my daughter to a table on the other side of the dining room.

"Where are you taking Joy —"

"Relax, Ms. Cosi. It's Clare, right?" Lippert asked.

"Yes," I nodded, my gaze fixed on my daughter.

"My partner just wants to ask the young lady a few questions in private," Lippert explained. He sat down across from me, his florid face and rust-colored comb-over blocking my view of the other table.

"I'd like to ask you a few questions, too," Lippert continued. His voice was warm, and through his sagging hazel eyes, he regarded me with a sympathetic expression. "We really need to find the person who committed this crime, and you might be able to help us do that."

His tone was urgent and earnest and kind, a pleasant change from Lieutenant Salinas's approach the previous night, which veered from downright suspicious to mildly hostile. I was relieved that Detective Lippert was treating me like a witness, not like a criminal

— or an accomplice.

"I'm sorry to have to do this, Ms. Cosi. I know you've had a bad experience tonight." Lippert tilted his head slightly. "But if you can answer my questions, it would be a really big help. It's best if we talk now, while the memories are fresh, and we can get as accurate a timetable as possible. It would probably be the most important thing you could do for us to help us catch the killer . . . But if you'd rather not, if it's too trying to talk about right now . . . I certainly understand."

Lippert paused expectantly, a notebook in one hand, a pen in the other.

"Of course we can talk," I said. "I want to help you find the killer. Tommy Keitel was no saint, but he certainly didn't deserve to die like this."

The detective smiled. "Good. Let's start at the beginning. Tell me everything you think is relevant, starting with why you and your daughter were here after hours in the first place."

I explained to Lippert about my daughter's leaving the restaurant earlier in the evening and then coming back for her knives. I explained to Lippert that Joy had only returned to the restaurant to pick up her stuff, and that I came here to meet her.

When Lippert asked me what my daughter's relationship was with the deceased, however, I clammed up.

"She works for him," I said. *That's all you need to know right now. You need to find Keitel's killer, not focus on Joy.*

"Joy worked for the victim. I see," Lippert said. "And is that all they were to each other? Just employer and employee?"

"She was an intern here for the last three months." I kept my answer short and only slightly evasive. "Her culinary school can confirm that."

Then I switched the subject pronto and began telling Detective Lippert about Brigitte Rouille and her violent outburst. I also mentioned that Tommy Keitel was feuding with the restaurant's owner, Anton Wright, about something. I brought up that shady character named Nick and told Lippert about Keitel getting some kind of mysterious missive in a glossy black envelope.

"It sounded like Chef Keitel received more than one of these envelopes," I said. "And whatever was inside angered him tremendously. It could have been a threat, even blackmail of some kind."

"Blackmail? Hmmmm. And why do you think that, Ms. Cosi? Because the letter came in a black envelope?"

I stared at Lippert. "I think it's something you should look into."

"I see . . ."

Detective Lippert continued to listen to me talk, he even took some notes, but then he went right back to Joy. He asked what "stuff" my daughter had come for so late, and I told him about the things in her locker and her expensive knife set.

"You're talking about the knife kit spread out on the counter beside the deceased?" Lippert asked.

"Yes." I nodded. "It's Joy's."

The luggage tag attached to the set had my daughter's name and address right on it. Unless they were idiots, the detectives had to know it was Joy's already.

"Maybe Chef Keitel was packing up Joy's knives when the killer arrived," I theorized.

"And the killer used your daughter's knife to kill him?"

"I guess it was the closest blade in sight —"

Lippert's expression turned thoughtful then mildly puzzled. "In a kitchen full of knives? There are blades and meat hammers and skewers hanging all over the place in there. Why would some stranger just happen to grab your daughter's knife?"

Clearly, Detective Lippert was playing

with the idea of Joy as the killer. I wasn't surprised he wanted to explore this angle, but I was sure I could talk some sense into him.

"Listen," I said quickly. "It's important that you find Brigitte Rouille as soon as possible. I'll bet she still has bloodstains on her. I wasn't sure before, but now it makes perfect sense. She's on drugs. Her life's been spinning out of control for weeks now. Brigitte tried to stab Joy yesterday, in the restaurant. I witnessed that myself. I think she has a grudge against my daughter . . . and if you scratch the surface, I'll bet she had a past with Tommy Keitel. I remember someone saying that they'd known each other a long time. And Tommy *is* a womanizer. Brigitte could have been jealous of Joy, addled by the drugs . . . Lots of people saw the woman threaten my daughter. Ask them. I'll bet that's even why she used my daughter's knife to kill Tommy. She wanted to make it look like Joy committed the crime . . ."

I closed my eyes, realizing for the first time that Vinny Buccelli might have been killed for the very same reason: to frame Joy.

My God, I realized, *I'll bet Brigitte even knew about Tommy and Joy using Vinny's apartment for sex!*

"But why would this Brigitte person kill her boss?" Lippert asked.

"Because Tommy wasn't her boss anymore. Chef Keitel fired Brigitte this morning, banned her from his kitchen. At this stage of her career, it could ruin her. Any future work would have relied on a good recommendation, and it sounded like Solange was the last chance she had. Isn't that a strong enough motive for her to kill Keitel?"

Lippert shrugged. "Sure it is, Ms. Cosi, but your daughter was the one who was here. She had the opportunity."

"But Joy's got no blood on her —"

"Soap and water will clean blood. And since Keitel was killed in a kitchen, the killer would have had easy access to a sink to clean up. As for bloodied clothes, those are easy enough to change out of, aren't they?"

We went around like that for a few minutes when Detective Tatum rose from the table where he'd been sitting with Joy. He walked to the center of the dining room, caught Lippert's eye, and waved him over.

I saw Joy wiping her eyes at the table across the room. But she didn't look overly distressed anymore. In fact, her expression was a little calmer, as if she'd just unloaded her burden on a really sympathetic friend.

258

Oh, no.

I could feel the dread creeping up my spine. Two uniformed officers were still standing over her. They seemed too close. I made a move to go to her, but a policeman hovering near me put his heavy hand on my shoulder. I hadn't noticed him back there.

"Please stay in your seat, ma'am," he said. "Detective Lippert will be back in a moment."

I watched the detectives confer. They spoke quietly, not glancing at me or my daughter. They talked for at least ten solid minutes, glancing at their notebooks to compare facts. Finally the two men nodded.

Frowning, Detective Lippert returned to my table.

"What were you talking about?" I demanded. "What's going on?"

Lippert sat down across from me again.

"Calm down," he said tersely.

"What do you mean, calm down?" I said loudly. "What do you intend to do?"

"With you? Nothing," Lippert replied. "You're being released, Ms. Cosi. We're not charging you for illegal entry or trespassing, though we can. Nor are we charging you as an accessory to murder."

"But what about my daughter?"

Joy's shrill cry interrupted us. "*No!* Are

you people crazy? Don't —"

Two uniformed officers gripped Joy by the arm. Then Detective Tatum began handcuffing my daughter's hands behind her back.

"No, please," Joy's voice was desperate, terrified. "Listen to me. Why won't you listen? I didn't do anything. Please! You've got it all wrong!"

I moved to go to her. The uniformed officer standing behind me grabbed my arm. "Let me go," I warned him. "Let me go to my daughter." But the policeman held on. With a curse, I elbowed the officer, right in the gut. I heard him grunt, felt his grip relax. I broke free, ran across the dining room.

"Joy!" I was less than two feet from my daughter when a new pair of officers grabbed me, restrained me. "Let my girl go. Please! She didn't do anything!"

But Detective Tatum wasn't listening. With a neutral face, he loudly intoned the words that froze my blood:

"Ms. Joy Allegro, you are under arrest for the murder of Tommy Keitel."

"No!" Joy cried. "I didn't do it!"

As the uniformed officers began dragging her to the police car outside, she turned her head, and her eyes met mine. "Dad's right, Mom," she said. "We can't trust the police!"

I struggled against the officers holding me, but they were stronger and slightly crueler in their determination to keep me restrained, having seen what I'd just done to their buddy in blue.

Detective Lippert stepped in front of me, blocking my view of Joy. His warm, friendly demeanor had gone dead cold. He glanced at the two uniformed men restraining me then met my eyes.

"If you assault another officer, we'll arrest you, too."

"Why are you doing this?!" I demanded, wincing at the forceful grip the men were applying.

Lippert pointed to the pages of his notebook. "Ms. Allegro herself supplied all the evidence we needed to make the arrest. She gave Sergeant Tatum one of the strongest motives I've ever heard. Tommy Keitel was her lover. The man jilted her today and also fired her, humiliating her in the process. Ms. Allegro confirmed that the murder weapon belonged to her, which you did, as well, Ms. Cosi. And you also confirmed that when you arrived, your daughter was already here and the victim already stabbed, which meant Ms. Allegro had the time and opportunity to commit this act."

Detective Lippert closed his notebook. "I

don't think I have to look any further for a prime suspect. Do you, Ms. Cosi?"

Sixteen

I returned to my closed, dark coffeehouse and dragged myself up the back stairs to the duplex. My body was exhausted and bruised from the manhandling by Detective Lippert's men. The door to the master bedroom was wide open, the room empty. It was after three in the morning. Matteo was still out clubbing with the Waipunas.

I tried Matt's cell and was sent immediately to voice mail. That's when I remembered how he'd warned me to stop calling earlier because his cell battery was about to die.

So what else is new? I thought. For far too many years, Matt was unavailable to me when I'd wanted him. *Why should tonight be any different?*

Then it occurred to me that I really didn't *want* Matt at all. I wanted to inform him what had happened to our daughter, sure. Given Breanne's connections, he would know what high-powered lawyer to call, so I'd leave that to him.

The man I actually wanted and needed was Mike Quinn. A little desperate to hear his voice, even if it was only on a digital recording, I picked up the phone and dialed his apartment's number.

I knew he was still on duty, so I wasn't surprised when I got his answering machine. I left a long, rambling, semicoherent message with every detail I could think of about Joy's arrest, ending with "Please, please, Mike, call me back."

Then I stretched out on the narrow couch. I tried to sleep, but visions of what my daughter was probably experiencing played through my imagination like a waking nightmare. I recalled my grim trip to Riker's Island when Tucker had been falsely charged of a crime and arrested. I wondered if they'd put Joy on a bus to that terrible place, shackled beside some crack dealer or small-time felon.

The phone rang beside my ear, and I bolted upright. Daylight streamed through the living room's French doors, and I realized I'd nodded off. I glanced at my watch: *8:15.*

The phone rang again. I snatched the receiver off the hook.

"Yes?"

"Clare? It's Mike."

"Thank you. Thank you for calling. I'm sorry I phoned you so late, but I didn't know who else to turn to —"

"Sweetheart, it's okay. You did the right thing." His voice was tender and reassuring, a splash of light in my darkest hour.

"So you got my message?"

"As soon as I heard it, I started making phone calls. All I got were voice mails, so I caught a few hours' sleep. Ray Tatum at the Nineteenth just returned my call."

"Yes, I remember Detective Tatum," I said. "He's the one I wanted to throttle when he handcuffed my daughter. What did he say?"

There was a long pause. "It's not good, Clare, but it's not the end of the world, either."

I took a breath. "Tell me."

"The medical examiner on the scene estimated that Tommy Keitel was murdered within an hour of the time his body was discovered. No one really knows when Joy arrived, because the burglar alarm hadn't been set, and the door wasn't locked."

"Is that good or bad?"

Mike sighed. "It's not great. If the alarm had been set, the time of entry and exit

265

could've been determined by checking in with the security monitoring company. As it is, we only have Joy's word to go on, and frankly, Tatum and Lippert don't believe her."

"Lippert," I bit out unhappily. "I tried to tell that man what I'd discovered. I outlined the other leads they could have investigated for Keitel's killer, but Lippert was obviously humoring me, buying time so I wouldn't disturb Tatum's interrogation of Joy."

"Don't beat yourself up, Clare. You've got a natural talent for investigative work, but you're not a trained interrogator. I know Ray Tatum well, and I know he's one of the best in the department. I don't doubt he sweet-talked Joy into crying on his shoulder, telling him everything."

"Incriminating herself, you mean?"

Heavy silence followed. Even across the phone line I could sense something bad was coming.

I cleared my throat. "There's more, isn't there?"

"Yes," Mike said. "There's more, Clare."

His voice was quiet and steady, as if he was about to tell me that someone had just died. "The handle of the murder weapon was wiped, but there were two fingerprints lifted off the base of the blade itself. They were Joy's thumbprints. The match is perfect."

"Mike, *listen* to me. My daughter did *not* kill Tommy Keitel."

"Clare . . ." There was an exhale and I could just picture the man running his hand through his sandy hair. "She had a motive. She had an opportunity. It could have been a crime of passion —"

"I can't believe you're saying this! You've met Joy. Does she look capable of stabbing a person to death? I know my daughter, Mike. I saw her right there in the kitchen moments after she discovered the body. She didn't do it!"

"Okay, Clare. Take it easy. I do believe you. I had to ask."

I calmed, realizing Mike's years as a detective weren't going to vanish just because of a personal relationship. The possibility of Joy's being guilty was there, so he had to consider it. The man's pragmatism probably reached the molecular level.

"So now we move on," Mike said.

"Move on?" I whispered. "What do you mean, move on?" Was he giving up on Joy? On me?

"We move on to other suspects, Clare. Tatum isn't looking. He and Lippert firmly believe they've found their killer. So if you

267

want this crime solved, we're going to have to solve it ourselves."

"You're in this with me?" I said, close to tears.

"Of course."

"Oh, thank God."

"Good, because we can use his help. We can also use a theory, if you've got one."

"Brigitte Rouille," I said without hesitation. "She's my prime suspect."

"Okay, Clare. I'm listening."

"Well, Brigitte was Tommy's second-in-command. The woman had excellent knife skills, she was very strong physically, and she had a history with Tommy. He went out on a limb to give Brigitte a job when nobody else would. Two and two is four. With Tommy's womanizing ways, I'm sure he and Brigitte were lovers at one time."

"You think Brigitte is capable of murder?"

"Yes. Her behavior toward my daughter was off-the-charts hostile. She called her a brat and a whore and threatened Joy with a knife. There were plenty of witnesses to that, me included."

"Good."

"I believe Brigitte killed Tommy in a fit of anger. The man had just fired her for using drugs. She could have returned to the restaurant to have it out with him — or

268

maybe even throw herself at him, for that matter. Knowing Tommy's ego, he could have said any number of things to send her into a violent rage."

"Why use Joy's knife to kill him?"

"That was the sweetest revenge of all for Brigitte. It allowed her to frame her romantic rival for the man's murder while getting herself off the hook. And as for the fingerprints on the knife — well, it was *Joy's* property, so her fingerprints on the blade shouldn't be a revelation, should they? Brigitte could have wiped her own prints off or worn a glove."

Mike paused for a moment. "It's not a bad theory. Drugs can drive people to commit crimes they might not have considered sober."

"That's not all."

"Okay. I'm still listening."

"I think Vincent Buccelli's death points to Brigitte, too."

"How?"

"Tommy and Joy were using the boy's apartment for sexual encounters."

"Christ, Clare. What was your daughter thinking?"

"Don't even go there."

"Well, clearly *Keitel* went there. To Vinny's apartment, I mean. And if the head chef was disappearing with the pretty intern often enough, then people probably figured out what was happening, right?"

"Yes, Mike, exactly! If Brigitte still had feelings for Tommy — maybe even hoped to become his mistress again — how would she have felt seeing him carry on an affair right under her nose with an intern half her age? It probably drove her crazy to see the two of them disappearing in the afternoons for sex. I'll bet Tommy was even insensitive enough to tell Brigitte where she could reach him while he was gone! And . . . come to think of it, more than one person at the restaurant mentioned that Brigitte had it in for Vinny. She probably started picking on him when she realized he was allowing Tommy and Joy to use his apartment for their trysts!"

"Makes sense so far."

"Well, here's the kicker. On the night Brigitte threatened my daughter with a knife, she accused Joy of 'undermining' her rep with Tommy. That was the *very same* night that Vinny was murdered. I'm betting Brigitte cracked that night. She went out to Queens and killed Vinny, using a knife from Solange. I think she did it with the intention of framing Joy, who had a key to Vinny's place. Or even Tommy, since she knew he went there to sleep with Joy."

"I follow. An investigation would have eventually turned up their names. Both had access to Vinny's apartment, and both worked at Solange, so they had access to the murder weapon."

"I'm not saying it makes complete sense. But the woman wasn't making a lot of sense the night I saw her ranting. If we can find her, we might get her to confess to at least one of the murders."

"And Joy's a suspect in Vincent Buccelli's murder, too. Is that right?"

"She was interrogated but never charged."

"Who's the detective on that case?"

"Lieutenant Salinas."

"Hold on . . ." I heard some shuffling of paper. "Salinas is in Queens, right? Do you remember the precinct number?"

I told him.

"Okay, Clare. You've got solid theories — for both murders. I'm going to give Salinas a call . . ."

Mike hung up, and I rose from the couch. As I stretched my achy body, I felt painful needles shoot through my arms. That's when I noticed the nasty purple bruises where Lippert's men had restrained me.

On a furious exhale, I headed for the kitchen and slammed together a stove-top pot of espresso. I needed the dark kick — even though I was already disturbed enough to kick furniture.

I ground the Italian roast fine, dumped the black sand into the filter, filled the lower chamber with water, screwed together the two separate parts, and banged the Moka Pot onto the gas burner.

Within minutes, liquid began to boil inside the little silver pot. At just the right moment, the water shot from the lower chamber to the upper, forcing itself through the cake of packed grounds. That's when the stove-top espresso was born, suffusing the room with the intense aromatics of the darkly caramelized coffee beans.

I closed my eyes, and in the briefest flash of sense memory, the rich, earthy smell returned me to my childhood. I was back in my grandmother's grocery again, watching Nana stir her pots of minestrone, mix up her homemade pastas, bake her Italian breads and cookies.

A sturdy, practical immigrant, Nana had lived a hard life, losing sisters in the Great Depression, a husband and brothers in World War II. She had what they called "the insight" and was able to read coffee grounds for the women of the neighborhood, advise them, even perform the occasional ritual to

banish those cursed with the *malocchio* —
what the old Italians called the "evil eye."

Because my own mother had abandoned
me — and my father was too busy running
numbers, not to mention running around
with a succession of flashy women — my
grandmother was the one who made sure I
was raised right.

Nana was my mother, my friend, my
teacher, my shoulder to cry on, my fearless
defender. Until her death, just a few months
before I'd met Matt, she was the one person
whom I could count on to make a bad day
good again.

And now it's your turn, Clare.

Since Joy's arrest, my emotions had been
all over the map. But dread and helpless-
ness were no good to me now. It was time
to distill my fears down, concentrate them
into the essence of something useful.

I poured myself an ink-black shot and
bolted it back. I poured a second and drank
it down, too. The phone rang before I could
pour a third.

I snatched up the kitchen extension.
"Hello!" I blurted, a little too loudly. (The
caffeine was starting to hit.)

"I spoke with Lieutenant Salinas," Mike
began without preamble. "Got his home
number from the desk sergeant, since he

273

wasn't on duty. Got him out of bed, actually. But he wouldn't tell me much —"

"What do you mean, he wouldn't tell you much?" I paced the small kitchen, all set to fight somebody, anybody. "He's a cop. You're a cop. You're both cops, for heaven's sake —"

"Sweetheart, calm down —"

"Don't tell me to calm down! This is my daughter's life we're talking about —"

"Clare! Listen to me! Salinas is not Ray Tatum, whom I've known for years. Salinas is a cop in a different borough, and as soon as he realized I knew one of his prime suspects, he clammed up. He had a right to. But at least I got him to admit he sent a man to Brigitte Rouille's apartment. Unlike Tatum and Lippert, Salinas followed your lead. His detective found out that Ms. Rouille skipped out on her rent several weeks ago with no forwarding address."

"Then she's still at large!"

"But the trail is cold. Salinas started the initial paperwork on finding her, requested a warrant for her banks records, her ATM and credit card charges. But we're not officially on the case, so we're going to do it another way."

"Another way?"

"Yes, Clare. We'll find her another way. I

promise."

"I'm sorry, Mike." I massaged the bridge of my nose. "I didn't mean to yell just now. I —"

He cut me off with a terse, "Forget it."

After a long pause, I asked, "Where do we go from here?"

"We start wherever the trail ended. I have the last known address for Brigitte Rouille. It's in Washington Heights."

"Salinas is still suspicious of Brigitte, right?"

"Not anymore. She *was* a person of interest in the death of Vincent Buccelli, but last night he learned about Joy's arrest and the details of Keitel's murder. Salinas is now looking to charge your daughter with a second murder."

I closed my eyes, hating the sound of the inevitable. "Both men were killed in the same manner," I rasped, "chef's knives plunged vertically into the base of the throat. Both men had relationships with Joy — one a lover, one a friend. Joy found both bodies. Oh, Mike . . ."

The room started a slow spin. I sank into a chair at the kitchen table, dropped my forehead into my hand.

"Clare, listen to me. We're going to find Brigitte Rouille. We're going to do it together. Give me a few hours, and I'll pick you up at your coffeehouse. Okay?"

Mike's confident, assertive voice sounded far away, like it was coming from another solar system. The room was still spinning; I had trouble thinking, forming words.

"Clare! *Okay?*"

The detective's deep shout jolted me awake again. My mind began to clear; my focus returned. I lifted my head.

"Okay," I said.

We bade each other good-bye, and I hung up. Then I rose from the chair and bolted my third cuppa nerves. If there was a solution to this horrific mess, I *had* to find it for my daughter's sake. With Mike Quinn on my side, I might have a chance.

Putting down the empty demitasse, I turned to leave the kitchen. I had to shower and dress fast, get down to the Blend, and make sure there was coverage for the day. I checked the master bedroom. It was still dark and empty. The four-poster's pillows and comforter appeared undisturbed.

I knew from long experience that Matt could be anywhere at the moment: eating breakfast with the Waipunas after their long night of partying or waking up in a new bed with a hot young thing he'd hooked up with at a dance club. Either way, I had to watch for the arrival of my ex-husband.

Joy's father would have to hire the criminal defense attorney today, because Joy's mother was going into the field. Despite the expressed feelings of my daughter, I was about to put my complete trust in the police — or rather, one very special police detective.

Seventeen

Mike picked me up at noon in a battered beige Dodge sedan that he sometimes used for undercover work. We drove north to Washington Heights, on the hunt for an address near Wadsworth Avenue — the last known residence of Brigitte Rouille.

Washington Heights was a large Manhattan neighborhood located above Harlem. Gentrification had infiltrated the area, but the wealth was concentrated mostly around Yeshiva University (an area recently dubbed "Hudson Heights" by a canny local real estate firm eager to attract a more upscale clientele). Gentrification had not yet spread to the shabby street off Wadsworth that Brigitte Rouille had been calling home until only a few weeks ago.

The language on the streets was Spanish, with a Latino population dominated primarily by Dominicans. The sidewalks were cracked and pitted on Wadsworth, and potholes dotted its side streets. I observed more than one homeless person lurching along, shouting at phantoms, and strange, illegible graffiti was spray-painted everywhere: billboards, buildings, passing delivery trucks.

Now I knew very well that graffiti had been around for a few millennia. The ancient Greeks had it. So did the Romans. But the stuff we were passing now wasn't attached to 2,000-year-old historical relics. This wasn't even the artsy kind of graffiti I'd seen during the eighties all over Soho and the Lower East Side: the kind of street art that had launched major careers, like the powerful primitive images of Jean-Michel Basquiat or the lighthearted pop figures of Keith Haring.

These slashing, sloppy, angular marks were gang tags, something I knew in passing but Mike knew in practice. "Violent drug dealers use the symbols to claim territory and send messages," he informed me.

"Messages?"

"To warn away rival gangs."

"And a Hallmark card would have been so much more thoughtful."

Mike shot me an amused glance, but he didn't laugh. As we walked along the rundown avenue, I sensed a tension in him.

There was a slight wariness, too, in his gaze, as he continually scanned our surroundings. But what most radiated from Mike was a tremendous coiled energy. I couldn't help flashing on a sketch I'd seen in Leonardo da Vinci's notebook: a medieval catapult, pulled all the way back, ready to unleash hell at a moment's notice.

But, as it turned out, there was no reason to unleash it. No one bothered or threatened us in the least. And within minutes, we'd easily entered the shabby interior of Brigitte's former address, which was not marred in any way by graffiti. The six-story dirty brick apartment building was merely filled with bad smells and a clashing color scheme.

The second Mike and I stepped through the front door, the scent of cigars was distinctly recognizable. The bouquet of cheap tobacco became even stronger as we headed down one flight of metal stairs to the basement. And by the time we walked the narrow, lime-green hallway with mustard-yellow trim, I'd added stale beer, scorched garlic, and the reek of industrial-strength cleaning fluid to my stomach-turning aromatic profile of the place.

We passed four apartment doors at the basement level. Mike glanced at each one.

He finally paused at the very last door on the hall. Under the harsh fluorescent lights, we stood together, reading the crudely scrawled name.

FELIX PINTO, SUPERVISOR

Spanish television was blaring on the other side of the door. From another apartment, I could hear a man and woman arguing loudly, speaking a language I didn't recognize. *Filipino? Tagalog?* Somewhere else, a dog yapped continuously.

Mike's square jaw worked a moment before he glanced at me. I was wearing my low black boots, a pair of pressed gray slacks, a loose white sweater, and a long gray overcoat. Mike told me to look like a professional detective, and I made sure to follow his advice.

"I'll do the talking," he said softly. "Okay?"

I nodded.

He lifted his knuckles and knocked. Three firm taps.

"Usted se va," a muffled voice called from inside. *"Yo estoy comiendo mi almuerzo."*

Mike frowned, turned his fist to the side and pounded. His deep voice boomed loud enough to make me flinch. "Lunchtime's over, amigo! Open the door!"

"Vuelva a las dos," the voice replied.

"No. Not two o'clock. *Now!*" Mike roared. "This is the NYPD. *Policía!*"

I heard muttering, and then a bolt was thrown. The door opened a few inches, until it was stopped by a chain. A young man in his twenties with slicked-back hair and a pencil-thin mustache peeked through the crack.

"Sí?"

"I want to see the inside of an apartment belonging to one of your former tenants," Mike said.

"No hablo inglés —"

"You *habla* English just fine, Felix. I already spoke to the old lady — the one who let me and my partner into the building."

My eyes widened at Mike's brazen lie. There'd been no old lady. We hadn't talked to a single soul on our way in. No one had *let* us in, either. We'd just waited until a teenager exited the building and then we'd rushed the door before it locked again.

Felix Pinto frowned. "*Vieja perra* should keep her mouth shut," he muttered.

"Don't blame the old woman. I just showed her this" — Mike held up his gold shield — "and she let loose. She told me all about you, Felix."

Now the super looked nervous. "What do

you want, man?"

Mike folded his arms. "I want to see Brigitte Rouille's apartment."

Felix leaned his forearm on the doorjamb — a naked woman in a tropical jungle was tattooed down the length of it. "Some other cops came by yesterday," he said.

"How long did they stay in the woman's apartment?"

"They didn't show me no search warrant —"

"That's not what I asked you, Felix. I asked you *how long* the police searched Ms. Rouille's apartment."

The man shrugged. "Not long. A few minutes. That's all. They didn't do much searching. They just wanted to make sure she was gone, I think."

"And *is* Ms. Rouille gone?"

"Long gone, man," Felix replied. "Like five weeks ago. Skipped out on the rent, too, but that ain't *my* problem. New tenant's movin' in Monday."

"Any idea where Ms. Rouille went?"

"Probably moved in with her boyfriend. Why pay two rents when you can pay none?" He snickered.

"Who's the boyfriend?"

"Don't know, man. I don't ask junkies their names. They all act kind of twitchy, you know?"

"Do you know where this junkie lives?"

Felix shook his head. "Sorry, no forwarding address. Guess she didn't want the management company coming after her. Deadbeat bitch."

"I'll need the key." Mike held out his hand. "Unless you'd rather come with us? Then we can talk over some of those things the old lady told me."

"No, man. I don't need to come with you."

The super searched through a ring of keys attached to a chain on his belt. He finally detached one of them and handed it to Quinn.

"Four F," Felix said. "And don't bother waiting for the elevator, 'cause it don't work. Just slide the key under my door when you're done."

Then the super ducked out of sight, and the door slammed in our faces.

"I don't recall you speaking to an old woman," I teased as we hit the stairs.

"Every apartment building in New York City has an old lady who talks too much," Mike informed me, casually tossing the key and catching it. "Sometimes it's useful to talk to the lady herself, and sometimes it's just an easy way to get around that *'no hablo inglés'* crap."

"This is a side of you I haven't seen before."

Mike arched an eyebrow. "A cop on the street, you mean?"

"No, a big fat liar. The baloney you fed that super was prime cut."

"It's not baloney, sweetheart. It's procedure. Sometimes you have to bend the truth to get what you want out of an interrogation." His blue eyes speared me. "*You* never bent the truth a few times to get what *you* wanted?"

I shrugged. "Guilty. But I only lie for a good cause."

"What do you think I just did?" He held up the key and smiled. "We're in."

We'd reached the fourth floor. Mike held the heavy fire door open for me, and we exited the stairwell. Apartment Four F was right across the hall. He stepped in front of me and slipped the key into the lock.

We walked through a small entryway and entered the empty living room. It was a nice apartment, very spacious, especially for Manhattan, with polished wood floors and new light fixtures. But it was stuffy, the air stale and close. Two small windows faced the walls of the next building on the block. I stepped across the room, opened one of the windows. A cool, refreshing November wind stirred the stagnant air.

"There was a chair here," I said, pointing to a ghostly square of fast-dispersing dust bunnies on the bare wood floor. "She didn't leave in the dead of night. Looks to me like Brigitte took her furniture with her."

"Maybe," said Mike, opening a small closet. Inside, empty hangers dangled from a wooden rod. Several buttons lay on the floor.

"I'm going to check the kitchen," I said.

The kitchen was clean but small, a long and narrow space with a single sink, a miniature stove, a tiny window, and a Kenmore refrigerator that seemed too large for the limited space. I opened it. There was nothing inside.

I checked the drawers next. In one I found a few discarded utensils — an ancient and corroded potato peeler, a plastic spatula, chopsticks from a local Chinese take-out place.

Another drawer was stuffed with handwritten papers. Shopping lists, mostly, and a few recipes. There were some pieces of junk mail and an old wrinkled note, written in a flowing, delicate hand:

Toby,
Food in fridge!

Love, B.

"In here!" Mike called.

I stuffed the papers that I'd found into my oversized purse for perusal later and followed the sound of Mike's voice.

He was in the bath, perhaps the coziest room in the place, with coral pink tiles and a large tub. Brigitte had left behind her matching shower curtain. The scent of feminine soap clung to the water-resistant material.

Mike had opened the mirrored medicine chest. Inside I spied a few waterlogged bandages, an empty container of face cream, and a couple of brown prescription bottles.

"What did you find?" I asked.

"These bottles were all prescribed to Brigitte Rouille," he said, pushing the stuff around with his finger. "Pretty innocent stuff: an antihistamine, antibiotics."

Mike displayed a bottle he'd kept in his hand. "This prescription isn't Brigitte's, and it's not so innocent, either." he said. "It's a 'script for methadone, from a clinic on 181st Street."

"Methadone? Isn't that what they give addicts to wean them off heroin?"

Mike nodded. "This prescription belonged to someone named T. De Longe."

"*Toby* De Longe, perhaps?" I showed Mike the note I'd found in the kitchen.

"Good, Clare. There's an address on this bottle, too," he said, pocketing the note with the bottle.

It took only a minute to search the bedroom and its closet. They turned up empty.

"Let's go," Mike said, tapping his pocket. "I think we found what we came for."

As we locked up, another apartment door opened. A little chocolate-brown terrier trotted out of the apartment, followed by a fortysomething man clutching its leash. He wore a nylon Windbreaker and Yankees cap placed at such a strategically conceived angle that I was sure it covered a bald spot. He smiled when he saw us.

"Are you the new tenants?" he asked.

"No," I replied. "She's coming later."

The man zipped up his Windbreaker. Tail wagging, the dog circled the man's khaki-covered legs, tangling them with the tether.

"Easy, Elmo, settle down."

"When did the movers come?" Mike asked while the man untangled himself.

"Movers? What movers?"

"The men who moved Ms. Rouille's furniture."

The man rolled his eyes. "That woman's furniture has been rolling out of here for months, not to mention the china, silverware, and electronics. A television. A stereo. Blender and a big cake mixer —"

"Where did her things go?" I asked.

"Pawned, I guess," the man replied. "Or traded for drugs. That woman had a *problem*." He put his hand to his lips and whispered, "Cocaine. Her friends all had monkeys on their backs, too. I'm not surprised the little cook was behind on her rent."

"Did you know her boyfriend?" Mike asked.

The man shrugged. "She had a lot of friends. I didn't know them, though."

Impatient, the little terrier barked. "Okay, Elmo, let's go caca," the man said, heading down the stairs.

After the man's footsteps faded on the stairs, along with the *click, click, click* of little dog nails, Mike faced me. "You learn something new on this job every day."

"Such as?"

His blue eyes smiled. "Not every apartment building's biggest gossip is an old lady."

Just then, the tinkling tune of "Edelweiss" from *The Sound of Music* went off in my shoulder bag. I pulled it out, checked the tiny digital screen.

"It's Matt," I said.

Mike nodded. "Call him back in the car." He glanced up and down the hall. "You should talk to him in private."

"Okay."

We hit the street again, found the battered beige Dodge. Mike unlocked my passenger-side door. I climbed in, surprised Mike didn't get in with me.

"Private's private," he insisted.

As I hit speed dial, Mike walked to the corner to check out the headlines at a small newsstand. I watched him affably engage the Hispanic vendor. He appeared to be speaking in fluent Spanish.

I put the phone to my ear, listened to Matt's phone ring. My ex picked up right away. "Clare, I have some news from the lawyers —"

"Can I see Joy today?"

"No. Neither one of us can. She's on Riker's Island, and no one can see her but her lawyers."

"What about tomorrow?" I asked, my tone a little desperate.

"Same deal. Neither one of us can see her until her arraignment Monday."

"Monday?" My gaze fell from the bright

windshield. I stared unseeingly at the Dodge's dashboard. "Is that a normal amount of time?"

"There are complicating issues. The Vincent Buccelli murder might be tagged on, but it took place in Queens, and that's another borough, so it's another DA's office." He sighed. "They're sorting it all out, I guess — a lot of law degrees are involved."

I took a deep breath, released it. "She *will* get out on bail, right? What are the lawyers saying?"

"The judge will decide Monday downtown in criminal court."

I closed my eyes, not able to comprehend my Joy sitting behind bars for months and months before her trial would even come up on the docket.

"Anyway, Clare, I'll stay on the lawyers, keep you informed."

"Thanks, Matt."

"You should thank Breanne, too. This criminal defense firm is one of the best in the city. Bree has personal ties to the partner handling Joy's case. She made all the calls from Milan."

"I *will* thank her, Matt. I just pray we never have to *use* Bree's lawyer friend. If I get lucky today, Joy's case will never have to go to trial."

"You think you can nail Keitel's killer?"

"Vinny's, too. I think Brigitte killed them both. She's on the lam now, but Mike and I are on her trail."

"Keep following it then." Matt paused. "Look, I know I've been down on you in the past for butting in, for being a nose hound, but this is our daughter we're talking about, so . . . anything you can do, Clare, *anything* . . ."

"I know, Matt. I've been doing the best I can —"

My eyes lifted up just then. I noticed Mike in his long overcoat, turning away from the newsstand. He glanced back at the Dodge, met my eyes.

"— now let me get back to work."

EIGHTEEN

The prescription bottle carried an Inwood address, which meant we had to go even farther uptown, way above 125th Street — the last road most tourist maps bothered to show as part of Manhattan Island.

The neighborhood was largely residential. Most of its structures were town houses, apartment buildings, and two- and three-family dwellings. It was probably the most suburban of Manhattan's seventy-plus neighborhoods with three shopping districts, a hospital, and a public park.

Mike drove us up one quiet, tree-lined street and down another. When the car's direction twisted and turned in a particularly odd way, I was a little confused whether we were heading east or west.

"The lay of the land's different up here," I remarked, leaning forward to peer at the passing street signs. "There's no grid pattern."

"Right," Mike said. "Some of these streets are based on old Indian trails. They weren't laid out by city planners like the rest of Manhattan."

"Except not all of Manhattan has the grid," I reminded him.

"True . . ."

The lanes in the West Village, for instance, were far from straight. This often confused people, but without the legal protection of historic preservation, my neighborhood's one- and two-century-old town houses — including the four-story Federal that the Village Blend occupied — would have been razed by now and replaced with thirty-story apartment buildings, all lined up in the nice, neat pattern of the rest of the borough, with addresses that were standard, predictable, and all-conforming.

I leaned back against the car seat. "You know what? I'd rather have the Indian trails."

Ironically, the address we were currently after was on a wild frontier, just beyond the invisible border of Inwood's happy, middle-class Hispanic lives. Sherman Creek, a run-down subsection of Inwood, was located along a strip of the Harlem River. To get there we drove through a sprawling public housing project called the Dyckman

Houses.

The Saturday afternoon weather was pleasant, bright, and only mildly chilly, yet the grounds around the project appeared close to deserted. Benches along the sidewalks were empty, and a children's playground was lifeless. I wasn't surprised, since I recognized the name of this housing development as the center of a recent crime wave that had been reported on the news.

Sherman Creek itself was mostly industrial. When we arrived in the neighborhood, Mike gave me a quick rundown on the place. He said it was mixed zoning, with warehouses and businesses existing next to apartments and lofts, some of which were now inhabited by urban pioneers, an adventurous and hearty breed of city dweller that I'd always admired since they paved the way for further residential development and eventual gentrification.

At the moment, gentrification was a moot point for Sherman Creek. The businesses we drove by — construction and demolition companies, air-conditioner installation and repair, and automotive garages — were branded with more gang tags than we'd noticed in Washington Heights. As Mike parked, I pointed out the graffiti.

"Yeah," he said. "It's pretty bad. Then

again, you should have seen the Upper West Side fifteen years ago, when I was working anticrime."

"You were in an anticrime unit?"

"Yeah, and I did some antigang work, too. Then I moved to OCCB-Narcotics —"

"What's OCC —"

"Sorry. Organized Crime Control Bureau. It's how I earned my gold shield, but I still attend antigang seminars twice a month."

"So you're an expert. Then what's the deal with this one?" I pointed.

Most of the gang tags were a mess, aesthetically speaking. But the scarlet symbol I'd singled out had been done with admirable graphic flair: two stylized letter *R*s spray-painted together, one drawn backward. The artist even added a drop shadow. All things considered, it could have worked as a corporate logo.

"Whoever painted it has a decent technique," I said, tilting my head to check it out at another angle.

"That's the Red Razors," Mike replied, folding his arms and regarding me, regarding the tag. "Nothing but a pack of small-time punks peddling ganja. They wouldn't last a week against the gangs we faced back in the day. Stone killers like the Wild Cowboys, the Red Top Crew. But the worst of the bunch was the Jheri Curls —"

"The *what?* You're kidding me, right? There was *not* a gang named after Little Richard's do?"

"It's a real gang. I promise you. Funny name. Nothing funny about their methods." Mike turned and began walking down the sidewalk. "The address we're looking for is Rayburn Way," he reminded me. "It should be a few more blocks this way."

I caught up to his long strides. "So what did they do? The Jheri Curls?"

Mike continued to glance up and down the street, taking in our surroundings. "Rafael Martinez and his four brothers ran a major cocaine trafficking operation out of Washington Heights, committed several murders, including a gang-style hit of a witness."

"What happened to them?"

Mike shrugged. "Some undercover guys got the goods on their cocaine operation from the inside, and they were taken down. Rafe and his *hermanos* are behind bars for good."

There was something about the way Mike told me the story, the hint of pride in his voice. "You had something to do with that, didn't you?"

"No comment," he said, but the faintest

297

upturn at the edges of his mouth told me that he was glad I'd guessed. A second later, however, the grim line was back. "That's the trouble with police work. It's always one step forward, two steps back."

"I don't follow . . ."

"Within a year, the Wild Cowboys and the Young Talented Children had taken the Curls' turf and their business."

I frowned. "But Dean Martin warned us, didn't he?"

"Excuse me?"

"You never heard him sing, 'You're Nobody 'Til Somebody Loves You'?"

"The song?"

"Yes, Lieutenant. Most memorable line: 'The world still is the same. You'll never change it.' "

Mike thought it over, grunted. "Good line. Good song. I'll grant you that. But if you want to talk Rat Pack, my guy's Sinatra."

"I should have guessed. You've both got that Ol' Blue Eyes thing going."

Mike smiled, then he stopped us on a corner. The green street sign read Rayburn Way. Under it, a bright yellow metal sign warned the alleyway was a dead end, and under that I spied another Red Razor gang tag. Mike pulled the brown prescription bottle out of his overcoat pocket.

"The address we're looking for is seventy-nine," he said, squinting to read the tiny letters.

I stayed close to Mike as we entered the dead-end alley.

On the left of us were cinder-block buildings; on the right was a sprawling junkyard, surrounded by an eight-foot chain-link fence topped with barbed wire. There was a fence at the end of the block, too. Beyond it, I could see the cold, uneasy waters of the Harlem River.

My attention returned to the stark gray buildings on our left. They seemed to be decaying before our eyes. The nearest building was topped by a faded sign that read Big C Plumbing. Under that, a smaller sign proclaimed the space For Rent. The building itself had high, broken windows. Its door was shuttered by a steel gate splattered with graffiti. The building next door had housed a Rapido Washing Machine Repair and Service business, which had also gone bust.

"Are you sure we're going in the right direction?" I asked.

"Yeah," Mike said, his eyes busy scanning the empty street. "Look for the numbers. Big C Plumbing was seventy-three. This repair place is seventy-five. The building at the end of the block should be seventy-nine."

We continued down the dead-end street, and I noticed a gap between the buildings. Another structure had been here once, but it was torn down now, leaving a flat patch of dirt between the cinder block buildings. As we approached the empty lot, the bitter smell of woodsmoke floated lightly on the brisk wind. The second Mike smelled that aroma, he slowed his pace and rapidly unbuttoned his overcoat. But the sun was behind a cloud now, and the blustery temperature near the Harlem River was downright frigid.

"Are you *warm?*" I asked (naively, as it turned out).

Mike reached out, touched my shoulder, gently but insistently pushed me to his right side so that his body was now standing between me and the lot we were about to pass — *shielding* me, as I realized a moment later, when the loud *clang* woke me up to what Mike already knew.

Someone had whipped a beer can so hard it flew from deep inside the empty lot, all the way across the street, bouncing against the junkyard's chain-link fence.

We took a few more steps forward, and I finally saw the bonfire blazing inside the steel drum, the half dozen Hispanic-looking youths in black hoodies and red sweatpants gathered around it.

"Stay to my right," Mike whispered, continuing with easy strides, as if we were strolling through Times Square at noon.

One of the punks noticed me anyway and whistled. Other catcalls followed. I braced myself for some crude comments. These came in ugly succession. Then three youths broke off from the pack and approached us, the flunkies flanking their obvious leader.

The leader looked about seventeen. He had light cocoa skin, a wispy soul patch on his chin, long sideburns, and short black hair covered with a red knit cap. The punk on the leader's right was clutching a can of Mexican beer. The one on the left spun a long chain that dangled from his pants. The leader's hands were free, and he was clenching and unclenching his fists.

"Hey, *papá*," he said. "You lost, man?"

"No, *junior.* I know where I'm going. Do you?" Mike said, staring the leader down. That's when I noticed he'd carefully drawn back one side of his overcoat, making sure the punk saw the large-caliber handgun strapped to his shoulder.

The leader spied the weapon and stopped in his tracks.

301

The gangbanger with the beer stepped forward. "Screw you, man! You don't scare us! How would you like —"

"Don't do nothin', *hijo!*" the leader shouted. He rolled his eyes. "Dude's a cop."

At their leader's gestured command, the youths retreated back to their bonfire, where they eyed us warily as we approached the final building on the decrepit block.

Something in me still wanted to turn around, go back to those young men, ask them who was responsible for designing and painting that Red Razor gang tag. I wanted to tell the boy that he had potential, tell him he could have a life. But Mike would have strangled me if I'd tried anything close to a stunt like that.

I was naive sometimes, but I wasn't an idiot. I stayed to Mike's right, kept my eyes averted from the young men.

We finally reached the end part of this dead end. The building marked 79 was a three-story brick structure covered in soot. There were cracked windows on the ground floor that had long ago been painted over. Two of the upstairs windows were covered with cardboard; dirty curtains dangled from a brass pole in the third. The building itself had once been part of the electric company's massive holdings. This I knew because

of the words set in stone above the front
entrance:

RAYBURN WAY CONSOLIDATED EDISON
MAINTENANCE STATION 116

Another sign had been added to the black
steel door, painted in gleaming silver letters
in a delicate, flowing script:

THE SHERMAN CREEK ART COLLECTIVE

The door itself was rusty and pitted, and
looked like it hadn't been opened in decades. Mike tried the handle, pulled as hard
as he could, but it was locked.

We both spotted the mail slot beside the
door and read the names scribbled in no
particular order on white tape: Saul Maxwell, Dexter Ward, Maryanne Vhong, T. De
Longe, Nancy Roth.

Mike looked for a doorbell or an intercom,
but there was none, so he pounded on the
metal door with his fist. He was about to
knock again when we heard muffled sounds
from the other side, then the door opened.

A tall, rail-thin young man appeared,
wearing a black T-shirt and faded, paint-
spattered overalls. His long brown hair was
stringy and dirty; the scraggly King Tut

beard hanging from his chin was decorated with blue plastic rings. He clutched a paintbrush in one soiled hand, a dirty rag in the other. His ears were pierced and decorated with tiny silver earrings that looked like skulls. When he spoke, I noticed his tongue was pierced, too.

"You knocked?"

"Are you Toby De Longe?" Mike asked.

The youth shook his head. "I'm Saul Maxwell. Haven't seen Tobe in a couple of days. I reckon he's upstairs, sleeping it off."

"Sleeping *what* off?"

Maxwell shrugged.

"Do you *reckon* he's alone?" Mike asked.

The kid's eyes flashed. "You ask a lot of questions for some asshole who came knocking on my door."

Mike displayed his shield. "Let's talk, you and me. Asshole to asshole."

"Frenchy's with him," Saul Maxwell said, frowning.

"Who's Frenchy?"

"Toby's girlfriend, Brigitte. She's French Canadian, so we call her —"

"Step aside," Mike said, muscling past the man. I followed him through the door.

The layout of the first floor was still one large industrial space, illuminated by fluorescent ceiling lights, half of them burned out. There were visible holes in the concrete floor where factory machines had once been bolted. I noticed another steel door in the corner, beside a concrete staircase with steel tube railings.

The walls were gray and unpainted, except for one massive section that had been turned into an impressive mural depicting the Manhattan skyline as seen from the middle of the George Washington Bridge. The central image was the figure of a man clutching his head and wailing in despair — an impressive pastiche of *The Scream,* Edvard Munch's most famous painting.

In a corner I saw an ancient, avocado-hued refrigerator, beside it a card table with a hot plate, a roll of paper towels, plastic plates, and a Mr. Coffee machine with a badly stained carafe. A six-foot folding ladder, several easels, all of them covered, and another card table laden with bottles and jars of paint dominated the space under the mural.

I smelled something like burning roses and a perfumed tobacco before I noticed there was another person in the room. A diminutive Asian woman with short, bottle-bleached hair was sunk so deep into a beanbag chair that all I could see were her head and her legs. She wore bell-bottom

Levi's decorated with embroidered flowers, boots, and a black sweater.

The young woman was attached to an iPod, head bobbing to the beat pounding in her brain. She clutched a thin black cigarette between two ebony-manicured fingers. Sitting next to her on the floor was a mason jar with three long sticks of incense burned halfway down. Her eyes seemed glazed, and she didn't appear to even register our presence.

"Where can I find De Longe?" Mike asked the young man.

Maxwell pointed to the stairs. "Second floor. Last door at the end of the hall."

The kid dipped his brush in a cup filled with vermilion paint, faced the mural again. Mike took my arm and led me to the staircase.

"Be a gentleman and knock first, Officer Asshole," Saul Maxwell called over his shoulder.

I felt Mike tense. I tugged his arm. "Forget it," I whispered. "Let's find Brigitte."

The stairway was cracked concrete and lit by what little sunlight penetrated an insulated glass wall streaked with soot. The second-floor hallway was dark, and musty, too. Mike found a light switch and another bank of fluorescent lights sprang to life. Two rooms flanked the main corridor, one filled with art supplies, the other with a pile of assorted junk, which I realized after a moment's viewing was meant to be a sculpture.

The door we wanted was at the end of the hall. The aromas of burning incense and tobacco, which had been so strong downstairs, were now dissipating, and I began to pick up another smell, a vague putrid odor.

"Mike, be careful," I warned. "I don't know a thing about this Toby person. But I know Brigitte has knife skills."

Mike stepped up to the door and listened for a moment, then knocked gently. "Toby De Longe? My name's Quinn. I need to have a few words with you."

Silence.

Mike knocked again, harder. Then again, hard enough to shake the wooden door in its frame. Finally he grabbed the doorknob and twisted it. The door opened a few inches then caught on the security chain.

"Damn . . ." Mike muttered. He leaned close to the door, peered through it.

That putrid odor was a lot stronger now. "Can you see anything?"

Mike shook his head.

"What do we do?"

"This." Mike reared back a foot and slammed his broad shoulder against the wood. The chain broke loose from the frame with a splintered crack. The momentum sent him across the threshold, and he quickly caught his balance.

I hurried into the room after him, but he'd already turned around on me. Before I could see anything, he was pushing me back into the hall.

"Back, Clare. Get back!"

"What? Why?!"

As he continued to dance me backward, I struggled to peer around his tall body. We'd come this far; I wasn't giving up now!

The room looked stark and miserable from what I could glimpse around Mike's stubborn form. There were frayed beach towels on the floor in lieu of furniture, cardboard boxes for dressers and drawers, a futon against the wall. The rumpled bed was occupied — and that's when it hit me. The person lying on that mattress wasn't sleeping.

"Mike, stop it! Let me go in!"

"She's dead, Clare. They're both dead."

Hands on hips, I stared up at the man. "Are you forgetting I found two stabbing victims in two days? I can handle this. Now let me go!"

Mike released me abruptly, showing me his palms. "Fine, Clare. Go in, if that's what you want."

"Yes. That's what I want. I may not have a gun or a license, Mike, but I've brought more than one murderer to justice, and you know it."

Mike held my gaze for a long moment. He nodded. "You're right, Clare. You are." His tone was respectful if not apologetic. "Okay then. If you say you can handle it, then you can."

"I can."

I stepped through the doorway and began to cross the small room. The smell was pretty bad as I moved toward the futon. I tried my best to cut off air to my nose, breathe only through my mouth.

"Don't disturb the scene," he reminded me.

Toby De Longe and Brigitte Rouille were side by side on the floor mattress. Tongue lolling and black, face greenish red, Toby De Longe had obviously died first. A rubber ribbon had been tied around his biceps, and his forearm was black below the compressed flesh. A hypodermic needle was still sticking out of his arm; a singed spoon and a melted candle lay next to the bed. There were several small squares of creased blue paper, too.

"Some very bad heroin has come to town,"

I heard Mike say, rubbing a hand over his face. "It comes in those blue wrappers. We've been trying to get the word out, but . . ."

His voice trailed off.

I shifted my gaze to Brigitte. Compared to her boyfriend, she looked positively placid. One arm was thrown over her head, the other stretched out on the bed. Her long, black hair was loose now and splayed all over the sheets. She could have been asleep, except for the greenish cast to her face and neck and the purple marks where gravity pulled her blood toward the floor. I leaned close to see her face, trying not to inhale, but a whiff of something sharply sour passed the receptor cells in my mouth. I gagged, and the odors of the room rushed into my nose.

"What's that sour smell?"

"You mean other than the putrid rot of the decaying bodies? Looks like Brigitte vomited while unconscious. See how blue her lips are? She suffocated before the pills she ingested killed her."

I hadn't noticed the bottle clutched in her hand. "What did she take?"

"We'll let the medical examiner tell us that."

Mike knelt down on one knee, gently

touched Brigitte's pale arm. "Cold." He hung his head for a moment. "She's been dead for a long time."

I continued to stare at the lifeless woman. "Why did this happen?"

Mike rose, placed a hand on my shoulder. "My guess, from the look of the scene: De Longe was a junkie who tried to kick his habit and failed. He took the bad heroin, died, and Brigitte killed herself in grief."

"Damn!" a voice cried behind us.

Mike and I both turned. Saul Maxwell was standing in the doorway.

"Call 911," Mike commanded.

Maxwell shook his head. "Sorry, dude. Our phone service has been interrupted. Someone forgot to pay the bill."

"I'll call it in," Mike told him, reaching for the radio in his overcoat. Saul Maxwell retreated down the stairs.

"Maybe Brigitte was feeling remorseful," I said hopefully. "Maybe she was feeling guilty about killing Vinny and Tommy, and that's why she chose to kill herself."

Mike shook his head. "Sorry, Clare. I've seen enough corpses to know that Brigitte Rouille and her boyfriend here have both been dead for at least twenty-four hours, probably longer."

I stepped back; the nausea came over me

then. I covered my mouth, swallowing hard, forcing my lunch back down. Mike's words blew away any chance I saw to clear my daughter of murder.

"You could be wrong . . ." I challenged weakly.

"Sweetheart . . ." Mike sighed, eyes full of sympathy. "It's remotely possible Brigitte killed Vincent Buccelli. But there is no way in hell she murdered Tommy Keitel. I'm sorry, Clare. By then your prime suspect was already dead."

NINETEEN

Rayburn Way had been a dead end all around. We waited at the scene for the ambulance and police to show. Then we piled into Mike's weather-beaten Dodge and headed back downtown.

By six o'clock, it was already dark, and the temperature was plunging fast. Mike double-parked his sedan in front of the Blend and climbed out. Our good-bye was brief, because the Brigitte mess and then rush-hour traffic had tied us up for hours. Mike was barely on time for his job.

"Today was a bust, but don't worry," he said after opening the car door for me. "We'll find Keitel's killer, Clare. We will. It'll just take a little more time."

Standing on the sidewalk, looking up at him, I summoned a weak smile.

Mike's words were real; I knew he meant them. Even though I'd watched him feed baloney to that super in Washington

313

Heights, I could tell he wasn't just "handling" me now. I could hear the experience in his voice, the steely confidence that came from years and years of enduring as much failure as success. I could only imagine how many frustrating hours he'd gone through on investigations that dead-ended and got dropped into cold-case files.

I was willing to do almost anything now to keep Joy's case from going cold. But I wasn't a hardened professional with over a decade of investigative experience under my belt, so even with Mike's pep talk, I was feeling pretty discouraged.

"If you learn anything new, leave a message on my answering machine," Mike said. "I'll be on duty all night and into the early morning, but we can follow up any lead you come up with after my tour's over. We'll do it together, Clare. *Together.* Okay?"

"I'm grateful to you. I am. But you can't work double duty forever, Lieutenant. You have to sleep some —"

Mike swept me up in his arms, covered my mouth with his. For a few seconds, my feet were off the ground.

"Good night, Clare," he whispered.

Then he released me, and I was sinking again, back down to earth. My gaze followed him as he returned to his car, slid behind the wheel. I continued to watch as he restarted the engine, checked the rear-view to pull out. When he noticed me watching, he shot me a smile. I nodded from the sidewalk, unable to move until he drove away. Then I turned and pushed through the Village Blend's beveled glass door.

The coffeehouse was busy on this Saturday night. A fire was burning in the hearth, one of Gardner Evans's jazz CDs was playing over the sound system, and the aroma of our freshly brewed French roast was stimulating the air.

Esther Best looked up from a table she'd just cleaned.

"Welcome back, boss," she said, drying her hands on her blue apron. "How's it going?"

"Okay, Esther. How are you? Your big date's tonight, isn't it?"

"You know it! Tucker and Dante are in at seven, and then I'm gone!"

Esther regarded me through her black-framed glasses. I guess I must have been wearing my emotions on my face, because she frowned. "You okay, boss? I mean, I heard about Joy from Matt. I'm really sorry about that. You must be wrecked. You want to talk?"

I needed to unload, so I told Esther everything, starting with Tommy's murder, the details of Joy's arrest. I even told her about my futile search today for Brigitte Rouille, and the state in which we found the sous-chef and her lover.

By the end of my story, Esther's mouth was gaping. "Listen, boss, why don't you sit down, and I'll bring you a nice fresh espresso. After all you've been through, I think you need to relax. Decompress, you know . . ."

"But I was going to help out —"

"No need. Gardner's got the bar covered. And I've bussed the empty tables, emptied the trash, and restocked the coffee bar. Any espressos that need to be pulled between now and seven, Gardner can handle. Take a load off. Go sit by the fire."

Esther grabbed my long gray overcoat. "Let me hang this up, too."

"Okay. *Thanks.* I appreciate this," I said, and couldn't resist adding, "though it proves you must be in love; either that, or the Esther Best I knew has been replaced by a really sensitive and caring pod person."

"Don't tell anyone," Esther whispered. "Especially not Tucker. I've worked for years to cultivate *the image.*"

"What image?"

"Snark bitch extraordinaire, of course!"

Esther took off for the coffee bar; I crossed our wood-plank floor and dropped into an overstuffed armchair near the hearth. I stared at the flames for a few minutes, then Esther brought over my espresso.

I sipped it slowly, letting my mind have time to absorb the caffeine slowly, calmly, reasonably. In the end, I knew Esther was right. I needed to decompress.

When I heard my cell go off, I fished inside my handbag for it and was surprised at how stuffed the thing was. Then I realized it was still packed with the papers I'd snatched from the kitchen in Brigitte Rouille's Washington Heights apartment.

The phone was Matt again. He was at his mother's apartment, updating her on Joy's arrest and the lawyers' opinions. The latest legal word was that the district attorney's office would probably be throwing the book at Joy — second-degree murder, two counts — in hopes of getting her to plead down to manslaughter.

"But she didn't kill Tommy or Vinny. Why should she admit it to get a reduced sentence for something she shouldn't have been charged with in the first place?!"

My voice had gotten a little loud. A few customers glanced curiously in my direction. I slumped down in my chair.

"Clare, I'm not suggesting our daughter cop a plea. I'm just telling you the lawyers are discussing this as an option."

"I know, Matt. You're right. I'm sorry I bit your head off." I massaged the bridge of my nose.

"It's okay, Clare. I know you're stressed, worrying about her. I am, too. How did you make out today? Did you get any closer to finding Keitel's killer?"

"I hit a dead end . . ." I could hear the exhaustion in my voice, the disappointment, the dread. "But I'm not giving up. I'm not . . ."

Matt must have heard the shakiness of my own conviction because his voice suddenly sounded stronger. "Of course you're not giving up. You never gave up on me, did you? You saw me through my rehab. And you were always there for Joy, year in and year out; day in and day out; through the hard times and dull times — unlike yours truly . . . Clare, all I'm trying to say is . . . I know you; I know the stuff you're made of; and I know you won't give up . . ."

As Matt's voice trailed off on the digital line, I sat speechless for almost a full minute.

"Thank you, Matt," I finally replied. "I

mean it."

"I'll see you later, okay?"

"Okay."

As soon as I hung up, I moved myself, my espresso, and my bag stuffed with Brigitte's papers to an empty café table. With renewed determination, I pulled out the thick wad of wrinkled and dog-eared pages and spread them across the coral-colored marble surface.

Most of the papers were months and even years old — things that should have been tossed — shopping lists, directions, reminders to do this or that chore.

There were recipes here, too, some clipped from magazines, but most handwritten in a flowing, delicate hand. Some were simple fare: a peasant omelet, baby peas *à le française,* a sole *normande.*

Others were detailed instructions for preparing more complex dishes and even entire courses. I found a three-page recipe for *pâté en croute* featuring woodcock, foie gras, and truffles. A lengthy description of how to prepare *ballottine d'agneau,* stuffed and braised shoulder of lamb. Even instructions for a roasted pig stuffed with *boudin noir* and *boudin blanc,* black blood and white veal sausages.

I discovered several newspaper and magazine clippings in the mix — not about Solange, or even food. The articles were all about the New York art scene.

One recent clipping was a page from *Time Out,* advertising a Chelsea gallery exhibit of three new artists, one of them Tobin De Longe. Another clipping from a local paper featured a scathing review of the same show, singling out Brigitte Rouille's boyfriend for special scorn. Other clippings mentioned De Longe's artwork. The notices were either neutral or negative.

Finally I found a couple of pages covered with names, phone numbers, and addresses, written at different times with whatever ball-point, felt-tip, or pencil was within reach at the time. As I scanned the pages, one name jumped out at me. It was written in bold felt-tip and underlined twice:

Nick

"Nick?" I whispered. The address under the name was on Brighton Beach Avenue. I closed my eyes, remembering the shady-looking guy to whom Tommy Keitel had introduced me on the night that Vinny was murdered. *Nick from Brighton Beach,* Tommy had called him. This *had* to be the same man!

"I wonder if Mike's ever been to Brighton Beach . . ." I murmured.

"Brighton Beach?" Esther said, overhearing me as she set down a fresh espresso. "Did you just say something about Brighton Beach?"

"Yes . . . there's someone there I definitely need to find." I showed Esther the note with the address. "Part of my investigation for Joy."

"That's a coincidence," Esther said with a tilt of her head.

"What is?"

"Boris is taking me to Brighton Beach tonight."

Did I miss something? "Boris?"

Esther nodded. "Boris is taking me to Sasha's for chicken Kiev and blinis with caviar."

"Back up, Esther. I thought you were dating some rapper character named Gun. Who's this Boris?"

Esther rolled her expressive brown eyes. "Same guy. BB Gun is his handle, but his real name is Boris Bokunin."

"Your boyfriend is a *Russian* rapper?!" I asked excitedly.

"A Russian émigré slam poet and urban rapper," Esther corrected, raising an eyebrow above her black glasses. "They pretty

321

much broke the mold after they made my Boris."

My brain was racing now (and I hadn't even needed the second espresso). I remembered what Mike said about investigating new clues together, emphasis on *together.* But the man wasn't going to be available until tomorrow morning, and I doubted very much he spoke fluent Russian, anyway.

If Boris was a recent émigré, he probably could. At the very least, he knew his way around the population of eastern bloc expatriates in Brighton Beach, Brooklyn.

There was no time to waste, and now there was no reason to waste it. "Esther." I took hold of her arm. "Would you and Boris mind if I tagged along on your date tonight?"

Esther gagged. "Boss, puh-lease. I don't need a chaperone. I told you before, Boris is a good guy, a real gentleman, actually —" She stopped abruptly and covered her mouth. "I can't believe I just said that."

"Esther, listen. It's not that I think *you* need a chaperone. It's that *I* might."

"What?" Esther scratched her head. "Okay, now I'm existentially confused."

After I laid it all out, she told me she would be happy to help.

"Thanks, Esther. I mean it. And listen, I

hope I don't ruin your big date."

She shook her head. "I'll smooth things over with Boris. We'll just hit Sasha's a little later, after we find your mysterious Nick guy." She laughed. "Boris is the kind of dude who's up for anything. He's a real man of the world."

I excused myself to go upstairs, splash some water on my face, and check the apartment's machine for messages. When I returned to the Blend thirty minutes later, Tucker and Dante had already arrived to relieve Gardner and Esther. And Esther was waiting for me at a table with her date. He stood when I approached.

"Clare Cosi, this is Boris Bokunin," Esther said.

I recognized him as the same wiry, tightly wound dude I remembered from the other night. He was wearing the same spiky blond hair, too, and the same black leather blazer. But his baggy blue jeans and basketball shoes were now replaced with pressed black slacks and black boots. The T-shirt was gone, too. Tonight's shirt, peeking out from behind the black leather, was a bright red silk number. He stood and removed his sunglasses. He had close-set gray eyes filled with curiosity, a wide nose, and a genuine smile.

I offered my hand, but instead of a simple shake, Boris slapped it, squeezed it, waved his hand around, and slid his fingers along mine, then gave a high five. Finally he tucked his hands into his belt and struck a gangsta pose.

"Clare Cosi, Clare Cosi, a fresh urban posy, a fragrant flower with the power to make the Village rosy," he rapped. "How you do, how you do, so nice to meet you!"

"Uh, hi," I replied. "I guess Esther talked to you about my dilemma? I'm so sorry to ruin your date —"

He raised a hand to silence me. "To someone so phat, so perky and tender, I'm proud and glad to have a service to render, for the Cosi, Cosi, the Village posy."

I glanced at Esther. "Does he do that all the time?"

"You'll get used to it," Esther replied with a shrug. Then she grinned. "Now I want you both to make nice while I change clothes in the euphemism."

I found it very sweet and European the way Boris waited until I sat down before he sank into his own chair.

"So, Boris, what do you do for a living?"

"I'm a baker's apprentice," he replied. "It's a temporary thing, to make the Benjamins. Long term, I'm looking to hit it big

324

in the show biz thing, like Eminem. He da man. He da king. He da boss with da bling."

Boris slipped his sunglasses back on.

"Esther tells me you have lots of talent. But she didn't say how you got into this whole rapping thing."

Boris leaned across the café table. "It started once upon a *long* ago —" He moved his hand through the air. "Back, back when I was in school. See, Clare Cosi, I'm a practical guy. I want to be more than a baker someday. But to get ahead in this world, respect's what plays."

"Respect? What do you mean? Like good manners?"

Boris nodded. "Exactly! Here's my grandfather talking now: It's important to remember someone's name. It's the right and polite thing to do. Don't forget a man's name, or he might forget you. To remember is respectful. It will gain you his friendship. Or to put it the Russian way, it's for *blat.*"

"Excuse me?"

"*Blat.* That means having friends in the right places. Connections."

I scratched my head. The sentiments were actually fairly conventional. "I don't see what that has to do with rapping."

"Here it is, Clare Cosi. I am not so good at the memory thing, but I like the rap

325

music, and I remember the lyrics, and I can make them up, too. One day I discovered that if I rap a person's name, make it like a song, then the memory is locked here." Boris tapped his temple. "That way I never forget."

"There's a name for that kind of thing," I said. "Mnemonics? I think that's the term. I can't remember."

Boris stuck a finger in the air, nodded sagely. "Ah, but you would not have forgotten if you had rapped about it!"

"Ready to go," Esther declared.

I looked up, blinked in surprise. The transformation from barista to hottie date was stunning. Esther wore a little black, clingy dress that hugged her zaftig curves and dipped daringly down to reveal a Renaissance-era quantity of push-up bra cleavage. The hem barely reached midthigh, and she added matching black tights and stacked heels. Her black librarian glasses were gone, replaced with bright red cat glasses. Esther had applied scarlet lipstick to match the frames, and she'd lined her big, brown, long-lashed eyes with a sexy dark liner.

Boris grinned stupidly and practically stumbled to his feet. "Like a vision of night, her beauty takes flight! Like Jam Master's bling in the blazing sunlight. My lady, come ride with me on a silver streak of phosphorus bright."

"Huh?" Esther said, clearly baffled. "Could you maybe translate that one?"

"My SUV's parked right outside." Boris explained with a shrug. "It's the silver Subaru."

TWENTY

BB Gun parked his SUV on the street, and the three of us walked along Brighton Beach Avenue. Beneath the subway's elevated tracks, a gust of wind off the nearby Atlantic whipped at our coats and hair. In a sweet gesture, BB draped his arm around Esther's shoulders and pulled her close.

On the drive to Brooklyn, Boris had explained that we were coming to the "fast-beating heart of Little Odessa." And within a few blocks of his parked Subaru, I understood what he meant. The neighborhood was pulsing with life; the streets were busy; the markets, stalls, and shops glowing and crowded, even on this cold, dark November night. Everyone was speaking Russian, and most of the signs on storefronts and food stands were printed in Cyrillic lettering.

We soon found the address for Nick on Brigitte's note, a four-story yellow brick building with art deco trim and a small storefront at street level. Through a crack in the curtained picture window, I spied cloth-covered tables with neat place settings, and even though the sign painted on the glass was Russian, I definitely recognized one word: *café.*

"Let's go in," I suggested.

The interior was warm but not luxurious with cheap wood paneling and simply framed pictures of various Russian cities. Beside a muted television a large chalkboard was covered with Cyrillic writing — probably the menu. Swinging half doors blocked the kitchen, and another doorway was veiled by a black curtain. A large samovar occupied a wooden table between the two exits.

I counted a dozen tables. At the small register near the front door, a plump, florid-faced hostess in her forties greeted us in Russian. Needless to say, Boris did the talking, and we were led to a table in the corner.

A waitress soon appeared with a tray of water glasses, no ice, filled nearly to the brim. I didn't care; my mouth was parched, my lips chapped from the persistent winter wind. I took a huge, long drink — and thought I'd just swallowed *napalm.*

"This isn't water!" I gagged, my eyes filling with tears. "It's vodka!"

Boris lifted his own glass. *"Za Vas!"* he cried, draining it. Esther took a tentative taste, then a big swallow.

"Oh, that's good," she said, waving air into her mouth.

Boris ordered hot borscht for everyone.

"Beet soup?" Esther's nose wrinkled beneath her red cat glasses. "I hate beets, *and* I was promised *caviar.*"

Boris pulled her close. "And caviar you shall have, my tsarina, but try a little borscht first."

My eyes cleared, and my mind started moving.

Beets . . . beets are important. Why?

I suddenly flashed on the cut-up beets that had been scattered on the prep table around Tommy Keitel's corpse. And there'd been stock bubbling on the stove, too.

Tommy was preparing borscht, I realized, probably from a recipe the mysterious Nick had given him!

Could Nick be the chef here?

The scorching fire in my throat had turned into a pleasing warmth in my stomach. I took another taste of the superb Russian vodka and looked around.

The place was pretty dead, especially for a Saturday night. Only two other tables were occupied. One by a trio of young Russian men in black leather coats, with hair that stood straight up, giving their heads a distinctly angular appearance. Four very attractive young women sat at the other table, nursing cups of steaming tea. One polished her long fingernails; another leafed through a dog-eared copy of *Vogue.*

"They look like hookers," Esther whispered.

"They work here," Boris said. "This is *banya,* probably also Red *Mafiya.*"

Esther stiffened. Boris touched her knee. "It's all right. We're no threat. We're . . . how you say . . . *civilians.*"

A young man at the other table rose. Cup in hand, he crossed to the samovar. Boris watched him and suddenly called out.

"Leonid, Leonid, the music man, he books my band as fast as he can. The man with the power and the hour was midnight, we rapped so neat we gave Eminem a fright."

The man turned toward us, and his eyes lit with recognition.

"BB Gun!" he cried, rushing to our table. Boris rose, and the two men embraced like long-lost friends.

"Hey, guys," Leonid called to his comrades. "This is BB Gun. He played at Klub Bespredel, the big Halloween show. Really brought down the house. Good haul for the boss!"

"Ah, Leonid, but we both know why you remember me," Boris said. "That was the night I introduced you to my ex-girlfriend, Anya."

The man touched his heart. "What a night! And thanks for introducing me to Svetlana, too."

"Da . . . da." Boris nodded.

Leonid smacked his lips, thumped his barrel chest. "They're a pair of hot pistols, I'll tell you. Make me feel like *byki* — strong like a bull."

"I'm the guy who'd know," Boris boasted. "That's why they call me BB Gun!" Boris put his arm around Leonid's broad shoulder. "Homey, listen up now! I wrote this song about those two phat booties."

Boris launched into another rap, this time in Russian. The names "Svetlana" and "Anya" came up a number of times, and the references were obviously lewd. The men at the table guffawed. The women pretended to be shocked, but in the end they laughed, too.

When Boris finished, everyone applauded except Esther. Stewing, she glowered at her new boyfriend.

Leonid nudged Boris with his elbow. "So

what is the great BB Gun doing in our *banya?*"

"It's my new friend," Boris said, tilting his head in my direction. "She came to this place because of a mutual friend of Nick's."

"You know Mr. Pedechenko?" Leonid asked me, obviously surprised.

"If you mean Nick, then the answer is yes. I met him once."

"Ms. Cosi wants to ask Nick a few questions," Boris explained.

The man snapped his fingers. "Olga," he bellowed.

The woman who'd been painting her nails rose. She wore a tight blouse, and figure-hugging black Levi's. Waving her spread fingers to dry the nail polish, Olga approached us. Her hair was long and black as squid ink, falling like a curtain around her oval face. She was supermodel thin and had a good eight inches on me, at least half of which could be attributed to her four-inch heels.

"Take Ms. Cosi to see Nick," Leonid commanded.

Olga nodded. "Follow," she said, spinning on her giant heels.

"I'll be right back," I told Esther. She barely heard me. She was still glaring at Boris. As I followed Olga through the black-

333

curtained door, Esther clutched her boy-friend's arm.

"Who's Anya?" she demanded. "And who the hell is Svetlana?"

Behind the curtain, cubicles lined one wall of the narrow corridor, a bank of steel lockers the other. Each cubicle was veiled by black curtains that matched the one blocking the door.

"In there," Olga said, directing me to a cubicle. Inside there was a bench and a clothing hook.

"What's this?"

"Changing room," Olga replied. Her voice was deep and sultry.

"What am I changing into?"

Olga thrust a white towel and plastic flip-flops into my hands. "Put purse and valuables in locker. You leave clothes here."

"Wait a minute, why am I changing?"

"You want to see Nick," Olga said, hand extended as she admired her manicure. "Nick in *banya.* You want to see Nick, you go in *banya.*"

"*Banya?* What's a *banya?*"

Olga rolled her eyes, clearly frustrated with the slow-witted American woman. "*Banya* is steam bath."

Wrapped in nothing more than the barely adequate towel, with rubber flip-flops on my feet, I stepped out of the cubicle five minutes later. Olga was waiting for me at the lockers. She took my purse and watch and made a show of locking them up, then she handed me a key on a long white string, which I wrapped around my wrist.

"Follow," Olga commanded.

She led me to a stout wooden door, painted black, with a comically large metal ring for a handle.

"When I open, go right in," Olga instructed. "Nick don't like to lose heat."

Then the door opened, and a blast of steam washed over me. My eyes filmed, and I blinked to clear them. Olga placed her hand on the small of my back and shoved me over the threshold. The door slammed behind me.

The bath was incredibly hot, hotter than any health club sauna I'd ever sweated in, hotter than the hottest kitchen I'd ever cooked in. Hissing steam rose from stones piled around a black cast-iron stove in the center of the room. The only source of light was the flickering glow of yellow flames through the grate.

Someone had just dumped water on the rocks as I'd entered. Now much of the steam had dissipated, and I looked around. The concrete room contained ascending levels — essentially long, wide steps, rising up to the high ceiling. On each tier I noticed spigots with aluminum buckets under them.

My eyes adjusted to the gloom, and I counted eight men, all clad in white towels. Four were young and fit enough to be bodybuilders, the terry cloth around their loins hardly larger than hand towels. The rest were seated on the higher tiers. They had towels wrapped around their heads, obscuring their features.

"My name is Clare Cosi," I called out. "I'd like to speak with Nick."

"I'm here," a voice boomed from the highest tier. "Talk."

I tried to see the speaker, but between the steam and the shadows, he was no more than a silhouette. I didn't recognize the voice, but why should I? When I'd met Nick the other night, he'd barely uttered a sound.

"You may not remember me, but we met at Solange," I continued.

"I don't remember you," the voice replied from on high.

"Okay," I said. "Could you answer a few questions, then?"

"I suppose so, Clare Cosi," the voice replied. "Since I doubt very much that you're wearing a wire."

The others chuckled. Self-consciously, I

readjusted the towel, but the narrow strip of terry cloth was barely up to the task. *Don't freak. Keep your head. This is for Joy. You can handle this . . .* I stepped forward, which brought me so close to the heat source that I suddenly felt light-headed.

"Do you know about Tommy Keitel's death?" I asked carefully.

"I read the papers."

"You knew Brigitte Rouille, too. No point in denying it. I found your name and address among the papers she left behind."

"Yes. I know Brigitte. Why do you speak of her that way?"

"What way?" I asked.

"You say I knew her. I *know* her."

One of the bodybuilders rose and tossed a bucket of water onto the rocks. More steam filled the room. I touched my forehead. My skin was slick with sweat, my hair stuck in dark ringlets to my face and neck.

I cleared my throat. "I said *knew*, because Brigitte is dead, along with her boyfriend, Toby. It was suicide by overdose."

There was a long pause. One man bathed his face with a blast of cold water from a spigot.

"When you visit a Russian man, it is customary to bring a gift as a gesture of goodwill. Did you know that, Clare Cosi?"

337

"No. I didn't."

"All you have brought me is bad news."

The door opened behind me. A draft of chilly air ran over my flesh, giving me instant goose bumps. I looked over my shoulder as another bodybuilder entered. This one had tattoos on his forearms and across broad shoulders that tapered down to narrow hips and sculpted, powerful-looking legs.

"She's not a policewoman," the newcomer said, standing uncomfortably close to me. "I went through her purse. Ms. Cosi here runs a coffeehouse."

"Coffee?" the voice cried. "Bitter, black mud! Russian men drink tea!"

Oh, good God.

The bodybuilder brushed past me and plopped down on the bottom tier, clad in barely more than a wisp of steam.

Once again, I cleared my throat. "I'm not here to defend my trade," I told the man. "I want to know how you're connected to Brigitte Rouille. Are you a chef? A restaurateur? A vendor or importer?"

"I'm a businessman," he replied. "My business of selling *kaif* to the *kit* —"

"Sorry?" I said.

"I peddle recreational drugs to people with the cash to waste on them. Do you understand, Clare Cosi?"

"I understand you sold drugs to Brigitte."

"A long time ago. When I first met her at a Manhattan nightclub, she was just another customer. But I enjoyed her company, and Brigitte became very special to me. So special I cut her off when I saw that she could no longer handle the drugs. When she hooked up with that worthless artist who was always on the *kalol,* I refused to see her again."

"On the what?" It was so hot I was having trouble following his words.

"Toby De Longe was hooked on the injection. Heroin. When the *lavit kaif* goes that far, it's not fun anymore."

Someone else tossed a bucket of cold water on the rocks. The sizzling hiss was deafening. Rising steam swirled around me, and the heat started really getting to me. I felt myself losing balance, swaying on my feet.

"I . . . You . . ." I couldn't seem to form words. The room was too hot. My grip on the towel faltered, and I almost dropped it. My head began to spin.

"Feeling . . . dizzy . . ."

Nick said something to me in Russian. But I couldn't understand him, and then I saw a figure quickly scrambling down from the steam bath's highest tier. My legs started giving out. *Crap!*

I must have gone down, because the next thing I remember was coming back to reality by the shock of cold water. Someone had filled a bucket and dumped it over my head. I yelped and opened my eyes at the icy jolt. A large man with beefy hands and thick, muscular arms was holding me. His round head was shaved, but his shoulders, chest, and torso were covered with curly hair. He looked at me through brown eyes filled with concern.

"Are you all right, Clare Cosi?"

"Who are you?" I demanded.

"I'm Nick, of course. The man you came to see. Nikolai Pedechenko."

"You're not the man I met at Solange!"

"I've never been there. And we never met, Clare Cosi, because I would've remembered someone as attractive and determined as you." He grinned.

I disengaged myself from his grip. "This has been a *terrible* mistake. I'm sorry to have troubled you."

"No trouble at all," Nick replied. "But I believe I know the man that you are looking for. His name is Nick, too. And he was a friend of Tommy Keitel's, the chef at Solange."

That's him! It must be! "Do you know where I can find that Nick?"

"Let me find him for you. You go shower and cool down. I'll make a call."

"Okay, thank you," I said.

"Good-bye, Clare Cosi. It has been a pleasure. My *byki* will show you out."

The naked bodyguard took my arm and led me to the door. Olga greeted me on the other side. "Take a cold shower," she said, thrusting a glass of clear liquid and garlic cloves into my hand. "And drink that right down quick. You're dehydrated."

Inside the shower stall, I dropped the towel and stood under the cold flow for a good ten minutes. When I came out, I was trembling, as much from nerves as from the cold. The glass was waiting for me on the bench, beside a clean robe. It was vodka, not water. I suspected as much. I drained the glass anyway.

I did my best to dry my hair with the weak hair dryer supplied by the house. I used the key to unlock my locker — a joke, since it was clear my stuff had been rifled. Nothing was missing, not even Brigitte's note. Apparently Nikolai Pedechenko felt he had nothing to hide.

When I finally returned to the café, Esther was in a better mood than when I'd left. I'm sure the vodka helped, because she was obviously feeling no pain.

"Hey, boss, you're back," Esther cried, slurring her words.

I was glad to see Boris wasn't in the same state. He was stone sober.

"After the first glass, no more vodka for me," he explained. "Better not to drink and drive."

"Ain't he sweet," Esther giggled. "You should try the boss, borscht . . . I mean, try the borscht, boss. It's spectacular!"

I was about to suggest we leave when a man at another table caught my eye. Behind dark sunglasses I saw a pale face framed by long brown hair, thin lips, and a cleft chin. He removed his sunglasses and motioned me forward.

It's him . . . "You're Nick," I said.

"Yes." He rose, shook my hand. "I am Nick Vlachek. I recognize you. We met at Solange the other night."

He offered me a chair. "Please sit down, Ms. Cosi."

I was sure Nick knew that Tommy had been murdered, but he probably hadn't heard who'd been arrested for the crime. I decided to keep him in the dark. Keitel had introduced me as a friend of his. Nick didn't

342

need to know that I was also Joy Allegro's mother.

"What's going on?" he asked. "I got a call from Mr. Pedechenko. He said I should come right over and talk to you. He also suggested I bring some of my new shipment — a nice Caspian beluga."

"Caviar?"

Nick nodded. "I have a restaurant not far from here. And I import caviar, among other commodities."

"So you were one of Tommy's vendors!"

He nodded. "I met Chef Keitel a couple of years ago, after your country banned the sale of beluga caviar . . ."

"It did? I mean . . . we did? Why?"

Nick shrugged. "Because Black Sea sturgeon is on the endangered species list. Tommy wasn't satisfied with the substitutes. He wanted the real thing for his restaurant."

"And you could get it for him? Even though it's outlawed?"

"Tommy wanted the *real* thing," he said with pride. "I got it for him. No crime. What I call a crime is what some of my unscrupulous colleagues do. They import Finland burbot and pass it off as beluga."

"The business is that profitable?"

Nick nearly choked on his vodka. "The market value for beluga is ten thousand dollars a kilogram."

"Oh. I see. Well, that *would* be profitable then, wouldn't it?"

Nick nodded. "At least Tommy knew the value of the real thing."

A waitress appeared. She placed a basket of toast points, a bowl of chopped hard-boiled eggs, another of minced onions, a bowl of sour cream, and two glasses of vodka on our table. In the center she set a tiny bowl brimming with what looked like silver jelly.

Nick smeared caviar on a slice of toast with a tiny spoon made of mother-of-pearl. "Caviar should never touch metal or it will taste like metal," he explained.

He handed me the toast, and I took a bite. I wasn't a caviar eater. I couldn't afford it, and I'd never actually eaten really good caviar — not the kind Nick was offering me now, anyway. The texture was soft, the taste briny and salty and mildly fishy, too, with a subtle hint of acid, more layers of flavor than I'd expected.

"Beluga is prized for its large, pea-sized eggs," Nick said, chewing. "It can be silver gray, dark gray, or even black. The lighter varieties come from older sturgeon and are the most highly valued."

I reached for another toast point and

slathered on the caviar. "I think I could get used to this stuff."

Nick laughed. "Don't bother with the eggs or the onions. The best caviar needs no embellishment."

"No wonder Tommy sought you out," I said after I cleared my palate with a few sips of vodka. I was starting to feel no pain . . . but then I remembered my daughter.

"Nick, I have some questions for you about Tommy Keitel. I saw beets on the prep table where he was murdered. I smelled stock simmering on the stove. Were you there last night, Nick? Were you there when Tommy was murdered?"

"No. And if you're asking me if I murdered Tommy, the answer is also no. Friday is my busiest night of the week. I was running my restaurant until almost two in the morning last evening. Hundreds of people saw me. So you can believe me. More than that," Nick added, a shadow crossing his features. "I was going into business with Tommy. A profitable one. Why would I kill him?"

"What business? Importing?"

"No. Tommy wanted to learn Russian cuisine. I know some of the finest chefs in Moscow and St. Petersburg. I was paving the way for Tommy's move to Russia."

My jaw dropped. "He was moving to Russia?"

"In seven weeks, his contract at Solange was up. He said he was ready for a new challenge. He'd become bored with French cuisine. He wanted to learn how to cook authentic Russian dishes in Russia. Then he was going to return to America, and we were going to open a new restaurant together."

I heard the sadness in Nick's voice, not only over the lost opportunities, but because Nick had also very clearly lost a friend.

"These are bad times," he said.

Tell me about it. "Did you know Brigitte Rouille?"

Nick nodded. "Yes. And Nappy, too. Of course when I'd first met them, they were still lovers."

I blinked. "Lovers? I'm sorry, but . . . I'd assumed Napoleon Dornier was gay."

Nick laughed. "I think he cultivates that impression. Goes with his pumped-up French accent. But Nappy is definitely not gay, and he owed Brigitte — quite a lot. He was no more than a waiter at Martinique when she took over its kitchen. It was Brigitte who used her influence as executive chef to help him move to sommelier and then maître d'. That's why; Dornier always

346

took care of Brigitte, even after they broke up."

I told Nick about Brigitte's death, and he absorbed the news in silence. I saw his eyes glistening. There was such a heaviness of heart about the man, it was almost contagious. And between Joy's arrest and finding Brigitte's tragic corpse, I felt my eyes tearing up, too.

"I'm sorry to bring you this news," I said, touching Nick's arm. "And I'm sorry for your loss. In many ways, Tommy Keitel was a great man. I'd like to find out who killed him. Do you know if Tommy had any enemies who would want him dead?"

Nick shook his head. "Tommy had a big ego. He stepped on toes. He fooled around. I suppose he could have hurt the wrong person. But I couldn't tell you who. Tommy never discussed with me anything that caused him fear or dread. My friend was a happy man. That's how I'd like to remember him."

Nick drained his glass. "Well, Ms. Cosi. I must leave you now. My restaurant is busy, and I must take care of her."

I rose and thanked him, remembering how Tommy had referred to Solange as a "her," too. Then I returned to our table. Esther was leaning against Boris. She was snoring lightly.

"She had too much vodka," he said with a shrug.

"I think I had too much, too," I said, massaging my temples. "So before I pass out, let's get Esther back to the car."

TWENTY-ONE

I shuffled into the kitchen the next morning wearing tube socks, my oversized terry robe, and a St. Petersburg–sized hangover.

"Coffee?" Matt asked.

"Da." I nodded. "With aspirin."

He poured me a cup, handed me the bottle. Then he set a tall glass of clear liquid in front of me.

"Drink this, too," he said.

"I hope to God it's water."

"What else would it be?"

I shook my head, picked up the glass. "You told me to drink water last night, you know, and I still have the hangover."

"You didn't drink enough. You passed out too soon."

Matt was right. He'd been waiting up for me. I told him as much as I could manage about my night in Brighton Beach, then the room began to spin, and I was down for the count.

I drank the water, took the aspirin, sipped the coffee.

"Okay," I said, feeling the caffeine hit my veins. "Update me. Tell me what's happening on the legal end."

"Joy's arraignment is Monday —"

"I remember."

"And Bree's lawyers said they're sure they can get our girl out on bail, but there are probably going to be restrictions."

"Such as?"

"She'll have to give up her passport. She has a roommate in Paris, and nobody wants her flying out of the country before her trial."

"Sounds reasonable."

"Also . . . she may be released under our recognizance."

"I think we can handle that, right? Joy's not exactly a threat to society."

"Worst-case scenario — and this *is* a real possibility, so we need to be prepared —"

"Just tell me, Matt."

"House arrest with some kind of electronic monitoring, like a leg bracelet."

I sighed, sipped at my coffee. "Joy will hate it, but at least she won't have to rot in a jail cell, waiting months or more for a trial. Do you need me to do anything as far as the legal stuff?"

Matt shook his head. "I'm taking care of it. Don't worry. But you might want to stop by her apartment, pick up her mail, get some clothes and personal items. If she's released tomorrow under house arrest, the lawyer is giving them our address as the holding location."

"Okay, will do. I'll stop by her apartment later today — tomorrow morning at the latest."

I got up, poured myself more coffee, feeling a little better already, especially with the prospect of my daughter's being released from jail in just one more day. What I didn't feel good about was my investigation.

I'd hit a dead end with Brigitte Rouille and another one with Nick from Brighton Beach. I'd have to sober up fast and start thinking about my other leads. In the meantime, I was grateful that Joy had good lawyers on her side. And I knew who to thank for that.

"Okay, Matt, I never thought I'd say it, but thank goodness you're sleeping with Breanne Summour. That woman and I have had our differences, but she really came through for our daughter."

Matt nodded.

"She must really care for you," I said, giving him a little smile. Matt didn't respond.

His gaze fell to the pile of newspapers on the table in front of him.

"Got the *Times* there?" I asked, turning my thoughts to a certain someone who cared for me.

"Yeah."

"Would you mind handing over the real estate section?"

"Why?"

"I'd just like to look it over."

"Why, Clare?"

I hemmed and hawed, not really wanting to get into my plans with Quinn. But Matt finally pressed hard enough.

"Okay, okay," I said. "Friday night, before Chef Keitel was murdered, before our daughter was arrested, Mike Quinn stopped by downstairs for *a talk*."

Matt's eyes appeared to brighten. "He broke up with you?"

"Almost. He gave me an ultimatum. Move out or move on."

"Wow. That's harsh. But then . . ." He shrugged. "What else could you expect from a guy like that?"

"Like what?"

"A guy who locks people up for a living."

"He hunts down criminals and predators, Matt. He brings them to justice. He agonizes about making the world better, or at least a safer place for the innocent —"

"Spare me." Matt waved his hand.

I frowned, took a long sip of coffee. "I understand how Mike feels. I mean, I'd feel exactly the same way if his estranged wife popped up unexpectedly and started gallivanting around his apartment."

"Did you say *gallivant?*" Matt made a face. "I don't gallivant."

"It's just an expression. Anyway, I'm going to move out of here."

"What?! Why?"

"Because I don't want to lose Mike Quinn. Why do you think?"

Matt folded his arms, regarded me with a look of pure skepticism. "You're in love with the flatfoot?"

"I care for him. I want the chance to love him."

"What about us?"

"Us?" I blinked, rubbed my eyes. My head was still a little fuzzy. I wasn't sure I'd heard my ex-husband correctly. "Excuse me?"

"Us, Clare. You and me."

"I don't . . . I don't follow. I mean, in case you've been Rip Van Winkling on me, we've been divorced for *ten* years. There is no us."

"We're living together again."

I nearly spat out a fresh mouthful of joe.

"We're sharing a duplex. And you're hardly here."

"I could be here more often, if that's what you want."

I gaped at the man. "Matt, I can't imagine what's brought this on . . ."

"Well, I was just sitting here, thinking about us, and I think maybe we should be one big happy family again: you and me and Joy." He leaned forward, grabbed my hand. "Honestly, honey, listen to me. You and I have been through so much over the last year."

He raised his plaster cast just to remind me — as if I needed the reminder or the guilt trip.

"Matt, please —"

"We've worked so well together. You can see I've changed. I'm willing to change even more. I think we just need to try again."

"No." I gently extracted my hand. "Matt, how can I make you understand? The cocaine —"

"I'm not using anymore! I've told you a thousand times. I'll never use again. You can believe me —"

"Matt, *please!* This isn't about you. This is about me."

"You're using coke?"

"No! *You* were my drug, okay? It was a

high, loving you, a fantastic high, but down the line, there was always the crash — the terrible, devastating, heartbreaking crash. You let me down too often, Matt. It was a terrible way to live."

"Please, Clare. One more chance?" Matt's brown eyes were actually blinking hard.

Why are you making this so difficult?!

"Listen, Matt, I care for you. I do. And I always will. If you need me, I'll be there — as a friend. But I can't love you anymore. Not like I used to. You may have changed. I'll give you that. But I need you to *get* this, okay? I've changed, too. I want something more. Someone who can give me more. I want Mike Quinn."

Matt was silent for a long moment, his expression studying my own. Finally, I asked my ex-husband something that I knew would make him understand: "If someone wanted you to become an addict again, would *you?*"

"No. I wouldn't." Matt looked away. "But do you really think it's fair to compare a destructive, addictive drug to me? I'm the father of your child."

"She's not a child anymore. She's grown. She's an adult. These terrible decisions of Joy's have driven that point home to me like never before. She's going to fly, and she's going to fall. But I want her to be free . . . and I need to be free, too . . .”

“You’re leaving the coffeehouse business?”

“No! I love managing this coffeehouse. I love working for your mother. She’s like a mother to me, too, and always has been. I don’t see any problem with us continuing to work together. I’m not quitting the Blend, Matt. I’m just quitting *you.*”

Matt’s head jerked back, as if I’d physically slapped him.

I tensed, still stunned that he was taking this so hard. *This is ludicrous! There is no reason for him to act like this, to cling so tightly, especially given his address for the last solid month!*

“I don’t want to hurt you, Matt,” I quickly added. “I honestly didn’t think I could. You’ve been intimately involved with Breanne for almost a year, haven’t you?”

Matt looked away again. He was quiet a long moment. Then, finally, he sighed and gazed back down at the stack of papers in front of him. “I have some things to do, Clare.” His voice had gone cold. He ran a hand over his face, pushed back from the table. “I’ll see you later.”

“Okay . . .” I said. My grip tightened on the coffee cup. This had gone badly. I could tell. And I wasn’t happy about that. Matt wasn't just my ex-husband; he was also my business partner. I *did* have a future with him, too — just not a sexual one. *Oh, Lord. Did I just mishandle this whole thing?*

"No hard feelings?" I called to his retreating back.

He said nothing in reply, unless you wanted to count the slamming of the apartment's front door on his way out. I took a breath, drank more coffee — and my gaze fell on the pile of papers across the table.

I got up, moved over to Matt's seat, and began rifling the pile for the Sunday *Times* real estate section. That's when I noticed something on the top of the pile. One of New York's tabloids was open to a Gotham Gossip column.

I saw that Matt had made a number of doodlelike circles and triangles next to a small article, as if he'd been contemplating something for a long time after reading it.

My eyes scanned the newsprint.

. . . and an arrest has been made in the murder of **Tommy Keitel,** executive chef of acclaimed Upper East Side restaurant Solange. The young woman taken into custody late Friday was an intern in Keitel's kitchen and has been identified as **Joy Allegro,** daughter of *Trend* magazine editor **Breanne Summour's** hunky flavor of the month, **Matteo Allegro,** a fixture on the local club scene . . .

Crap.

I wasn't surprised to see the news about Joy. Keitel was a noted chef, and Solange was a popular restaurant. I'd already braced myself for some bad publicity for my daughter and our family, but I was stunned that the *New York Journal* chose to link Joy with *Breanne* through Matt. And the way they referred to my ex-husband was downright emasculating. The trashy gossip column loosely implied that Matt was one notch above Breanne's gigolo.

That "flavor of the month" jibe must have really irked Matt for him to suggest getting back together with me . . .

But then the media-celebrity culture did expect a certain progression in relationships. Breanne and Matt had been seen around town for a long time; and when that happens, people naturally anticipate wedding bells. When they don't get them, they start speculating — and speculation in a New York tabloid is never a pretty thing.

Just then, the phone rang, halting any further conjectures on my part about Matt, Breanne, and their publicity problems.

"Hello?" I said, picking up the kitchen extension.

"Hello? Is this Clare?" said a vaguely familiar female voice.

"Yes."

"It's Janelle. Janelle Babcock from —"

"Solange, of course! My favorite pastry chef."

"I heard about Joy, Clare," Janelle said, "and I was wondering how she was doing."

I gave Janelle a quick update. ". . . and she should be out on bail tomorrow. At least I'm praying she will. I could use the help in that department, if you're so inclined."

"She's already in my prayers. Tommy and Vincent are, too," Janelle replied. "Of course, I don't believe for a second that Joy killed anyone. Not Joy. No way, nohow."

"Thank you, Janelle." I rubbed my chin. "You wouldn't by any chance have any idea who *did* kill Tommy and Vinny?"

"I wish I did. Honest to God. I didn't know a lot about the man's personal life. But . . . now that you bring it up . . ."

"What?"

"Well . . . if you want to know more about Chef Keitel, maybe you should come with me this evening. I'm going over to the Kingston Funeral Home with the other line cooks. We're going as a group to pay our

359

respects."

"I see . . ." I thought it over a moment. "Do you think I should talk to the other cooks?"

"I think you should speak to Chef Keitel's wife. If she's not too broken up, maybe you two can discuss things, figure out who the man's enemies were. Who may have wanted to . . . you know . . . do what they did."

I nodded, checking my watch. "What time are you going?"

"You're coming?"

"I'm coming," I said, making the decision on the spot, and we quickly made plans to meet.

I still had Madame's green Valentino suit and her exquisite emerald necklace and earrings. It wasn't the traditional black, but then this wasn't a funeral; it was just a viewing. Madame's clothes were conservative, tasteful, and dripping with class; they'd be my perfect camouflage for the Upper East Side crowd.

Okay, so the designer suit didn't fit me perfectly, but with a pin here and there, I knew it would get the job done, just as it had the day before, when I'd pitched Dornier and Keitel on my Village Blend beans.

My God. It seems like a lifetime ago . . . I

360

froze and closed my eyes, realizing: *It really was a lifetime ago for Tommy Keitel.*

With a sigh, I reached for the coffee carafe to pour myself another. Chef Keitel's viewing was bound to have some uncomfortable moments, but it was likely to have some good leads, too. Either way, I was definitely going to need another big cup of nerve.

Twenty-Two

There he was. Tommy Keitel. Larger than life. Smaller in death.

The big man was dwarfed by his own casket — a huge, expensive affair of heavy metal camouflaged with a veneer of polished cherry wood that appeared to be the same fine grain as Solange's dining room tables. The handles were brass, the trim gold-plated, and the interior's lining of warm yellow silk looked as sunny as his restaurant's walls. It was quite a final resting place; but then why shouldn't a four-star chef get a four-star send-off?

The mortician had dressed Tommy's corpse in a dark suit. The terrible wound at the base of his throat was well covered by the starched white color of his dress shirt; and his tie was a beautiful royal blue that came close to matching the arresting blue of his eyes, which were closed now, so I couldn't exactly check my opinion on the palette match.

"I'm so sorry this happened to you, Tommy," I murmured, hands clasped together. "May you rest in peace. And I can only hope that wherever you are they're smart enough to give you a few ingredients and a good-quality range . . ."

Janelle and I had arrived ten minutes earlier by cab. The evening viewing was crowded, and we'd waited in line to sign the condolence book. We moved to the casket, where she'd said her prayer beside me. Then Janelle went off to find her line cook colleagues, and I stayed near Tommy's casket, contemplating my strategy for catching his killer.

The funeral home's viewing room was very large, and jam-packed with people. It was also packed with flower arrangements that spilled out into a second sitting room beyond.

The aroma was cloying, and if Tommy's spirit was really in that casket, it probably would have bolted upright by now to roar: *The long-stemmed lilies can stay, but will you people please burn those damn carnations! I can't breathe in this stink!*

". . . it's a tragedy, I tell you. The art of the restaurant has been lost to the public relations racket. People who just want to

363

make a quick buck . . ."

I overheard the familiar voice and turned to see a familiar face. The food writer and restaurant critic Roman Brio had entered the viewing salon. Roman was a heavyset man with the round, chubby-cheeked face and intensely luminous eyes of a young Orson Welles. I'd met him a month ago, at the same Beekman Hotel tasting party where I'd first met Tommy Keitel. He was a friend of Breanne Summour's, owing to his frequent flamboyantly written contributions to *Trend* magazine among other publications.

". . . there's a term I often use called 'palate fatigue,' " Roman continued to expound, his basso voice distinct over the buzz of conversations.

Palate fatigue, I repeated to myself. I'd heard the term before, but I wasn't entirely sure what Roman meant by it. I stepped a little closer to eavesdrop.

"That was the key to Keitel's greatness," he continued. "He worked very diligently to see that his customers never experienced an overabundance of taste. It was the reason he put no more than five or six bites on a plate. 'When there is too much food, the tongue isn't tasting anymore,' he once told me. 'And when the customer isn't yearning for just one more bite, boredom sets in with the dish.' Yes, boredom was anathema to Tommy Keitel . . ."

The last line got to me. *Boredom was anathema to Tommy.* The words looped in my brain like a Buddhist chant.

Nick had told me the same thing in Brighton Beach, about Tommy getting bored with French cuisine. It seemed Tommy bored easily in his personal life, too. I thought of his affair with Joy, how he'd gotten tired of her in a few months.

In his cheese cave, he'd given me that whole pitch about realizing how "young" Joy was, but on reflection now, in front of his cold, dead form, I wondered if it wasn't a quirk of his personality to find a reason, any reason, to dump a woman when he got tired of her. He'd described himself to me as a collection of unbridled testosterone — and then started hitting on me to prove it.

Now I began wondering about Tommy's wife. How did Faye Keitel *really* feel about her marquee-chef husband?

I turned from Tommy's casket, scanned the crowded room. I didn't even know what Faye Keitel looked like. *But I'll bet Roman Brio does. I'll bet he knows a lot of things about Tommy Keitel . . .*

I approached the acerbic writer. By now, Brio's audience had dwindled to a single young man with long sideburns and a shaved head.

". . . to never again taste Chef Keitel's *tartelettes* of rabbit liver on a *brunois* of young vegetables, or his panko-breaded escargot, deep-fried with parsley and star anise. It's a tragedy, young man."

"The king is dead," I said.

Brio turned to greet me, but his smile faltered a little when he realized who I was.

"Clare Cosi. My, my. This is certainly awkward. Here I am speaking to the mother of the presumed murderess in this drama, yet I'm oddly delighted to see you."

"I'm flattered."

"My motives are not entirely unselfish. I'd planned to look you up, and quite soon. I want that book deal, you see."

"What book deal?"

"Why, the inside scoop on the culinary crime of the century, of course."

The young man had wandered away. I had Brio to myself now. I took his arm and led him to a quiet corner. "Wouldn't you rather get the exclusive on how the culinary crime of the century was *solved?*"

Brio crooked his elbow and hugged his neck. "Now *that's* intriguing. You're saying the police have got it all wrong?"

"I'm saying my daughter is innocent, and

366

I'm going to prove it."

His face brightened. "Didn't I hear about you and that dustup after the UN fellow 'fell' from the Beekman's balcony? And before that, wasn't there a scandal involving David Mintzer's new Hamptons eatery?"

"Not me," I said.

"Ah, well, not all news makes the papers, apparently. Yet word *does* get around."

"A little information, please," I said. "Faye Keitel is where?"

Brio extended his little finger. "Over there, beside Anton Wright."

I followed his pinkie to a strikingly good-looking fortysomething woman in a black designer dress. Her upswept hair was a shimmering blond with golden highlights that reminded me of the color scheme at Tommy's restaurant.

"Tell me about her."

"They met during Tommy's Italian phase. She was a talented young line cook. They married, and when he became completely bored with Italian fare, Tommy swept her off to France, where he studied and she had babies. It was all very romantic, or so they told me when I interviewed them."

"Recently?"

Roman shook his head. "This was five years ago, right after Solange opened. They were living in Brooklyn Heights. I went over for a breakfast tête-à-tête. Tommy and Faye were there. I believe a child was present — I recall some irritating noise. Tommy served three homemade jams, freshly baked almond croissants, chilled ewe's-milk yogurt, and prunes infused with tea —"

"You were talking about *Faye?" And I thought I was food-obsessed.*

"Oh, yes. Faye . . . She was Tommy's roast chef, and a talented one, but their love was more important than her career, so she gave it up for him. They were still madly in love during those Brooklyn days. At least that was the story they told me."

"And now?"

"Tommy made his fortune, bought a big, beautiful home in Oyster Bay. Faye lives there now, seldom comes into the city. And Tommy? Well, look around. It's packed in here, elbow to elbow, but if they'd had his funeral on Long Island, no one would have come. Tommy's life was *here.*"

"And Tommy's womanizing? How did Faye feel about that?"

"You might ask her yourself."

I smiled, but it probably looked more like the smirk it was. "Only if you introduce me."

He took my arm and we crossed the salon. As we approached Faye, I heard the sound of a grown man crying. I turned to find Henry Tso being helped out of the room by Yves Blanchard and another one of Solange's line cooks.

"Chef Keitel was like a father to me," Henry sobbed. "I learned so much from him. I . . . I can't believe he's gone . . ."

Oh, my God. The sauté chef's losing it . . .

"Faye?" Roman called.

The woman turned, smiled graciously. "So nice of you to come, Roman."

"Sorry for your loss, my dear."

"Too kind," she said. "You're too kind to come at this sad time."

Her response is syncopated, I realized, suddenly flashing on a BB Gun rap lyric. Faye Keitel had memorized her grief response so that she could recite it on autopilot a thousand times in a row.

"This is Clare Cosi," Roman said. "Clare is the mother of Joy Allegro."

Ack. It was true, of course; but, given the circumstances, it wasn't the introduction I would have chosen!

To Mrs. Keitel's credit, she remained stoic and unflappable. She stepped forward and actually put her arms around me in a semblance of a hug.

"I'm sorry," she told me. "Sorry for what Tommy drove your daughter to do. Joy is so young and naive. Tommy's done this sort of thing before."

"That must have been hard on you," I said.

She shrugged. "He's been sued for sexual harassment a number of times. Stalked once, too, by some poor, deluded young woman who's probably locked up in Creedmoor now."

Faye frowned. "I don't want this to sound like it probably sounds. Tommy was a wonderful man in so many ways. You learn to put up with the bad things, because there was so much good in him."

Despite her earnest tone, I could easily see that Faye was not at all broken up about her husband's death. I could understand her emotions because of my own experiences with Matt. After all the things that Tommy had put her through — the infidelities, the petty social humiliations that resulted from them — any love she may have had for the man had withered and died. Now that Tommy was dead, I doubted she felt anything more than relief.

Anton Wright approached and touched Faye's arm. "The deputy mayor is here. He'd like to express his condolences."

"Excuse me," she said, resting her hand on my arm. "Please, if there's anything I can do."

I nodded, and Anton led her away.

Brio had drifted off, observing us from a distance, no doubt. Now he was speaking with Robbie Gray. Across the room, I spied Janelle Babcock standing with Napoleon Dornier. I could see the displeasure on the man's face as I approached.

"Can you believe Henry Tso?" Janelle whispered. "Before tonight, the only two emotions he ever displayed were arrogance and anger."

I smiled. Dornier looked away.

Janelle sensed the tension. "Excuse me," she said.

Dornier moved to leave. "I have to go, too."

"Stay," I insisted. "I'd like to speak with you."

Dornier finally met my gaze. "We have nothing to talk about, Ms. Cosi —"

"I know you were Tommy's friend. But you also have to know that Joy is innocent."

Dornier frowned behind his amber glasses. "That's not what the police think. They interviewed me about the murder. I told them all about Joy's relationship with Tommy."

"You knew?" I said.

"Everyone did. There are no secrets in a

371

place like Solange. Of course your daughter killed Tommy. Who else would do it?"

"Hold on there a minute, Nappy."

The man winced, taken aback by my brazen use of his nickname. *Good,* I thought, because I wanted him off balance.

"I can think of at least one other suspect," I told him. "Do you remember that black envelope Tommy received the day he was murdered? The letter he told you to burn, like the others? Don't you think that's a little suspicious? Did you mention those letters to Detectives Lippert and Tatum?"

Dornier looked away, adjusted his glasses. "Lippert and Tatum were only interested in what I had to say about your daughter and her relationship with Tommy."

"So you didn't even mention the letters, did you? Tell me what you know," I said. "*Please.* You know Joy. You know she has a good heart. She genuinely cared for Tommy. She admired and respected him. Now she's facing prison for a murder I can assure you she did not commit."

"You're her mother. Of course you think —"

"If it's *possible* that someone else did this, at least tell me who it might be."

Dornier shifted on his feet and sighed. "The man behind those letters is Billy

Benedetto. He's the beverage manager at a club called Flux —"

"The place on Fourth Avenue. The club that used to be a church, like the old Limelight?"

Dornier nodded. "For months now, that man has been sending letters, demanding money from Tommy. I don't know why. The chef would never discuss it. The letters would come, all of them in those black envelopes, and Tommy would tell me to burn them. It got to the point where it was routine."

"Routine? How many have there been?"

"Over twenty. Two a month, since January —"

"Like an overdue bill notice."

"Exactly."

"So what did Tommy owe this man?"

"If you want to know that, ask Benedetto yourself," Dornier replied. "Tommy would never discuss it, so I have no idea."

Despite Dornier's surly tone, I thanked him, and we parted. Then I found Janelle, said good-bye, and headed for the door.

On the way, I noticed Faye Keitel and Anton Wright standing together in an alcove. Their heads were together, and they were whispering. Anton nodded and touched Faye's hand. It was a comforting touch, but then it appeared to change. His fingers ran up and down her bare arm in a gesture that looked more like an intimate caress. It didn't last long. Had I misjudged it?

I wondered if there was something sparking now between them . . . or if something had sparked long ago, before Tommy's death. The two didn't stay together long, and there wasn't much else to see, so I moved along.

My best lead now was this man named Billy Benedetto, and that's who I was going to see. I checked my watch. It was too early in the evening for a dance club to be open, so I'd have to cool my heels for an hour or two. Then I'd head to Club Flux and ask to speak with the beverage manager. What would I say next? I wasn't sure, but as I stepped onto the frigid uptown sidewalk, a chilling thought occurred to me. If Benedetto believed that Keitel owed him, maybe the debt had just been collected.

Twenty-Three

Purple light illuminated the granite walls of the former Fourth Avenue Episcopal Church. The cathedral was no longer a house of worship. The stained glass windows with religious scenes had been replaced by massive laser light displays that morphed and shifted with the relentless rhythms that filled the century-old sanctuary.

A winding sidewalk outside the entrance to the Gothic structure had once been the path to Sunday services. Now those same stones were buried under the spiked heels and polished loafers of at least one hundred flashily dressed revelers, waiting to be admitted to the club's inner sanctum.

In recent weeks, this gray stone structure had been rechristened Club Flux. Now there was a new breed of faithful flocking here, the type that willingly followed the leaders of the hip, the trendy, the terminally chic. If this brand-new nightspot was the location of the season, these dedicated pilgrims would line up to adulate.

I, on the other hand, just wanted to get in and out of the darn place as quickly as possible, but the length of the line at the door was irritating beyond belief. Moving past the crowd, I approached the velvet rope. Three bouncers guarded this draping gate, each bigger and tougher-looking than the last.

Seeing them here, it occurred to me that if you put Armani on a trio of football thugs, they still looked like football thugs, only dressed in Armani. I approached the least intimidating linebacker in the group — least intimidating because his shoulders were only broad enough to rival the span of the Brooklyn Bridge, his neck thicker than my waist.

"Hi," I said, loud enough to be heard over the music. "Could you tell me how long I'll have to wait on this line? I'm guessing at least an hour?"

I'd just exited a too-warm taxi, and my long gray coat was still unbuttoned. The big man eyed me from the top of my French twist to my green silk heels. The Valentino suit screamed class, and his gaze lingered a long moment on the exquisite emerald necklace, which shouted, *"Money, honey!"*

If any dame was going to buy up all those four hundred dollar bottles of Cristal inside, it was going to be the one wearing *this* necklace.

The bouncer winked at me and unlocked the velvet rope, which was exactly what I was banking on. People on the line booed, but not too loudly, since no one wanted to risk being shunned by the Gatekeepers of Gargantua.

After the rope guy moved aside, I strode up to the club's door, where another WrestleMania candidate held open the slab of heavy oak.

I stepped over the threshold, took off my overcoat, and tried to speak with the woman staffing the coat check, but she cupped her ear and shook her head, pretending not to hear me over the pulsing electronica flowing off the club's dance floor.

With Madame's green beaded clutch in my hand, I entered Flux's massive interior. It appeared exactly as I'd expected: flashing lights and jam-packed bodies writhing to a pounding, relentless beat.

I moved through the crowd, avoiding the central dance floor. A young man jostled me, excused himself, and I realized — as he flashed a toothy Hollywood smile — that this dude was a fairly famous television actor. I searched for other familiar faces, half expecting to see Madame here with her new, "younger" flame (she did say they were going clubbing Saturday. Maybe they'd come out Sunday night, too?).

But the only familiar face I noticed was on the crowded dance floor: Anton Wright, Solange's owner. He was clad in the same outfit he'd been wearing at the funeral home: a tailored black jacket over a black, open-necked shirt. And he wasn't alone. The man was dancing with a young woman in a daring red dress.

Oh, damn . . . another theory shot to hell . . .

Earlier in the evening, at Keitel's viewing, I'd suspected Anton was getting a bit too cozy with Faye, but now I could see I'd been wrong. Anton was dancing with this young woman, but he was also touching her suggestively, occasionally kissing her. Clearly, he was interested.

Wright hadn't seen me in the packed room and probably wouldn't have recognized me if he had. Nevertheless, I moved quickly along to the largest bar, which was located in approximately the same spot that the church's altar once stood. It took me a few minutes to push through the milling, thirsty mob and get the attention of a bartender.

"Where can I find Billy Benedetto?" I yelled. "I believe he's the beverage manager."

The man nodded. "Billy's expecting you."

I frowned. *How can he be expecting me?* Because of the loud music, it took me a moment to register the fact that the bartender hadn't asked my name. Obviously, Benedetto was expecting someone else to ask for him. *Oh, well. Too bad. I'm in.*

"It's through that door there. It's unlocked," the bartender said, pointing to a section of the mirrored wall next to the bar. I saw a knob and turned it; a door swung inward.

"Go to the top of the stairs. Billy's office is the first door on the left. If you walk into the control booth, you've passed it."

"Got it." I stepped through the opening, and the door closed behind me.

The dark space was soundproofed, the music muffled to a muted throb. The narrow corridor and the staircase beyond were surreally illuminated by ultraviolet lights, the black walls covered in psychedelic patterns reminiscent of retro sixties pop art.

At the top of the stairs I saw several doors, including the door to the control booth at the end of the dark hall. It was open, and I could see banks of dials and switches for the laser lights and sound system. I found Benedetto's office easily enough; his name was displayed on the door. I knocked, and a voice boomed.

"Come in!"

I pushed through the door.

The beverage manager's office was small: a desk and computer, a couple of chairs. One wall held shelves crammed with bottles of all shapes and sizes, many tagged with labels that read Sample Only: Not for Resale. The wall behind the desk was dominated by six full-color monitors, each displaying live security-camera footage from each of the club's serving stations.

Crowded and tight, the office was further reduced by the impressive girth of its occupant. Billy Benedetto was a large man — at least as large as one of the linebackers outside the club and much bulkier than the lithe Russian bodybuilders at Pedechenko's *banya.*

I guessed he was over sixty, but the age thing was iffy. Judging from his bloodshot, sad-sack eyes and the deep lines on his puffy face, Benedetto could easily be a hard-living fiftysomething. Tonight he was swathed in a loose-fitting Hawaiian shirt, decorated with little art deco rocket ships. His gray hair was worn long and tied back in a ponytail.

One ear was pierced with a diamond stud.

The second he saw me, Benedetto scowled. But then the man *was* expecting someone else.

"Who the hell are *you?*"

Charmed. "I'm Roman Brio's collaborator."

The scowl immediately vanished. "Roman Brio, the food writer and restaurant critic?"

"The same. Roman and I are working on a lengthy piece exposing the peccadilloes of Chef Tommy Keitel. You've heard, haven't you, that he —

"Kicked? Bought the farm?" Benedetto's sad-sack eyes brightened, and his face actually broke into a grin. "Yeah, honey. I heard."

I noticed the man had been writing on something when I walked into the room. Now Benedetto lifted the item. It was a white label. I watched him affix it to a glossy black envelope, the same size and shape of the envelope I'd seen Tommy open the day he was murdered.

So, I thought, *Dornier told me the truth . . .* I was relieved to be on the right track, but a part of me tensed, knowing full well that I might have just placed myself in a room with Keitel's murderer. *But he had a motive to kill Tommy. He's not going to kill an associ-*

ate of Roman Brio's, so just keep up the act, Clare . . .

"You don't seem too broken up about the news of Chef Keitel's demise," I noted carefully.

Benedetto laughed. "That's because you didn't know Tommy like I knew Tommy. Consider yourself lucky. The great chef didn't live long enough to stab *you* in the back."

Benedetto tossed the black envelope aside, leaned back in his chair, and sighed heavily. "So who are you? You work with Brio, but what's *your* name?"

"Clare Cosi. I'm here looking for background so Roman can write his piece. He may want to call you, even take you out to dinner. Would that be all right with you?"

Judging from the man's girth, I figured that was a pretty good carrot. And I wasn't wrong.

"Well, now," Benedetto said, lacing his hands over his belly, "this is turning out to be one pleasant weekend. Tommy Keitel gets sliced up like red meat, and I get offered a plate of it. That's rich!" He tossed his head back and laughed; then his gaze came back to me. "Okay, I'll bite . . . What do you want to know about Keitel? I've got *lots* to tell you."

Benedetto gestured to a chair opposite his desk. I sat down and crossed my legs. *Motive. I need the motive . . .*

He regarded me. "Don't you have a notebook or tape recorder?"

I did my best to channel the amazing BB Gun — "I keep it all up here," I said, tapping my temple.

The man's bushy, gray eyebrows rose. "You have that good a memory, eh? Well, all right, here's something to remember. Tommy Keitel is a son of a bitch who ruined me and my whole family. How do you like that for something to remember?"

"Good. Very good. Please go on . . ."

"The restaurant he ruined was more than a business. It was three generations of my family's blood, sweat, and tears." He held up three sausage fingers to make his point.

"I was born in the apartment above the place. My father died in his bedroom. Now it belongs to a damn health club chain — the house my grandfather built with his own hands."

He shook his large gray head; the ponytail swayed. "That place was everything to me. When my grandfather died, we needed a new chef. Keitel was that man. We paid his asking price, put a fortune into renovating the place, and it worked. Keitel's new

383

menus were the talk of the town. People waited for weeks to eat his food. Then one day that arrogant prick woke up and said he was 'bored' with cooking Italian and wanted to learn French cuisine instead. On nothing more than a whim, he left me and my family high and dry. What a complete and total asshole. I watched the business my grandfather built wither and die right in front of my eyes. Tommy wouldn't even sell us his recipes. His contract was ironclad. He owned the recipes. So he took them with him, and the prick never even *used* them again!"

Benedetto locked his sad eyes onto mine. "The heartbreak killed my mother, God rest her soul. The pressure ruined my marriage, too. I lost everything because of that egomaniac. All I ever wanted out of Tommy was some amends. But do you think he'd give it to me?"

"Give it to you?" *Okay, now we're getting somewhere . . .* "I don't understand. You weren't threatening Chef Keitel in some manner, were you?"

"Threaten him!" Benedetto bellowed so loudly I flinched. "You're damn right, I threatened him!"

I tensed in my chair. *Uh-oh.* I'd obviously pressed the anger button.

"That son of a bitch was a millionaire! Solange made him famous! All I wanted was a loan, or even just for Tommy to lend his name to a new restaurant I'm trying to open. It was the least he could do. But the prick wouldn't even answer the phone when I called, had me thrown out by that prissy little maître d' of his when I paid him a visit."

I cleared my throat, tried to appear completely calm and cool and unperturbed, which wasn't easy. This man was shaping up to be the killer — of Keitel, maybe Vinny, too, although I couldn't imagine the motive there, but if I could keep him talking, who knew what I could get? I was so close now. I didn't want to blow this.

Just stay on his good side, Clare. He thinks you're in his corner. Just keep him thinking that.

"Everything you've told me is heartbreaking," I said, shaking my head in sympathy, not unlike Detective Lippert had done with me. "It's awful what Keitel did to you and your family . . ."

"Your damn right it's awful."

"Roman will be very interested in these details, Mr. Benedetto, but . . . I must ask. You don't strike me as the kind of man who would dare take no for an answer, especially from a man as arrogant as Chef Keitel. Didn't you do anything to drive your point home with him?" *Like the point of a knife maybe?*

"You have me there, Miss . . . Cosi, was it?"

I nodded.

"I did something, all right. I wrote to the man."

"You wrote to him? Is that all? Doesn't sound like much."

"What do you mean by that?"

I shrugged. "Just one measly letter?"

Benedetto threw back his head and laughed. "Try twenty-one — *at least.* I sent the man bills for exactly what he owed me."

"And did he ever pay up?"

Benedetto grinned, displaying an uneven row of sharp yellow teeth. "He's dead now. I'd say he's paid in full."

My mouth went dry. "Did you kill him?"

"What?"

I leaned forward, put a finger to my lips. "Don't worry. I won't tell, but did you . . . you know . . . do the deed?"

"What kind of a question is that?" He eyed me warily now. "Are you a cop?"

"No."

"Well, I don't like the look in those cat green eyes of yours. I think you should get out of here. Roman Brio can call me if he wants a story. If you really work with him, you tell him to contact me himself. And *another* thing, nobody gets something for nothing in this world. If Brio wants my Keitel story, then he's going to have to pay."

"Pay?"

"Yes. I just got a backer for my restaurant. And when it opens, I expect Brio to be there reviewing it. And I expect a *rave.*"

"I see." *Brother, this guy's whole life is about extortion.*

"What's 'I see' mean, missy? Do you agree?"

"Sure. What's the restaurant?"

"You'll find out soon enough. My backer's coming up here tonight to finalize the plan." He glanced at his watch.

"And who is this backer? Does he own other restaurants? Does Roman know him?"

"It's someone with deep pockets. That's all you need to know."

I could tell he wanted me to leave, but this mysterious "backer" story had me intrigued. Benedetto was so open about his past with Keitel. Why clam up now?

"How can you be sure your backer isn't going to back out?" I pressed.

"Oh, he's not backing out, missy. This one *has* to come through for me, or he's in big trouble. I've got something on him. Something big. Something bad. And there's no way in hell he can afford to cross me now."

"What do you mean by that exactly? That you have something on him? Because it sounds a little like blackmail."

Benedetto scowled at me and pointed to the door. "I want you *gone* right now."

"But —"

"Do you want me to call my security team?"

I flashed on the linebackers in Armani guarding the velvet gate. "No. I'm going."

I left the man's office and descended the stairs.

If anyone was bitter and angry enough to kill Tommy Keitel, I'd just met him. The only thing that niggled at me was the murder of Vincent Buccelli. It didn't make sense. *Yet.*

I resolved right then to wait at the bar and watch the mirrored door. If Bendetto's mysterious backer was going to show, then I was going to wait and see who it was.

I didn't expect to recognize the person on sight. But my gut told me that if Benedetto wanted Keitel dead, and Keitel ended up that way, then he may have hired someone to do it. And in that case, I wanted to know what this "backer" looked like, if only to be able to recognize him out of a mug shot book.

When I opened the soundproof mirrored door at the bottom of the stairs, the wall of pulse-pounding noise smacked me in the face. Despite the din, I collared the bartender, pointed at a pale blue drink a young woman was dangling in her manicured hand.

"One of those . . ." I didn't know what the heck it was, but I liked the color.

The drink came, I paid for my eleven-dollar cocktail, and snagged a stool at the bar, watching and waiting for Billy Benedetto's mysterious backer to arrive.

Five minutes passed. Then ten. Then fifteen. But not one soul entered that room. While I kept watching the door, I'd been nursing what turned out to be a blueberry martini. After twenty minutes of very slow sips, my tapered glass was finally empty. I was about to order again when a sweet, male voice spoke close to my ear.

"I'd like to buy you another, if I could."

I turned. Beside me at the bar, a fashionably dressed man at least fifteen years my junior smiled down at me. He was model handsome, far more striking than the Hollywood celebrity I'd collided with earlier. He was tall and tanned with black hair worn slicked back like Wall Street's Gordon Gekko, only this guy was closer in age to Gekko's son.

"Simon Ward," he said, offering me his right hand. I shook it, and he rested his left hand on top of mine. I got the distinct impression he'd done that so I could see the Rolex on his wrist.

"My name's Clare," I said.

"Clare." His smile broadened. "Clare. I like that name."

Upon second glance, I decided that the man's tailored suit was much too trendy for a stodgy brokerage house, and he was far too young to be a power player in the financial world, anyway. I figured him for a scion of a wealthy family, some trust fund baby who'd come to the new Club Flux on a lark. New York City was full of that type: young, well-educated, sophisticated urbanites who never had to do a lick of work, unless boredom with partying set in. Why? Because they were smart enough to come out of the right birth canal.

"Now, how about that drink?" he asked.

"I think I may have had enough," I replied, charmed and somewhat bemused by this too-young man's attention but also aware that my thoughts were turning edgy. *Probably a result of this relentless dance music pounding through my head.*

Simon Ward frowned, but the expression of eagerness never left his bright eyes. "Come on, the night is young! Have another drink, on me."

I sighed. There was *still* no sign of Benedetto's backer.

Clearly, I had a stakeout on my hands, and I could *almost* hear Mike Quinn's voice: *You're not going anywhere at the moment, anyway, Cosi. So talk to this guy. He's a good cover. And this bar's not exactly democratizing its luxury, so let the man pay.*

I glanced up at Simon. "Sure. If you'd really like to treat me, why not?"

"That's the spirit." He took my nearly empty glass, slid it across the bar, and ordered another.

I managed to avoid his unwavering gaze while we made polite conversation. At one point, I spied a woman at least my age, in a too-daring banana-yellow tank dress with a short skirt and plunging neckline. She was fairly tall and strongly built with severe features, and her ebony hair was slicked back into a tight ponytail. To my surprise, the woman was openly glaring at me.

Whoa, what is her problem? She can't possibly be jealous. This kid's not much older than my daughter!

That's when I remembered Tucker giving me the lowdown on a recent social trend. *Tadpoling,* he'd called it, insisting older women were hooking up with young men all the time now.

Simon passed me the drink, and our fingers touched. I looked up and met his gaze. His eyes widened, and he took a breath.

"Sorry," he said, seemingly embarrassed.

"What are you apologizing for?"

"I was struck a little speechless, that's all," he replied sheepishly. "Yeah, I know it sounds corny to someone as sophisticated as you obviously are."

"Excuse me?"

He nodded. "Your beautiful hair, your wonderful clothes . . . I'm a fashion designer, and I knew from just one look at you that you possessed an impeccable taste —"

I nearly choked on my martini. The irony was hilarious. It wasn't my taste he was admiring. It was Madame's. And I had to agree with him on that score. Her taste always had been impeccable.

"Just look at those green emeralds around your neck. See how they shimmer. Do you realize those gems are an exact match for the gorgeous green shade of your bright eyes?"

I gulped a hit of my martini. *This guy's really pouring it on. Has he been drinking excessively?*

That's when I noticed a man finally going through the mirrored doors next to the bar. It wasn't an employee. And it wasn't an unknown. The man going in to see Billy Benedetto was Anton Wright.

Anton Wright is Benedetto's backer.

My God. I'd scored big coming here. *Huge.* I was now absolutely sure I'd found Keitel's killer. Benedetto wanted Keitel dead, but I was willing to bet that Anton Wright was in on it somehow, too. What else could Benedetto possibly have on Anton?

I'll talk to Mike first thing tomorrow, I decided. *With his help, I'm sure we can come up with a plan to collar Billy Benedetto and free my baby girl!*

A grin split my face, and I felt like celebrating. Simon glanced over, saw my expression. "Hey, now," he said. "Look at that beautiful smile —"

Just then, someone tapped me *hard.* I turned. An Amazon of a woman in a dress covered in red rhinestones placed a manicured hand on my shoulder.

"There you are, girlfriend!" she gushed. "I

393

see you've hooked up. So have I. But before I go home, I want you to join me in the powder room."

I blinked, baffled. Did I *know* her? Was she a customer from the Blend?

I took a closer look at the woman. My goodness, she was large. Was there a WWF for women? If there was, she'd have mopped the floor with every opponent. In her late thirties, she had a longish, slightly horsey oval face, and she wore her very short blond hair in tight curls against her scalp. I didn't recall seeing her at the Blend, and I certainly would have remembered this Wonder Woman stand-in.

She smiled, batted her heavily made-up eyes.

"Look!" she cried, acting a little tipsy. "There's my guy, over there." She clutched my shoulder and pointed insistently.

I looked in the direction of her gesture, and my body froze. The man she'd pointed to was Mike Quinn. The lieutenant was waving at me from across the room.

Mike? I blinked, more than a little confused. *What in heaven's name is going on?*

Twenty-Four

I moved to go to Mike, ask him what was happening, but the blond Amazon acting like my best friend actually restrained me with a fairly powerful grip.

"Come to the ladies' room with me, *please*, Clare," she said.

How does she know my name?

Before I could ask, Wonder Woman turned to my eager young suitor. "You don't mind, do you?" she asked. "I promise, Clare will be right back as soon as we're done with our girl talk."

I glanced at Mike again, and he nodded. Something was going down here. He wanted me to play along.

"Okay," I said, nodding to the big blond. I handed my martini to Simon Ward. "Would you hold on to my drink, Simon? I'll be right back."

"Please hurry," he replied, appearing a little annoyed.

I followed the woman across the room to the ladies'. But as soon as we stepped through the door, I turned on her.

"Okay, what's going on?"

She immediately reached into the bodice of her rhinestone dress and pulled out a gold shield. "Detective Lori Soles, NYPD. I'm on Lieutenant Quinn's task force."

"You're hunting the May–September gang?"

I could have kicked myself the second I'd blurted that out. Mike had told me that in confidence.

The woman blinked, surprised. "Lieutenant Quinn told me you were a private detective. You are, right? You have a license?"

"I, ah —"

"Quinn also told me to tell you that he thinks you can *handle* this. He said I should emphasize that for some reason. Something about a conversation you had with him at a crime scene recently?"

Oh, God.

"He also told me that you solved some pretty hairy homicides, and this should be a walk in the park. Are you up for it?"

The door opened again, and another woman entered. I recognized her at once: the jealous one with the too-daring banana-yellow tank dress and the slicked-down ebony ponytail. She'd glared at me earlier, when Simon first began talking to me. I noticed she was clutching an oversized black handbag under one arm that in no way matched her outfit.

"This better work," she grumbled. "I turned on the charm for forty minutes, then *she* walks in and the freakin' perp dumps me!"

She appraised me, shook her head. "The little bastard is obviously going for the emeralds."

Detective Soles rolled her eyes. "This is my partner, Sue Ellen Bass," she said.

"Well, is she going to do it?" Detective Bass demanded.

"Calm down," said Detective Soles. "I haven't explained the sting yet."

Before I could ask them, "What sting?" or even make an educated guess where this conversation was going, given Quinn's current task force goals, the door opened, and two exceedingly tipsy young women entered the ladies', tittering loudly.

"Into my office," Detective Bass commanded. She shoved us into a marble-walled bathroom stall and locked the door behind us. The stall was quite spacious, a mercy, considering there were three of us crammed in there.

"Are you going to wear the wire?" Detective Bass whispered to me.

"The wire? What for?"

"That guy, the one who was chatting you up? He's our prime suspect."

"That kid, Simon? You're telling me he's a May–September gangster? He said he was a fashion designer —"

Bass snorted. "*Simon,* huh? And he's a fashion designer? That's real funny, because he told me his name was Richard, and he worked on Wall Street."

"Sounds suspicious to me," Soles agreed.

"Or the SOB is married," Bass replied. "In which case, the situation's even more pathetic than I originally figured, because it means I can't even get a lowlife scumbag to be straight with me."

"Please, Sue Ellen . . ." Soles shook her head. "Let's not delve into your dating habits —"

"Easy for you to say. You're a happy newlywed."

Soles rolled her eyes. "And you're the one with the commitment problem!"

"True." Bass shrugged. "But there are too many cute guys on the force. Like Lieutenant Quinn out there. He's pretty hot, but word is he's taken."

"Already?" Soles asked. "He just split with

his wife."

Sue Ellen shrugged. "Whoever the lucky lady is, the man's got it bad for her."

Oh, Lord.

Her partner hushed her, faced me. "Look, Ms. Cosi. We really need you to do this. Lieutenant Quinn told me to tell you something else. He said he wouldn't ask if he didn't need this."

I nodded. The man had gone out on a limb enough times for me. The least I could do was return the favor. "Okay. I'll do it."

"There's a risk," Detective Soles warned. "These guys have been violent in the past. We'll be on you like glue, but you could still get roughed up if we drop the ball —"

"We won't," Detective Bass declared.

"But it's a possibility," Soles added.

"What do you want me to do?"

Detective Soles glanced at her partner. "I told you she'd do it. This one can take care of herself."

"You're going to wear a wire, honey," Sue Ellen Bass said as she reached into her bag. "Ask simple 'Simon' out there to escort you home. You live in the Village, right? We'll monitor your conversation after you leave the club. We'll follow you, too. If he tries to rob you, or rape you, or even look at you funny, we'll know it and come running."

"What if he's *innocent?*"

Sue Ellen yanked a radio, battery pack, and a tiny microphone on a long wire out of her bag and untangled it. "Then you have nothing to worry about."

Detective Soles fumbled with the buttons on my blouse.

"Excuse me? What are you doing?!"

"The wire goes *under* your clothes."

It took several minutes, but eventually I was ready. The transmitter was tapped to my belly, the microphone wire running up, under my bra, to the microphone itself, which was nestled between my breasts.

"Did you bring a coat?" Bass asked, checking out my breasts.

"Of course. It's freezing outside."

"Well, don't button it; you might cover the mike."

"Okay, Ms. Cosi. Say something." Soles commanded, slipping a headset over her tight blond curls.

"Say what?" I asked.

Detective Soles listened and nodded to her partner. "It works. Now we need a panic phrase —"

My eyes widened. "A what?"

"Something you say that lets us know that you're in real trouble," Sue Ellen replied in an exasperated tone, as if I should know this stuff already.

"Oh, sure, a panic phrase," I replied flatly. "How about 'Help, help, I'm being mugged'?"

Detective Soles rolled her eyes. "That won't work. What if he's holding a knife on you? If you yell that, he'll just finish you off."

"Can't you just follow me and see that I'm in trouble?" I said.

"We can try to keep a visual on you," Soles said, "but what if he pulls you into the shadows where we can't see you? Or takes you into some private lobby, where our presence would tip him off?"

"We have to rely on the wire," Detective Bass insisted.

"And the panic phrase," Lori Soles reminded her. Then she looked down at me (a long trip) and put her large hand on my small shoulder. "If something bad starts to go down, and you want us to rush in, you have to say something that's not at all appropriate, something that will confuse the perp long enough for us to move in. We'll need about fifteen seconds, at least, and that's enough time for a guy like this to kill you."

"Okay, I'm convinced," I said. "Like what?"

401

"Just say 'Carnegie Hall,' " Soles replied. "We'll understand."

"Carnegie Hall?" I smirked. "Are you sure I don't have to practice first?"

Soles laughed, glanced at her partner. "This one's quick. I think she's gonna do it for us."

"Okay, honey," Sue Ellen Bass said, slapping me on the back. "Get out there and break the little scumbag's heart, so I can crack his skull."

Detective Soles and I left the bathroom together. I could tell she was relieved to see that Simon Ward was still waiting where we left him. She made a big show of saying good-bye, making sure to mention that I would be going home alone now.

"Thanks, Clare," Detective Soles said, squeezing my shoulder reassuringly as she pecked my cheek. "I've got to go find my man."

I took the blue martini from Simon and drained it in one gulp.

"You're friend seems a little . . . scatterbrained," he said.

"She is." I nodded. "She might be a little tipsy, too."

"You've finished your drink in a hurry. *You* may feel a little tipsy soon, too."

"That's why I'm going home," I told him.

Simon frowned — until I took his arm and added, "But not alone, I hope. You know, I don't live far at all, but I could use a chaperone on the walk home."

Simon grinned and patted my hand. "I'll be your *escort* — how's that? I have far too many designs on you to be an effective chaperone."

I laughed, only half faking it. I had trouble believing Simon was anything more than a charming young man who had a way with the ladies — which was also *(eesh)* a fairly accurate description of a May–September gang member, come to think of it.

We waited a few minutes at the coat check. Simon retrieved our stuff. As he helped me into my coat, he leaned close and gave me a light kiss on the back of my neck. I stiffened, remembering Mike was watching this — or, at the very least, listening.

Outside, the line was still long, but it was colder than I remembered it. We stepped onto Fourth Avenue, and a blast of arctic air hit us.

"Too cold." Simon groaned, reaching for a cell phone. "I'll call my driver."

He hit a speed-dial button and waited a moment. "Bring the car around. I'm outside Flux on Fourth Avenue." He paused. "What do you mean, *traffic?*" He faced Fourth

Avenue. It was jammed with cars. "Fine," he said, sounding annoyed. "I'll meet you on Broadway."

Simon pocketed his phone and took my arm a little roughly.

"This way," he said, leading me down shadowy Eleventh Street. It was late, and all the businesses were closed. A block ahead, I could see traffic moving along Broadway, but where we were now, between Fourth and Broadway, it was the twilight zone, completely deserted.

"So where do you live, Clare?" Simon asked, his tone back to upbeat and pleasant.

"Above a coffeehouse, actually. On Hudson Street. I'm —"

The sucker punch came out of nowhere — which is probably why they call it a *sucker* punch. One second I was walking along, chatting away; the next I was reeling, down on my knees, thrown by force into a shadowy alley.

"Ca —" I began, but couldn't get the word out! In about a nanosecond, strong hands grabbed me, lifted me up. A forearm was shoved against my throat. *I can't talk!* Simon's face loomed close. "Don't fight," he whispered, jamming a knee between my legs. I could smell his alcohol-soaked breath, hear the sound of a car pulling up.

"Come on, man! We got your back!" I heard someone call. "Bash her head in and let's go!"

God, this guy was strong. He had me pinned against the wall like a butterfly to a board. But then his free hand moved toward my neck. *He's going for Madame's emerald's!* The pressure on my windpipe finally loosened. Now was my chance.

"Carnegie Hall!" I shouted.

"Huh?"

"Carnegie Hall! Carnegie Hall!"

The hard smack seemed to come a moment later, a fist striking flesh, and my attacker was sprawled on the ground. Free now, I stumbled, almost going down myself when a pair of strong hands caught me.

Around me I heard shouts, feet pounding pavement, squealing tires. A police car rolled up to the curb. Another appeared at the end of the street, siren blaring, blocking the getaway car.

In the flashing red lights, I looked up, saw the rugged face. Finally, I understood. I was in Mike Quinn's arms.

"It's over, sweetheart," he said, smiling. "You were wonderful. The way you handled that perp, reeled him in. It was textbook, Clare. Thank you."

I clutched his neck, pulled him close, and whispered into his ear.

"Next time, we've *got* to have a better panic phrase."

Two EMTs checked me out, but I didn't need more than an ice pack. I would have accepted a stiff drink, too, but nobody was offering me anything stronger than Coke (the kind that came in a cold can).

Mike had paperwork, interviews, instructions for the detectives under him, who were handling the bookings. And then he was off, and we were free.

"You didn't have to wait for me," he said as we exited the Sixth Precinct house.

"Yes, I did. I've got some good news . . ."

I told Mike everything. How I went to Keitel's funeral home viewing and questioned his wife. How I heard from Dornier about the threatening letters in the black envelopes. When I got to the Club Flux part, he was mostly caught up.

"I remember your debriefing," Mike told me. "You said you went to Flux to speak with the beverage manager, Billy Benedetto."

"He's Keitel's killer, Mike. I'm sure of it. He has a very strong motive: Keitel ruined his family's business, and it led to a lot of heartache. Benedetto also has a history of threatening Tommy. And here's the topper: Dornier was a witness to it. He saw the threatening letters. He saw how often they came and how many."

Mike nodded, put his hands on my shoulders. "I think you did it, sweetheart. I think you saved your little girl."

"But how are we going to get him, Mike? We need proof, don't we? I've heard you tell me that a thousand times."

"We'll get it. We'll find a way. We can start by going to Ray Tatum tomorrow — you and me together. Tatum will give me some leeway, I think. We can get warrants for Benedetto's computer and cell phone. We can find incriminating evidence, use it for an interrogation, pressure him to confess. We might have to use you to bait him. Do you think you can handle that?"

"Sure. I already baited Benedetto once. I'm willing to do it again with you listening."

Relieved beyond belief, I closed my eyes then. Mike misunderstood.

"Listen, sweetheart," he said. "Tomorrow's another day. You look tired. Do you want me to walk you back to the Blend?"

"No." I opened my eyes. "I'm not tired at all. My daughter will be out on bail by this time tomorrow, and once we nail Benedetto, she'll be free of this nightmare for good. I feel like celebrating."

"Is that right? Have anything special in mind?"

I nodded. "Your place."

Mike's own expression had looked a little weary, but the sun dawned fast at my suggestion. He smiled down at me; then his smile became a grin. He slipped his arm around my waist.

"Let's go," he said.

We took a cab to Alphabet City. We could have walked to the next neighborhood, but neither one of us wanted to waste time. Mike paid the driver, grabbed my hand, and pulled me into his apartment building.

The place was eight stories, a converted factory with high ceilings and new windows.

"Nice building," I said in the elevator.

"It's spartan inside," he warned.

"But you *do* have a bed? I remember you saying something about —"

"A nice big one, sweetheart." Mike winked. "No worries on that score."

I laughed, so did he, then I waited a week for him to unlock his apartment. We moved inside, closed the door, and the moment he threw the dead bolt, I was pulling on the lapels of his overcoat, insisting his mouth cover mine.

That was the extent of the preliminaries. There was no need for more. We'd had a month of them already. It was finally time to get on with it.

Mike groaned and pulled me closer; then my feet were off the ground, but not by a few inches; this time my legs were swept fully off the planet. He carried me across his living room, where I failed to notice much — not the parquet floor or the high ceiling, not the lack of rugs, pictures, or furniture. All I remembered about our short trip was Mike's hungry kisses, my racing heart, and the slight bump of the man's shoe as it impatiently kicked at a half-closed door.

Now we were inside Mike's bedroom: a chest of drawers, a wooden nightstand, a small table piled high with books and papers, and, just as promised, a nice, big, king-sized bed. The frame was no-frills. There wasn't even a headboard, but the sheets were soft and clean, and the thick, new comforter was the color of sky.

He laid me down gently, resting my back against a heavenly cloud, and then things weren't so gentle anymore. I tore at Mike's overcoat, jerking it off. Next came the sport jacket, the tie. When I reached to unbutton his dress shirt, he stilled my fingers. He took care in removing his shoulder holster, wrapping the leather straps around his service weapon, resting it on the nightstand.

The shirt came off next. I lightly touched his heavy muscles, softly kissed some old scars. Mike swallowed hard, pushed me back against the pillows, wasted no more time separating me from my clothes. When he saw the nasty purple bruises on my upper arms, he stopped.

"My God, Clare. Was this from tonight?"

I shook my head. "When Joy was arrested. Lippert's men . . ."

He quietly swore, pressed his lips to the hurt, and then we were both completely naked, stripped down until there was nothing more that could come between us.

The only thing left to take off was the exquisite string of emeralds around my neck. I moved my hands to undo the clasp. Mike stopped me, capturing my wrists and bringing them together above my head. His gaze moved slowly over my bared curves, taking me in for the first time. I held my breath, self-conscious for an instant, until his shining eyes met mine.

"So beautiful . . ." he whispered.

I smiled, and so did he. Then Mike and I

were finally together, and for the next few hours, the rest of the world went away.

Twenty-Five

The sound of ringing woke me. For a moment, I thought it was an alarm clock, and then I realized it was the bedside phone. There was movement next to me on the mattress, and that's when I remembered —
Mike.

I opened my eyes. He was there, beside me. His spartan bedroom was bathed in morning light, the sun rays pouring in through the half-closed miniblinds.

"Hello?" his deep voice murmured.

I was about to answer when I realized Mike was talking into the phone receiver. His long arm had allowed him to grab it off the nightstand without even sitting up.

"No. It's okay. I asked you to . . ." he said to the unknown caller. "What did you get?"

I started to sit up off the pillows; Mike instantly pulled me back down. His free arm wrapped around me, urged me close against his long, strong form.

"Uh-huh . . . and?"

I tucked my head into the crook of his shoulder, rested my hand on his bare chest. Mike's body was solid, the muscles well-defined. There were scars here, and I lightly outlined an angry-looking slash — a knife wound was my guess. Then I touched some healed incisions from surgeries, which looked like entry points from multiple gunshot wounds.

Mike's free hand stopped stroking my hair. His fingers moved lower, to the nape of my neck. His massaging was sweet and leisurely, his finger pads slightly calloused, a texture that made me purr.

Mike shifted slightly, cleared his throat. "Go on. I'm listening . . ."

I pressed my lips where my hands had just been. Mike took in sharp breaths of air, feeling my mouth on his skin. Then his free hand moved down my body on a mission to mess with my focus, too.

"Okay," he finally said. "I'll be in later."

He punched the Off button and tossed the phone away. The call may have ended, but Mike's touching was just beginning.

"Who was that?" I asked.

"Who cares," he growled.

I was wide awake now, but getting up wasn't an option. It would be well over an hour before the man would let me out of his bed.

"So . . ." Mike said as I poured him a cup of coffee, "do you remember that phone call I got?"

"Phone call? What phone call? That was over an hour ago. So much has happened since."

Mike laughed. He was sitting at the cheap card table in his kitchen; four creaky folding chairs completed the less-than-elegant set. The kitchen itself was new and clean with faux marble counters, a full-sized fridge, and a good gas range. As I expected, the larder was spare, but he did have a coffee-maker, a small grinder, and some of my Village Blend beans. It was gratifying to see I'd had *some* influence on the man, after all.

In the fridge were bottles of a good Mexican beer, a few limes, a carton of half-and-half, Chinese mustard, and one egg.

While Mike showered, I'd thrown on one of his T-shirts, made us the coffee, and rifled a cardboard box I'd found sitting on the counter. Someone had written *Mike* in big letters with a Magic Marker along with the address of this place. I got the impression from its contents — a collection of pans, dishes, cups, a small spice rack, and some unopened grocery items — that this was a box from his old Brooklyn brownstone, the one he'd owned jointly with his wife.

Mrs. Quinn was now living on an estate on Long Island with the Wall Street whiz whom she intended to marry. I figured she had no use for these things from her old kitchen, and the movers delivered them here with Mike's clothes and the few other items in the place — obviously very few.

I dug out a cardboard container of corn-meal, a small sack of flour, some baking powder, and sugar, stirred them together with the egg, the half-and-half, and a bit of oil. I poured the batter in a square pan and baked it at 400. The timer was set for twenty, but Mike was out of the shower in twelve.

Now he was sitting across from me at the table in gray sweats and a faded blue T-shirt, his feet were bare, and his dark blond hair looked even darker now that it was wet and slicked back against his squareish head.

I wanted to kiss him again.

It took a few gulps of hot coffee to *focus* and remind myself that Mike's mouth oc-casionally did something other than that.

". . . and I need to talk to you about it," he was saying.

"Huh?"

"The phone call, sweetheart."

"The call. Right. Was it serious?"

"It was a colleague calling with some news." He leaned forward in his folding chair. "Billy Benedetto's your prime suspect in Keitel's murder, right?"

I nodded.

"Well, this man named 'Simon,' who hit on you in Flux and then *really* hit on you in the street, was a perp with a lot of aliases. After a long, hard night of questioning, the little jerk spilled his guts to the interrogating detectives. He gave up Benedetto."

"Wait. You're telling me that Benedetto was running the May–September gang?"

"Yeah. He helped set up dozens of robberies. He was the beverage manager for three different nightclubs. He used security cameras at each club to select whales for his crew of young robbers to harpoon."

"Where's Benedetto now?! Don't you have enough on that creep to arrest him?"

"Of course. My guys are looking for him as we speak."

"Why didn't you tell me an hour ago?"

Mike shrugged, sipped his coffee. "I didn't want to break the mood."

Beep! Beep! Beep!

Mike sat up, looking around as if an emergency alert had just gone off. "What the hell was that?"

"It's your oven timer."

"My *what?*"

I rolled my eyes. "Don't bake much, do you?"

There were no oven mitts in the cardboard box, so I used a dish towel to pull the pan out. My knife got busy, and I set the warm, fresh squares of corn bread on a plate between us.

Mike stared at me as if I'd just dug a five-carat diamond out of his sink.

"Where did you get that?"

"What? The corn bread?"

"Yeah."

"You had the ingredients. I whipped it together."

He stared at me, still a little dumb-founded. "I had the ingredients? In *this* apartment?"

I laughed. "Try some."

I didn't have to suggest it twice. Mike grabbed a square, inhaled the aroma of the warm, sweet bread, and shoveled it in. "Hungry . . ." he said, as if he'd just re-alized it. He ate the entire square in about three bites and reached for a second.

"The standard recipe calls for skim milk, but I prefer using half-and-half anyway. It gives a much richer mouthfeel to the product, don't you think?"

"Yhemmmh Immm thimnk so . . ." he replied. He swallowed the second square and reached for a third.

Finally, I thought, *a man who has no issues with palate fatigue!*

"So this Benedetto May–September gang thing . . . That's good news, isn't it?" I pressed. "I mean, once you get the man into custody, you can go over his computer files and papers with a fine-tooth comb, look for clues that he killed Keitel or hired someone to do it."

Mike chewed, swallowed, and winked. "Piece o' cake."

Just then the phone rang. Mike got up, went into the next room for a few minutes. When he came back, he looked strange. I couldn't read him — and that was unusual.

"What's up?"

"My guys couldn't find Benedetto at his apartment, so they started checking the clubs where he worked. They finally found the man about thirty minutes ago — or his corpse, anyway."

"What do you mean his *corpse?*"

"He's dead, Clare."

"Benedetto's dead?" I rose from the table, paced the room, tried to process this. "Benedetto's dead? Benedetto's dead!"

Finally, I stopped pacing and faced Mike. "Where was he killed? Which club?"

"Club Flux. They found him in his upstairs office."

"And *how* was he killed, Mike?"

"That's the bizarre part. Someone slipped the man a Mickey. They found a half-empty bottle of champagne with two glasses. There are traces of the drug in Benedetto's glass. They're dusting for prints now."

"The drug killed him?"

Mike shook his head. "When Benedetto passed out, the killer slit his throat."

"Another murder with a *knife?*"

"Listen, Clare, I want you to think about your meeting with this guy. Did you pick up anything from Benedetto, any lead on who might have wanted him dead?"

"Billy Benedetto said he was expecting a backer. This mysterious backer was going to put up money for Benedetto's new restaurant. The reason, according to Billy, was that he had something *on* this guy — and it sounded to me like —"

"Blackmail?" Mike said.

"Anton Wright!"

"What?"

"The owner of Solange! That's who I saw go up to see Benedetto after I left him, which means Benedetto had something incriminating on Anton Wright. 'Something big. Something bad.' Those were his very words."

"What did he have, Clare? What's your theory?"

"I believe Billy and Anton conspired to kill Tommy Keitel. Anton's a polished entrepreneur now, but Keitel told me the man started out in life as the son of a butcher — so he must have had knife skills."

"You think Anton was the one who stabbed Tommy Keitel to death. And he did this for or with Billy Benedetto —"

"Yes, Billy had a very strong motive to want Tommy dead. But then Billy must have turned on Anton and blackmailed him. Anton obviously decided to get rid of blackmailing Billy by drugging him and slashing his throat. I can't prove it yet, but I'm sure I'm right."

"Murder needs a motive, Clare. And while your scenario gives a motive to Anton Wright for killing Benedetto — if he was in fact blackmailing Anton for some reason — it doesn't answer the motive in the murder of Tommy Keitel. It comes down to a simple question. Why would Anton Wright want to kill Tommy Keitel?"

"Motive, motive . . ." I drummed my fingers on the tabletop. "Why would Anton kill Tommy?"

"He wouldn't. Tommy was the jewel in the Solange crown. No sane man throws away a jewel, Clare. He goes to great lengths to hold on to it."

Mike paused just then; his blue eyes met my green ones, held them for a long, sweet, unnervingly suggestive moment, and I got the distinct impression that he wanted us to remember the emeralds from last night, the one's I'd worn naked while we —

I cleared my throat. Any thoughts in that direction weren't going to solve Tommy's murder and free my daughter.

"I've got no answer for Anton Wright's motive, Mike. I'll grant you that. But Anton and Tommy were feuding about something. So I'm *not* clearing him off my suspect list. Not yet."

Mike nodded, sipped his coffee, and smiled inappropriately — probably at my use of the term *suspect list.*

"What's with you, Lieutenant? Half the time when I talk to you about my theories, I catch this little smile on your face. Do I *amuse* you?"

Mike leaned back. "You really want me to answer that?"

"No." I rolled my eyes, glanced at the clock. "Listen, I better get dressed and get out of here. I want to shower and change back at the Blend. Then I have to go up to Joy's apartment, pick up some of her clothes and personal items. She should be out of jail today, and she'll be coming back to the Blend to stay with Matt and me until her trial. Even if the judge doesn't put her under house arrest, I'm guessing she'll just want to crash with us for the moral support."

"I'll go with you," Mike said, rising from the table. "You can use the help carrying her stuff, right?"

"I'd love you to help me. But don't you have to go in to work?"

"I do. But there's no hurry." He shrugged. "The ME's office won't get back to us for a few more hours, and it's not like I have to rush in to interrogate Benedetto. The only investigator getting info from that scumbag now is the doc who's performing his autopsy."

TWENTY-SIX

"Where are we going, exactly?" Mike asked.

"Tenth Street and fifty-second."

"Hell's Kitchen?"

I nodded. "Joy moved into the two-bedroom about six months ago. It's not too far from Restaurant Row — a prime location for two aspiring chefs."

Mike laughed. "Two chefs living in Hell's Kitchen. Funny."

"Believe me, the irony was not lost on Joy's roommate. Yvette's family owns the Ice Castle ice cream franchise, and they subsidize her lifestyle here in New York and in Paris, where she's interning now."

Outside, the sun was bright, and the air was crisp but thankfully not too cold. It was Monday morning rush hour pretty much everywhere on Manhattan Island, but once we were in the car, the trip wasn't too heinous, owing to the fact that Mike seemed to know exactly how to get around most traffic snarls. The man had skills. And apparently a penchant for conjuring parking spaces because, miraculously, we found a spot right in front of Joy's building.

I paused in the large lobby to pick up my daughter's mail, which had piled up in her box since Friday. I noticed a large envelope in the mix. The return address was Solange. A rubber-stamped note indicated the missive was hand-delivered by messenger service this morning. I tore into the envelope and found an invitation inside.

Mike peered over my shoulder. "What's it say?"

" 'Dear employee or vendor of Solange,' " I read. " 'You are cordially invited to a memorial dinner to celebrate the life and legacy of Chef Thomas Keitel. A four-course meal will be prepared by Chef Robbie Gray and his staff. As part of this celebration, hosts Faye Murray Keitel and Anton Wright will make an exciting announcement concerning the bright new future of Solange, New York, and its sister restaurants.' "

"Sister restaurants?" Mike said.

"There are no sister restaurants. And since when has Solange been called Solange, *New York*?" I faced Mike. "This is it! "This is why Tommy Keitel was murdered! Anton

Wright and Faye Keitel are going to franchise Solange. That must have been their plan all along —"

"Whoa, Clare. Slow down."

But I was too pumped to slow down. "Don't you see, Mike? Wright spent millions opening three restaurants, but Solange was his only success. Naturally he'd want to capitalize on it. He probably told Chef Keitel his plan, and Tommy went ballistic. He wasn't interested in French cuisine anymore. Tommy wanted out. He wanted to move to Russia. He just wanted to be free again."

"But other chefs can cook Keitel's dishes, right? Why did Anton even need Keitel?"

"They're *signature* dishes. According to Tommy's contract, he owned all of Solange's recipes, not Anton."

"Why couldn't Anton buy them?"

"Because Tommy was too much of an egomaniac to sell! Billy Benedetto told me that Tommy refused to sell him the Italian recipes he'd invented for his eatery, even though Chef Keitel never used them again." I shook my head. "If Tommy wasn't attached to a restaurant any longer, he simply didn't want them serving his dishes. Period."

I waved the invitation in Mike's face. "Don't you see? Anton wanted to expand,

Tommy didn't, so Anton murdered him, then made a deal with Faye Keitel to use Tommy's name and recipes for his franchise."

"You could be right, Clare, but you don't have any proof —"

"I have a *theory!* That's more than I had an hour ago. Now I have to *get* the proof."

"You have to build a case. Which means you'll have to go to this memorial dinner, for starters. When does it take place?"

"Tonight at eight o'clock."

Mike looked at the invitation. "This must have been sent out as part of a mass mailing."

"For sure." I nodded. "Someone in Anton Wright's office probably just used a staff list. Joy was still on it, so she got the invite."

Mike grabbed my arm. Only then did I notice that others had gathered in the lobby. "Let's go," he said. "We'll talk upstairs."

We climbed four flights in silence. I unlocked the door, and a blast of stale air hit us. I crossed to the window and opened it. I was relieved to find the place neat and tidy. Joy used to be a real slob when she had me to pick up after her, but it was apparently different now that she had her own place. I took the neatness as a sign of her budding maturity and I said so to Mike.

426

"I just wish she'd been this tidy in her personal life, then she wouldn't be in so much trouble right now."

On my way to the bedroom to gather up some clothes, I spied a blinking light in the living room: Joy's and Yvette's answering machine. The digital display indicated there were nine messages.

I sighed and pressed Play.

"Message one. Thursday, twelve fifty-five pm," the electronic voice announced.

"Bonjour, mon amie," chirped Yvette. "I'm sitting in an outdoor café on the Left Bank, up to my chin in *hommes, hommes, hommes.* More fool you for interning in New York City, where all the men are married or unemployed actors. *Oo-la-la!* I'll take Paris. Call me — and don't forget to water the herb garden."

"I'd better do that before I go," I reminded myself.

"Message two. Thursday, eight nineteen pm."

There was a pause. I heard breathing on the digital recording, from a man who was no longer breathing. Then came the voice of a ghost. A dead man. "Hey. It's Vinny —"

"Mike, listen!" I cried.

"I'm here," he said.

427

"Joy, I have to talk to you," Vinny said. "I left a message on your cell, too. When you get off work, come out and see me, okay? Something happened last night when I stayed late to do all that prep work Brigitte assigned to me. I was in the walk-in fridge for a long time, so long that Anton Wright thought he was alone. Well, I overheard Mr. Wright in the kitchen —"

There was a long pause, and my heart stopped, thinking the time had run out on the message.

"Anton was talking to someone on his cell," Vinny continued. "He and this person planned on doing something bad. Stuff you wouldn't believe. Listen, Joy, you have to come see me. I can't go in to the restaurant. When Anton saw me, I ran. And now I'm scared to go back. Chef Keitel is, like, *never* there anymore, and I don't have his cell number, so I don't know how to warn him what Anton's planning, but I know you see him. *You* have to warn him. He'll listen to you. Then maybe he can tell me what I should do, too! You have to talk to him before it's too la —"

"End of message," the digital voice declared.

"There's the proof," I said. "Vinny heard Anton plotting the murder of Tommy Keitel. He tried to tell Joy so she could warn Tommy."

Mike shook his head. "That's what you thought you heard, but to anyone else, that message is inconclusive."

"You're crazy —"

"Listen to it again, Clare. Then imagine how a jury might hear it. And how a defense attorney might spin it as referring to something completely innocent."

I played the message again, and my shoulders sagged. "You're right, Mike. There's no real proof here."

"No, there isn't." Mike folded his arms. "But I think I know how we can get it."

"How?"

"Last night you went out on a limb for me. Do you think you could do the same thing for Joy?"

My eyes met Mike's. "I think we both know the answer to that."

I arrived at Solange at seven fifteen, almost an hour before the festivities were to begin. I flashed Joy's invitation to the man at the door.

"Madame, you're —"

"Early, I know. But I wanted to speak to Mr. Wright and Mrs. Keitel."

I breezed past the doorman, strode into

the dining room.

The tables were set, complete with name tags. Members of the waitstaff were still bustling around. I didn't recognize anyone, but why should I? For this event, Solange was staffed by men and women from Robbie Gray's restaurant, Anatomy. The crew from Solange was on the guest list.

I spied Faye Keitel in the middle of the dining room, speaking with a tall maître d'. She looked stylish in a designer gown that put Madame's green Valentino suit to shame. Her highlighted blond hair was coifed in an elegant French braid, her makeup perfect. Beside the pair, I saw Anton Wright in black tie. He held a wine bottle at arm's length while he read the label.

Faye tensed when she noticed my approach. Anton sensed her reaction and set the bottle aside.

"Remember me?" I said.

"Oh, hello," Faye replied, forcing a smile. She glanced at Anton. "This is Clare Cosi. She's —"

"The mother of Joy Allegro, the innocent girl you framed for murder."

The maître d' did a horrified double take. Faye and Anton didn't even blink.

"Please excuse us, Matthew," Faye said.

"Very well," the maître d' replied, then disappeared into the busy kitchen.

Anton stood beside Faye, arms folded over his chest. Faye Keitel peered down her nose at me.

"You've gotten our attention. Say your piece," she demanded.

I ignored her, faced Anton Wright. "I know all about that phone call the other night. You planned Tommy Keitel's murder in Solange's kitchen. Vincent Buccelli told me all about that conversation — before you murdered him."

"You're crazy," he said unconvincingly. Clearly Anton was rattled. But Faye Keitel regarded me through a gaze like ancient ice.

"Why would Anton kill his golden goose?" she asked.

"Because the goose was about to fly the coop. Tommy was bored and wanted a new challenge."

I faced Anton again. "Tommy told you he was gone when his contract expired, which messed up your plan to franchise the Solange name, didn't it? How could you find backers without Tommy's reputation to peddle?"

Anton sneered. "I already had the investors, because I'd already sold the idea. I'd

431

signed the contracts and taken the money
—"

I blinked. "My God, no wonder you were so desperate."

"I took a bath on those other restaurants," Anton said. "Solange was a moneymaker, but it didn't make up for my losses. I needed the cash, so I sold the franchise idea. All Tommy had to do was sign on to the deal, and he'd be a millionaire ten times over —"

"But he wanted nothing to do with your scheme. He wouldn't even sell you the recipes, would he?"

Anton winced, and I knew I'd struck a nerve.

"What do you want, Ms. Cosi?" Faye asked.

"The same thing Billy Benedetto wanted," I replied.

When I mentioned the late Mr. Benedetto, even Faye seemed rattled. I took some satisfaction in that.

"Oh, yes. I spoke with Benedetto, too. Before Anton murdered him."

"What do you *want?*" Faye repeated impatiently.

"My daughter is going to cop a plea for Tommy's murder," I replied. "She'll spend six or seven years in prison. When she gets out, you are going to back her restaurant to the tune of six million dollars."

"Now why would we do that?" Anton asked. "You can't prove your ridiculous claims."

"I don't have to prove anything," I replied. "All I have to do is talk to Roman Brio. He'd certainly be interested in my tale, interested enough to ask questions, maybe write an exposé. What would happen to your deal then?"

Anton locked eyes with Faye. "With Benedetto gone, I thought we were through with blackmail —"

"Shut up," Faye said softly.

But Anton wouldn't. "There's precious little profit in this as it is. We can't slice off another piece of the pie. That's why we got rid of Benedetto —"

"I told you to shut up, Anton."

"I should have never listened to you, never let you seduce me, talk me into this," Anton said.

"Excuse me, Anton," I said. "But you wouldn't be the first sucker who let his mistress talk him into murdering an inconvenient husband."

"I didn't kill Tommy!" Anton replied. "Vinny, yeah, because I had to. And Benedetto because he was costing me money.

But it was *Faye* who killed Tommy. She couldn't wait."

Faye howled, and I whirled to face her. She had a steak knife in her hand, lifted from one of the place settings, and she lunged at me!

I managed to deflect the blade with my forearm, which saved my life. It plunged deep into my shoulder instead of my throat.

"Carnegie Hall! Carnegie Hall!" I yelled while I continued to wrestle with the crazed woman.

The police who'd been waiting outside poured into the restaurant. Detective Lippert cuffed Anton Wright. Ray Tatum pulled Faye Keitel off me and disarmed her.

I stumbled backward against a table. I was a little dizzy. My shoulder hurt like a son of a bitch, and I felt something warm flowing down my arm. My knees buckled. Before I hit the floor, Sue Ellen Bass and Detective Soles caught me, one on each arm. They cleared a table and stretched me out on the white cloth. Detective Soles pressed a stack of napkins against my wound to stanch the bleeding.

They were asking me questions, but their voices were whispers. And they both seemed so far away. From my position on the table, I could see Solange's gargoyles were still up there, on their high perches, but the detectives were closer . . . and they looked like angels, floating against the restaurant's sunny yellow walls. I blinked, my vision going fuzzy.

Mike Quinn strode across the room. "We've got it all on tape," he announced, glancing around, looking for me. Then Mike saw me on the table. He saw the blood. "Son of a —"

"Mike?"

"Clare! You're hurt! My God!" His rugged face loomed over me. He looked scared.

"What's wrong, Mike? Didn't we get them?"

"We got them, sweetheart. *You* got them."

"Good . . . Okay, then I can close my eyes now . . . finally take a rest . . ."

"No, Clare! Stay awake! Please, sweetheart!"

Mike's booming voice began to fade. I saw him shouting at the female detectives. "Keep pressure on that wound, do you hear me? Where are the paramedics? Is the ambulance here? Dammit! Get the paramedics in here!"

"Sorry, Mike. I'm just a little tired . . ."

Then someone turned off the lights.

Epilogue

"Night, boss," Esther called, waving at the door of my hospital room. "Take care of that shoulder now. And go easy on the meds."

"My lady knows of what she speaks. So listen, Clare Cosi, and don't be weak."

"Okay, Boris." I tipped my hat to the hippest Russian rapper in the country — or at least on this floor of the St. Vincent's Hospital. "I'll keep it real."

It was late, close to the end of visiting hours, and Esther and BB Gun were the last to depart. They'd just helped me polish off a sinfully delicious box of Chef Jacques Torres's handmade chocolates that Janelle Babcock had delivered earlier in the day.

My daughter and ex-husband were back at the Village Blend by now. Madame had gone off to meet her beau for a late dinner — that mysterious younger man I had yet to meet. And I'd been entertaining an endless stream of visitors all day long: Tucker, Gardner, Dante, Detectives Soles and Bass. Even Napoleon Dornier had dropped by to see how I was doing.

Now that Joy was cleared of Tommy's murder, there was no more tension between Nappy and me. In fact, he confided that he'd already found a backer for his own restaurant. He was taking Tommy's entire staff of cooks with him — Ramon included. And he was hoping I'd consider supplying the coffee beans.

Janelle was the only Solange staffer to decline Dornier's offer. She'd found a position with one of the most prestigious cake makers on Manhattan Island, a job that would easily double her pay (which was one reason she said she'd splurged and bought me the gourmet chocolates).

I yawned and fell back against my hospital pillows. The room was full of flowers and cards, balloons and stuffed animals. The angry stab wound to my shoulder still smarted, and the meds were still necessary, but the surgery had gone well, and the doctors said I'd be leaving the hospital in a day or two.

"Knock, knock?"

"Is that the start of a joke?" I called. "Or a visit?"

"It's a visit . . . from a visitor who has his hands full!"

Mike.

I'd last seen the man hours ago in his detective jacket and tie. Now he was back, in worn jeans and a distressed-leather bomber, apparently bearing gifts.

"What have you got there?"

One hand held a huge thermos, the other a stack of paper cups. "Since you can't go to the Village Blend, I brought the Blend's coffee to you."

"Oh, Mike, you're a savior! I'm dying for a cup!"

"I figured you would be about now. 'Cause I know hospital coffee. You're talking to a real vet when it comes to line-of-duty injuries."

I remembered the scars I'd seen on the man's naked chest. And I remembered what had happened after I'd seen those scars . . . and touched them, and kissed them. But that line of thought wasn't going to let me sleep tonight, not without a bucket of icy cold *banya* water dumped over me.

"So . . . how did we do, Lieutenant?"

Mike moved my rolling tray next to the bed and poured me a cup of French-roasted Kenya AA from the thermos. "We got it all on tape, sweetheart," he began, handing me

438

the steaming cup then pouring one for himself. "Anton's admission that he killed Vinny and Benedetto, his statement that it was Faye Keitel who murdered Tommy. It was a thing of beauty what you did — including deflecting that knife." He reached out, caressed my cheek. "It saved your life."

"Yeah. But I shouldn't have ended up in here at all. I should have remembered what Roman Brio told me about Tommy's wife."

"What?"

"Before she'd dropped her culinary career to have Tommy's kids, she was the man's roast chef!"

"His what?"

"It's the position in the brigade that's responsible for roasting meat. Like Anton, the son of a butcher, Faye Keitel definitely had knife skills. She was a cool customer, too. The thing I don't get is what made her snap."

"I listened to the tape about fifty times, and I can tell you why. Faye Keitel snapped the moment Anton Wright turned on her. You heard the saying 'no honor among thieves'? It's true among murderers, too."

"She should have stabbed Anton then!"

"No, Clare. In more ways than one, you put yourself between them."

As I sipped my dark cuppa, Mike updated

me on the case. The detectives from the Nineteenth were handling the follow-up investigation. They'd legally confiscated and then examined the cell phones, computers, and personal files of Faye and Anton, and in short order they found evidence of their conspiracy to murder Chef Keitel.

"There are e-mail exchanges and phone messages that document it all," Mike told me. "Their alibis don't hold water, and because of Faye Keitel's attack on you, we've gotten a confession out of her with a plea deal in the works. Anton's hanging tougher, but we're working on him. Worst-case scenario, Faye will have to testify against him at his trial as part of her deal."

"That should bring the man to heel."

"We're looking at Anton for Benedetto's murder, too, thanks to what you observed at Flux last night." Mike regarded me over his coffee cup. "You've been one busy homicide detective, Clare Cosi."

I raised an eyebrow at my partner. "I had a *little* help."

Mike laughed.

"There's only one thing I'm still puzzling over."

"Mmmm?" said Mike, swallowing his fix.

"What in the world did Billy Benedetto have on Anton Wright? I mean . . . he was obviously blackmailing the man. But unless Benedetto was psychic — which I sincerely doubt — I can't figure out how he knew where to pin Tommy's murder."

"Billy Benedetto actually *saw* Faye Keitel come out of Solange the night of the murder. And Benedetto knew enough about the couple to realize that Faye would never set foot in her husband's restaurant. He also knew Anton was seeing Faye on the side. When Benedetto heard the details of Tommy's murder, he put two and two together and solved it before us. Unfortunately for him, he didn't try to bring them to justice. The opportunity for extortion was just too tempting. The threats and e-mails from him were among Faye's and Anton's personal computer files. Benedetto claimed he'd go to the police with what he knew unless Anton backed his restaurant. Good old blackmailing Billy was willing to let Joy rot in jail so he could get a bona fide backer."

My fingers tightened around my cup. "Since you put it that way, I can't say I'm sad that Benedetto's off the planet."

"Well, he is. And Joy's free. So how's she doing?" Now that the talk had turned personal, Mike relaxed a little more, sat down on the edge of my bed. "Is she okay?"

"Joy's fine. She's a strong girl."

Mike rested his hand on my leg. "I can't imagine where she gets that."

I placed my hand on top of his. "She's very relieved, Mike. But I can't say she's happy. The man she loved and admired is dead. Her good friend was needlessly executed, and the scandal has embarrassed her culinary school. We just found out today that she's being expelled."

"Even with the dropped charges?"

"Her affair with Tommy was considered 'conduct unbecoming.' That she can't dispute."

"The poor kid. After all she's been through . . ."

"It's a blow. This was her internship year. It should have been her best year ever. Now it's her worst."

"But she does have the training, even if she doesn't have the piece of paper that proves it. And don't you think, Cosi, when it comes down to the wire, that someone's ability to *handle* any situation is more important than a piece of paper?"

Mike's blue eyes were spearing me. I shook my head. "Why do I think you're referring to something other than a diploma from a culinary school?"

"You could get a PI license, Clare. If you ever want one, I can help you apply."

"Maybe someday, Lieutenant. Not today."

Mike shrugged. "I just think if you're going to keep getting yourself mixed up in murder, you might want to think about carrying a gun."

"I'd rather think about a new Asia-Pacific blend. Matt's getting some new beans in next week."

Mike laughed, glanced down at our hands, interlaced his fingers through mine. "So is Joy going to work for you now? At the Blend?"

"God, no. She'd hate that." I smiled. "Madame and Matt and I all agreed to send her to Paris after the holidays. Yvette's invited her, so she already has a place to crash. And we've come up with the money to stake her for six months. She can polish her French and find a line cook's position, and decide if she wants to stay there for a spell longer or come back to New York and start fresh."

"That's got to be hard for you, Clare, to send her away."

"Harder than you know. But it would be worse to see her suffer here. There are too many terrible memories. She needs to make new memories, have fresh, exciting experiences. When I was in Italy at her age, I met my . . . That's where I met Matt."

The mere mention of his name seemed to frost Mike's edges. "Let's hope she meets a better guy."

I nodded, although down deep I didn't really agree. True, Matt had put me through some pretty bad times, but he was no Tommy Keitel. And he'd really come through for Joy and me in this round.

Still, with Mike's blue eyes smiling at me now, I knew *I'd* found a better guy. In many ways Matteo Allegro was an amazing man. But Mike was the kind who'd stay with you through the boredom — not just the thrills.

I leaned forward then and kissed Mike Quinn. I kissed him sweetly then hotly, leisurely then hungrily. I could see that he needed it — and, frankly, I was getting tired of talking.

We came up for air when my bedside phone rang. And after all that delectable kissing, I had a little trouble finding my voice.

"Hello?" I croaked.

"Clare, something awful has happened . . ."

"Hold on a second, okay?" I covered the receiver. "It's Madame," I whispered to Mike.

He smiled, caressed my hair, pressed his lips to my forehead. Then he lifted his chin toward the hallway. "I'll come back."

"No. You don't have to leave."

"It's okay." Mike winked. "I'll be right outside when you need me."

I smiled. That pretty much summed up Mike Quinn for me, all right. I watched him leave, the easy, powerful length of him; then I took a breath and pretended I could actually focus.

"Okay, Madame, tell me," I said. "What's the matter?"

"It's Matteo . . ." Madame sounded stricken, like someone she loved had just been diagnosed with a terrible disease. "He's gotten himself into a terrible fix, and he's going to need our help like never before."

"Anything, Madame. Tell me what's wrong?"

"He just left me a message, Clare. He's getting *married.*"

"Married! Matt?"

"In a few short months, Matt plans to wed himself to Breanne Summour. But he doesn't love that woman, Clare. And I won't let my boy make that kind of mistake with his life."

"But, Madame . . ." I closed my eyes, massaged my forehead. "It's *his* life."

"Oh, please, Clare! Do you think you're

the only mother who knows how to butt in?"

"What are you saying?"

"I'm saying Matt may *think* he's getting married, but I'm going to find a way to stop this wedding. And you, my dear, are going to help!"

I closed my eyes. *Oh, God. Here we go.* "I think you'll just have to accept it, Madame. Matt's marrying Breanne Summour."

Madame's voice went down to a subterranean octave. "Over my dead body," she vowed.

■ ■ ■ ■

RECIPES & TIPS FROM THE VILLAGE BLEND

■ ■ ■ ■

Visit Cleo Coyle's virtual Village Blend at
www.CoffeehouseMystery.com
for coffee tips, coffee talk,
and an easy recipe for tarte Tatin.

RASPBERRY COULIS

A coulis is a thick and evenly textured French sauce made from pureed and strained vegetables or fruits. Coulis can either be sweet or savory, depending on what it is meant to accompany, and it is popular both with classically trained French chefs and practitioners of fusion cuisine.

A vegetable coulis is generally used with meat or vegetable dishes, or as a base for soups or other sauces. Fruit coulis are generally used with desserts, but savory fruit coulis may also be used to accent roast meats. Herb coulis are becoming popular, and mint coulis often accompany roast lamb.

This classic sweet coulis is made with raspberries, but an equal amount of another fruit, such as strawberries or mangoes, can be substituted.

2 pounds raspberries, fresh or frozen

1/2 cup sugar
1/2 lemon, juiced

Combine the raspberries, sugar, and lemon juice in a saucepan over medium heat. Simmer while stirring, until the sugar dissolves, about 10 minutes. Strain through a mesh sieve. Add additional sugar or lemon juice, to taste.

In France, raspberry coulis is often served with poached apples, but it may also be served with ice cream or pound cake, artfully drizzled on a plate or pooled next to the food it accompanies. Different types of coulis can appear on one plate, for varying flavors and colors.

Coulis should be kept in the refrigerator and can be frozen for future use. Chefs keep coulis in a squeeze bottle, so that it can be quickly applied when needed.

CHOCOLATE POTS DE CRÈME

The classic French chocolate pots de crème are not your typical chocolate pudding. They're sinfully chocolaty and truly delightful — and they're relatively easy to make, too. This recipe will yield approximately six 6-ounce servings.

12 ounces semisweet chocolate (chopped or chocolate pieces)
2 cups heavy cream
3/4 cup milk
6 egg yolks (extra large or jumbo eggs)
1/2 cup confectioners' sugar
1 tablespoon pure vanilla extract
1/8 teaspoon salt

Preheat the oven to 300°.
Put your chopped chocolate (or chocolate pieces) in a metal or glass bowl. Then in a medium saucepan, heat the cream and milk until it's just about to boil (but not

yet boiling). Pour this hot liquid over your chocolate, and let it sit for about a minute until the chocolate is softened. Then stir this mixture until it's smooth. This will take between 1 and 2 minutes.

In a second bowl whisk the egg yolks together (or use an electric mixer instead for this entire step). Gradually whisk in the sugar until smooth. Whisk in vanilla and salt. Now gradually whisk the chocolate mixture into these egg yolks.

Strain this custard through a fine-meshed sieve. (Tip: pour mixture into a container with a pouring spout.) Divide the mixture among six 7- or 8-ounce custard cups[*] (or even ovenproof or stoneware coffee cups), and place the cups in a 9″ × 13″ baking pan. Fill the pan with boiling water until it reaches about halfway up the sides of the custard cups (or coffee cups). Cover with foil and pierce in several places so that steam can escape.

Bake for about 30–45 minutes in the center of your oven until the tops of the pots de crème look solid, but the custard still

[*]Authentic French pots de crème cups include tiny lids for each individual cup. For variations on this recipe, as well as a recipe for a crème Chantilly topping, visit www.CoffeehouseMystery.com.

jiggles slightly when you shake it. Don't worry, the custard will firm up as it cools. Note: the deeper your cup, the longer your custard will take to set. If the custard still has a liquid top after 30 minutes, increase oven temperature to 325° and bake another 15 minutes.

Now remove the pots from the oven and the hot pan and let them cool to room temperature before placing them into the fridge. Make sure to *cover* these with plastic wrap to prevent a skin from forming. The custards should be chilled at least 2 hours before serving and will store well for up to 2 days. Try serving with a dollop of whipped cream. For added flare sprinkle with shaved chocolate.

NICK VLACHEK'S BORSCHT

Borscht is a soup prepared with fresh beets that is popular in both Russia and Poland. It's traditionally prepared using a variety of vegetables, a meat stock, or both. It can be served hot or cold and is always garnished with a dollop of sour cream. This recipe uses lamb, which results in a particularly rich and savory version of this traditional dish. Beef may be substituted.

Serves 10.

3 tablespoons olive oil

6 cloves garlic, peeled and finely chopped

1 1/2–2 pounds lamb stew meat, cut into pieces

1 large yellow onion, peeled and finely chopped

1 1/2 pounds green cabbage, chopped

1 1/2 pounds ripe red tomatoes, diced (use fresh, no need to peel)

2–3 pounds red beets, rinsed, peeled, and
  diced (small cubes)
3 quarts beef stock, fresh or canned
1/4 cup red wine vinegar
1/2 lemon, juiced
2 bay leaves
1 teaspoon sea salt
1 teaspoon freshly ground pepper
1 quart sour cream
1 bunch fresh dill, chopped

Heat a 12-quart pot; add the oil and garlic.
  Brown the lamb, and add the onions;
  sauté until onions are tender. Add the cabbage, tomatoes, beets, stock, vinegar,
  lemon juice, bay leaves, salt, and pepper.
  Bring to a boil, then reduce heat to a simmer. Cover and cook for 2 hours. Dish
  into bowls; serve with one or two teaspoons of sour cream and chopped dill for
  garnish.

COQ AU VIN

Chicken in red wine with braised onions, mushrooms, and bits of tender pork. Sounds simple, right? Don't be fooled. Classic coq au vin is a complex dish that requires advance planning and multistep preparation. It's time consuming, but you'll find the taste well worth the trouble.

Serves 4.

STEP ONE: BLANCH THE PORK

3/4 cup (6 ounces) of 1/4-inch strips of slab bacon or salt pork

Drop the pork into a saucepan; cover with 2 to 3 inches of cold water. Bring to boil over medium heat, simmer 5 to 8 minutes, drain. Refresh the pork in cold water, then pat dry with a paper towel.

Step Two: Prepare the Beurre Manié

1 1/2 tablespoons Wondra flour
1 1/2 tablespoons butter

Blend flour and softened butter into a paste. Chill for at least 30 minutes.

Step Three: Prepare the Ragout of Chicken

3 pounds frying chicken, cut into parts
2 tablespoons butter
1 tablespoon olive oil
Sea salt to taste (Baleine Mediterranean coarse crystals recommended)
Freshly ground pepper to taste
2 large cloves garlic, pureed
1 bay leaf
1/4 teaspoon thyme
1 large, ripe red tomato, chopped (or 1/3 cup canned Italian plum tomatoes)
4 cups young red wine (Chianti, Zinfandel, Macon)
1 cup chicken stock
3 tablespoons freshly chopped parsley

Sauté the blanched bacon or salt pork with the 2T of butter in a heavy-bottomed 12-inch frying pan, then remove to a side dish, leaving the fat in the pan. Brown the chicken over medium-high heat, add olive oil to fat if necessary. (Be sure the chicken is completely dry or it will not brown evenly.) Place chicken pieces skin side down. Don't crowd the pan; the chicken needs room to vent. (Make two batches, if necessary. And if you do, separate dark meat from light; it takes a little more time to brown dark meat.) Turn chicken every 20 to 30 seconds to ensure even browning. To finish the cooking, cover pan, lower the heat to moderate, and cook for about 6 minutes, turning once.

Baste the chicken in the rendered fat. Season with sea salt and pepper, then add the garlic, bay leaf, thyme, parsley, and tomato. Pour in 3 cups wine and enough stock to barely cover the ingredients. Bring to a simmer, cover, and cook for 20 minutes. Remove the chicken to a side dish.

STEP FOUR: BRAISE THE ONIONS

12–18 white boiling onions (peeled)
Clarified butter or olive oil
Chicken broth
1 cup red wine
Sea salt

Sauté 12 to 18 peeled white boiling onions in clarified butter or olive oil. Swirl the pan to brown them, or they will not braise evenly (approximately 12 minutes on low heat). Add chicken broth and a cup of red wine to half cover the onions. Season *lightly* with sea salt. Cover and simmer slowly for 25 to 30 minutes, until onions are tender but retain their shape when pierced.

STEP FIVE: SAUTÉ THE MUSHROOMS

1 tablespoon butter
1 tablespoon light olive oil or cooking oil
3–4 cups fresh mushrooms, trimmed, washed, dried, and quartered
1/2 tablespoon chopped shallots (or scallions)
Freshly ground pepper to taste

Set a 10-inch nonstick frying pan over high heat with butter and oil. When the foam from the butter subsides, add the mushrooms. Toss frequently for a few minutes while the mushrooms absorb the butter. In a minute or so, the butter will reappear; then add the shallots (or scallions) and ground pepper to taste and brown lightly.

STEP SIX: FINISH THE SAUCE

Pour the pan juices into a saucepan. Clean the frying pan you started with (you'll need it again). Boil down the juice a bit to concentrate the flavors. Remove from heat and whisk in the beurre manié to make a slightly thickened sauce. Bring briefly to simmer. Return the chicken to the clean pan; coat pieces with sauce.

STEP SEVEN: ASSEMBLE THE DISH

Strew a portion (to taste) of the pork lardons, all the braised onions, and all the sautéed mushrooms over the chicken. Baste with the sauce and simmer for a few minutes to blend the flavors. Serve with warm bread (to dip in that delicious sauce).

CLARE'S CORN BREAD

A delightful dish for a cold winter morning, especially tasty if served warm, with or without butter, along with your favorite coffee. Traditional recipes use skim milk and less sugar. Mine's sweeter, and the half-and-half brings a slightly richer texture to the party.

1 1/4 cups all-purpose flour
3/4 cup yellow cornmeal
3 teaspoons baking powder
1/2 cup sugar
1/2 teaspoon (dash) salt
1/4 cup vegetable oil
1 cup half-and-half
1 egg, beaten

Combine flour, cornmeal, baking powder, sugar, salt. Stir in oil, half-and-half, and the egg. Mix until dry ingredients are moistened. (Don't overmix!) Pour batter

463

into a greased 8-inch square pan and bake in a preheated 400° oven. Bake 20 to 25 minutes, until golden brown and a toothpick inserted in the center comes out clean.

ABOUT THE AUTHOR

Cleo Coyle is the pen name for a multi-published author who collaborates with her husband to write the Coffeehouse Mysteries. Although they did not meet until adulthood, Cleo and her husband had very similar upbringings. Both were children of food-loving Italian immigrants; both grew up in working-class neighborhoods outside of Pittsburgh, Pennsylvania; and both held blue-collar jobs in food service before moving to the Big Apple to begin their post-college careers: Cleo as a journalist and children's book author; and her husband as a magazine editor and writer. After finally meeting and falling in love, they married at the Little Church of the West in Las Vegas. Now they live and work in New York City, where they each write books independently and together, cook like crazy, haunt local coffeehouses, and drink *a lot* of joe. Among their many co-authored projects are the

Haunted Bookshop Mysteries, written under the pen name Alice Kimberly.

Cleo enjoys hearing from readers.
Visit her virtual Village Blend coffeehouse at
www.CoffeehouseMystery.com,
where she also posts recipes and coffee news.

We hope you have enjoyed this Large Print book. Other Thorndike, Wheeler, and Chivers Press Large Print books are available at your library or directly from the publishers.

For information about current and upcoming titles, please call or write, without obligation, to:

Publisher
Thorndike Press
295 Kennedy Memorial Drive
Waterville, ME 04901
Tel. (800) 223-1244

or visit our Web site at:

http://gale.cengage.com/thorndike

OR

Chivers Large Print
published by BBC Audiobooks Ltd
St James House, The Square
Lower Bristol Road
Bath BA2 3SB
England
Tel. +44(0) 800 136919
email: bbcaudiobooks@bbc.co.uk
www.bbcaudiobooks.co.uk

All our Large Print titles are designed for easy reading, and all our books are made to last.